More Oklahoma
Renegades

More Oklahoma Renegades

KEN BUTLER

PELICAN PUBLISHING COMPANY
GRETNA 2007

*The word "Pelican" and the depiction of a pelican are trademarks
of Pelican Publishing Company, Inc., and are registered in the
U.S. Patent and Trademark Office.*

Library of Congress Cataloging-in-Publication Data

Butler, Ken, 1926-2005.
  More Oklahoma renegades / Ken Butler.
    p. cm.
  Continues: Oklahoma renegades.
  Includes bibliographical references and index.
  ISBN-13: 978-1-58980-464-7 (pbk. : alk. paper) 1. Outlaws—
Oklahoma—Biography—Anecdotes. 2. Frontier and pioneer life—
Oklahoma—Anecdotes. 3. Oklahoma—Biography—Anecdotes. I.
Title.
  F699.B963 2007
  976.6'050922—dc22

                                        2007017863

Printed in the United States of America

Published by Pelican Publishing Company, Inc.
1000 Burmaster Street, Gretna, Louisiana 70053

To Maurine

Contents

7

Preface

More Oklahoma Renegades is an anthology of twenty-eight articles written over the course of several years since my first book, *Oklahoma Renegades: Their Deeds and Misdeeds,* which was published in 1997. Most of the stories (now chapters) have been published in a different form in one or more of the following periodicals: *True West* magazine, *Oklahoma State Trooper* magazine, and the *Oklahombres* and *OKOLHA* journals.

These intriguing tales of murder and mayhem are of the lesser-known outlaws, bandits, brigands, gangsters, hellions, and bad guys (and gals) who roamed the highways and byways of my home state of Oklahoma from the 1880s to the mid-1960s—nearly one hundred years of outlawry. This collection tells the stories of the lawbreakers as well as the lawmen who pursued them with determination. While some of the characters were "horseback outlaws," others were "wanted" criminals during the Roaring Twenties and the depression. They are individuals whom I found to be unique, and their careers included many interesting escapades. Each chapter is a complete story, and they are arranged in chronological order. In some cases, the same character will appear in more than one chapter.

In 2004, I learned that I had developed an eye disorder known as macular degeneration, which meant that, for all practical purposes, I would never be able to read regular newsprint again. This pretty much ended my researching activities. As for writing, however, I realized that by enlarging the print size of my articles' computer files, I could see well enough to revise and expand upon them. Therefore, I was able to prepare the chapters in this book. Although I have included my bibliography, I was unable to provide notes relating to specific material in the text.

I hope that my love of history, especially the history of outlaws and lawmen, will find a place in the reader's heart and mind and provide many, many hours of reading enjoyment.

Acknowledgments

I would like to express my gratitude to the many people who provided information and helped in the assembly of this work. Among those who did so are:

Jim Rabon, Oklahoma Department of Corrections, Oklahoma City; Anne Diestel, Federal Bureau of Prisons, Washington, D.C.; Phillip Steele, Springdale, AR; Bette Williams, Checotah, OK; Charles F. Loefke, Deputy Court Clerk, Lawton, OK; Meg Hacker, Southwest Regional Archives, Fort Worth, TX; Chuck Parsons, Luling, TX; Nancy Samuelson, Sacramento, CA; Al Ritter, Ponca City, OK; Ron Owens, Oklahoma City; Herman Kirkwood, Oklahoma City; R. D. ("Ron") and Naomi Morgan, Haskell, OK; Mollie Stehno, Shawnee, OK; Steve Bunch, Mooreland, OK; Terry Whitehead, Blackwell, OK; Diron Ahlquist, Oklahoma City; Dee Cordry, Piedmont, OK; Michael Koch, Tulsa, OK; Michael Tower, Elmore City, OK; and David Murray, Inverness, Scotland.

Thanks to the Oklahoma Historical Society and its wonderful staff, including Laura Martin, Delbert Amen, Scott Dowell, Brian Basore, Nancy Laub, Chester Cowen, and Lily Tiger; to the Western History Collection at the University of Oklahoma, Norman, OK; and to the staff at the Oklahoma Publishing Company, Photographic Archives Division.

A very special and loving acknowledgment to my wife,

Maurine ("Rene"), who endorsed my efforts and the many hours that I had devoted to this project; and, last but not least, to my daughter, Doris Tomlin of Oklahoma City, who reviewed my writing and offered corrections.

More Oklahoma Renegades

Depictions of five events in the life and death of Wesley Barnett. (Illustrated by and with permission from Western artist Al Napoletano)

CHAPTER 1

Wesley Barnett

Wesley Barnett was a notorious outlaw in the Creek Indian Nation during the late 1880s. The passage of more than a century since his demise has faded the recognition of his name, until now it is doubtful if anyone can recall ever having heard of him. The few currently available copies of newspapers that were published in Indian Territory during his time provide fragments of information about Wesley Barnett. These old newspaper articles focus on reports of his villainous escapades and his encounters with various law enforcers.

A previously published account of Wesley's misdeeds provides some bits of information concerning his youth. From that source it seems that he was born circa 1870 and his parents were full-blood Creeks. Young Barnett's typical boyhood was extensively altered when his father died. Following that disruption, Wesley was sent to Haskell (a boarding school for Indian boys) at Fort Lawrence, Kansas. Sometime after he had left "The Territory" and was attending school, his mother remarried. Several months later, she died, rather mysteriously. Thus began the saga of Wesley Barnett, the Terror of the Creek Nation.

When Wesley received word of his mother's death, he hastened home. Upon returning to Indian Territory, he began to pick up information about his mother's second marriage and her death. He learned that she had been abused by her new husband and had left him. Wesley was advised that his stepfather had attempted reconciliation with his mother. Numerous people revealed their suspicion that when she refused to rejoin him, he had killed her. Wesley accepted their speculation and deemed it his duty to avenge his mother's death. He then set forth to "do in" the guilty party.

Hiding in the brush near his stepfather's cabin, young Barnett awaited his chance to perform his evil task. Perhaps the man felt that danger was lurking, because he remained alone inside the house as if hiding. Wesley was determined to carry out his mission, and so he stayed at his post. His perseverance prevailed and, after a lengthy period, his mother's second husband opened the door and stepped into the yard. Wesley shouldered his rifle and fired three quick shots, ending the man's life.

Suspicion that Wesley had committed the homicide immediately arose; however, proof was lacking because he had carried out his mission with utmost secrecy. Many of his neighbors and acquaintances who were familiar with the case, suspected young Barnett's involvement, but they considered that justice had been rendered. No one was charged with the murder of Wesley's stepfather.

From that venture, it was said that Wesley Barnett developed a compulsion to kill. He would find that compulsion to be a useful trait as he entered his new career, stealing horses. When Wesley began to swipe livestock, he limited his larceny to the better quality animals and took only those that were owned by white men.

Barnett was described as a light-complexioned Indian who was small in stature. He wore his hair long, in the typical manner of that era, and he walked with a limp. His most noticeable feature was protruding front teeth. There was nothing in his physical makeup to indicate his criminal proclivities. Wesley was quick and accurate with pistol and rifle. He was a tireless rider, and at his choosing he roamed the countryside, day or night, despite all obstacles, man-made or natural. It was said that he crossed the Arkansas and other rivers in the area at any point, regardless of rising water or foul weather. His actions were indicative of a reckless rebel who seemed to be endowed with a talent for coping with hidden dangers.

As his reputation for stealing horses from white settlers spread, he became a popular figure among his tribesmen. Others of his ilk joined his enterprise, and soon a gang of Creek rogues was riding with the young outlaw on his forays. As Wesley gained experience in this field, he became cannier in his operation.

Later, Barnett's greed prompted him to forego his self-imposed restraint of filching only from white folks. With his new outlook, the entire Creek Nation became his hunting ground, without regard to the owner's ethnic background. As a result, the adulation that many of the Indians had held for Wesley waned, when they realized that they too might be subject to his prowess.

Wesley's betrayal of his blood brothers was soundly demonstrated when he and his raiders stole several horses from Mutaloke, a tribal leader. A group of Creek citizens led by Mutaloke then formed a band of vigilantes to rid the nation of this blight. They intended to stop the plundering of Barnett and his outlaw gang.

The vigilantes were unable to locate the band of robbers, so they decided that when found alone, they would arrest the individuals and enforce the law. Using this method, they could rein in several of the known horse thieves.

Noah Partridge was one of the older members of Barnett's gang. The vigilantes posted an observer to watch the Partridge homestead. A few days later, the horse thief was sighted riding toward home. As darkness fell that evening, Mutaloke and his followers gathered at Partridge's house and called him out. The suspect's arrogance toward the vigilantes further agitated the

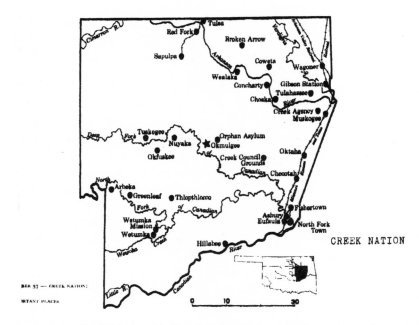

Map of the Creek Nation, Indian Territory, showing the major settlements, circa 1890. (Author's collection)

self-appointed officers. Harsh words were exchanged, and Partridge was gunned down. When Wesley and his gang learned that the vigilantes had killed their cohort, "they made another bold raid." Mutaloke led his men in pursuit of the fleeing outlaws, but as before, they did not overtake the gang.

L. C. Perryman had recently taken office as governor of the Creek Nation. One of Governor Perryman's first acts was an attempt to persuade both sides of the troubled tribe (the outlaws and the vigilantes) to disband. At first, it seemed that the new governor was effectively influencing the two factions to cease their warfare.

After Mutaloke had been charged in the Creek Nation for the murder of Partridge, he went into hiding in the Seminole

Nation. Mutaloke's departure lessened the intense conflict between the two factions in the Creek Nation. However, that slack period didn't last long. Within a few weeks, it was reported that Barnett had become obsessed with revenge for the death of his fellow henchman and that he was vowing to personally bring retribution to Mutaloke for Partridge's murder.

Meanwhile, Mutaloke had decided to settle the affair legally and arranged a meeting with attorney Thomas Adams and Judge John Freeman. He then returned to the Creek Nation to resolve the pending murder charge. After discussing the case, the three men traveled to Tulsa in order to consult with Governor Perryman (who had not yet moved to Okmulgee, the tribal capital). They arrived at the governor's home during the morning of January 10, 1888, and the four men started to his office to discuss the matter.

The cold north wind chilled their bodies as Perryman, Freeman, Adams, and Mutaloke briskly walked toward the governor's office. Suddenly, the icy air of the winter morn was unexpectedly disrupted by a man's voice. Looking for the source, their attentions were drawn to a house only forty feet away, where they saw Wesley Barnett standing in the doorway. The startled men then heard the young outlaw shout, "I'm ready." The three professional men (Perryman, Freeman, and Adams) scurried away, but Mutaloke stood staunch and firmly replied, "So am I." Without further words, Barnett brought forth his rifle as Mutaloke grasped his pistol. Wesley fired four shots into Mutaloke, who fell upon the frozen ground. The wounded man had manipulated his pistol twice. His first shot had whizzed past Barnett and while falling he had triggered the second cartridge, sending an errant slug through the brim of Governor Perryman's hat. As life drained from Mutaloke's fatally wounded body, the unblemished Barnett hurried to his saddled horse and fled. Having witnessed Wesley Barnett kill a loyal tribal leader, Governor Perryman ordered the tribe's police force, called lighthorsemen, to pursue the "Terror of the Creek Nation" with all possible haste.

Barnett's blatant attack upon Mutaloke furthered the personal controversy about his character among the members of his tribe. Those who deemed Barnett's assault to be courageous spoke proudly of his bravery. Many, however, considered that the young villain had merely committed another murder. After the attack, Barnett and his gang vanished into the hills where they resumed their chosen careers.

At some point later, Wesley's brother Waite joined him. No information is available about Waite Barnett. Wesley and his cohorts had recently entered into another criminal activity, having become involved in the illegal liquor trade in the Indian Territory. This violation brought the deputy U.S. marshals, as well as the Creek Lighthorsemen and tribal vigilantes, into the search for the gang.

A green corn dance, a local Indian festival, was held on Saturday night, June 30, 1888, at Thopthlocco. In attendance at the dance were Deputy U.S. Marshal John Phillips and his friend William Whitson (whom he had deputized). Two prisoners had escaped from these officers the day before, not far from where the dance was being held. The lawmen had a hunch that the escapees were still in the vicinity. Phillips and Whitson (one account identifies him as McLaughlin) had arrived at the dance early, and about 9:00 P.M. they gave the impression that they were going home. Instead, they traveled only a short distance and stationed themselves at a well-known watering hole. The officers thought it likely that the two escapees (if still in the area) would attempt to obtain water from the spring during the night, and if so, they would be in position to recapture the "wanted men."

After the lawmen had left the dance, the Barnett brothers arrived at the scene of the Saturday night entertainment. Likely their interest in the affair was to peddle some whiskey and perhaps steal a horse or two, rather than frolic to the tempo of the music. About midnight, Wesley and Waite Barnett left the dance and went to the spring. As they neared the hidden officers, Deputy Phillips called out to them, "Halt and identify yourselves." Each of the brothers immediately pulled his revolver and began shooting. One of their first shots struck Phillips in the head, inflicting a mortal wound. The gunfight continued until both Whitson and Waite Barnett had also been fatally injured. Leaving his lifeless brother behind along with the two dead officers, Wesley Barnett, the unscathed sole survivor, left the field of battle and returned to the dance.

Arriving back at the festivities, Wesley did not mention the deadly encounter to anyone. The merrymakers had not heard the shooting and were unaware of the violence that had preceded his return. A few minutes later, Wesley confronted one of the dancers, Bunny McIntosh, and accused him of setting up the ambush at the spring. Bunny was not cowed by the young renegade and when Barnett drew his pistol, he quickly grabbed the weapon. The one shot that Wesley was able to trigger grazed Bunny's arm and incited him to hold on desperately. Barnett was unable to extract his gun from the grip of the stronger man, and McIntosh gained control of the weapon. The disarmed, dejected outlaw immediately slunk away, into the darkness.

Wesley Barnett was not a character who would willingly accept the humiliation that he felt Bunny McIntosh had heaped upon him. After leaving the Saturday night gathering, he went to a house in the nearby vicinity and obtained a Winchester. With rifle in hand, Barnett returned to the dance for the purpose of accosting McIntosh. Upon his arrival at the gala event, he learned that the "hero of the night" Bunny McIntosh had been taken to his home in Eufaula. The rearmed and now brazen desperado commandeered a wagon and team, along with two men at the dance. Wesley directed the hostages to drive to the nearby spring. Flaunting the rifle, he ordered the men to load his brother's body into the wagon. Shortly before Sunday morning dawned, Wesley left his hostages at the site of the triple killing, where the two officers still lay, and began the journey that would be his brother's final trip home.

On Monday morning, July 2, 1888, Wesley drove the stolen conveyance to Okmulgee, where he purchased a burial outfit for his brother. The much-sought-after bandit encountered no lawmen in carrying out this errand into the Creek Capital. It is assumed that Waite was buried near whatever abode Wesley then called home.

Most everyone who was aware of the incident that occurred at the dance expected Barnett to go into Eufaula to settle the conflict that had developed from his encounter with Bunny McIntosh. However, this event did not come to pass. Even though deputies from the Fort Smith marshal's office, Creek Lighthorsemen, and tribal vigilantes searched for Barnett, they were unable to locate him. Wesley and his outlaw band continued to steal horses and sell whiskey. It appeared that his brother's death had made Wesley even more daring in skirting the law.

It had been rumored throughout the Creek Nation that Wesley would lead his gang into Okmulgee while the Tribal Council was in session. Most did not take the report seriously, never considering that he would undertake such a venture. In typical Barnett fashion the young hellion and his cohorts rode into Okmulgee, on Sunday evening, October 7, 1888. Shortly after the outlaw gang arrived at the Creek Capitol, they fired twenty-six bullets into the building, then rode away. Two days after this incident, the council authorized the appointment of a special ten-man police force to patrol and keep order in Okmulgee during the remainder of the session. The special force would be empowered with the same authority as the Creek Lighthorsemen, and each of the new officers would be issued warrants at the rate of two and a half dollars a day.

On November 8, 1888, a squad of thirty-five lighthorsemen departed from Okmulgee, heading north toward the location where Wesley Barnett and his rustlers were reported to be in

Creek Capitol Building, Creek Nation, Indian Territory, as it appeared on October 7, 1888, when the Barnett gang shelled it. (Photo courtesy of the Archives & Manuscripts Division of the Oklahoma Historical Society)

hiding. The following morning as they approached the suspected area, they divided their forces into three posses and began searching houses in the vicinity of Wealaka.

When the posse that was being led by Capt. Will Lerblance approached the home of Abe Carr, gunfire erupted from the house. During this initial barrage, Moses McIntosh was killed, and Captain Lerblance and another officer were wounded. This surprise attack and unexpected casualties forced the lighthorsemen to fall back. Tribal reinforcements soon arrived to support the posse. Gunfire by both forces continued throughout the day, with a mutual cessation falling over the area that night. When morning came, the tribal police found Carr's house vacant. Barnett had killed again, and as usual he was "long gone" when the lawmen arrived.

This escape of the outlaw gang raised questions about the

competence of the tribal lawmen. Abe Carr, owner of the home which had harbored Wesley Barnett and his gang, was believed to have been a friend and willing partner in the conspiracy and armed conflict. Holes and scars left by some four hundred bullets were plainly visible at Carr's splintered and badly damaged house, yet it could not be ascertained that any of the outlaws had been wounded during the numerous salvos of gunfire.

Moses McIntosh, who had been killed when the posse rode upon the outlaws, was a highly respected and well-educated young full-blood Creek who had recently been elected to the "House of Warriors" (one source relates that Moses and Bunny McIntosh were brothers). Moses was a member of the Creek Lighthorsemen, and at the time that he was killed, he was acting in the capacity of a deputy U.S. marshal. Therefore, his murder placed those responsible for his death under the jurisdiction of the Western District of Arkansas at Fort Smith, which was commonly referred to as "Judge Parker's Court."

Following the escape of the Barnett gang from Carr's cabin, a number of posses spread out across the Creek Nation in another attempt to bring the outlaws to justice. Two days after Moses McIntosh had been killed, a squad of lighthorsemen located Barnett and some of his rogues near Checotah. The ensuing gunfight resulted in four of the young renegades being captured by the tribal lawmen; however, their leader (Wesley) had again escaped. The four men were thought to have been with Barnett at Abe Carr's cabin when Moses was killed. The captives were identified as Joe Tulsa, Wan-saw-sa, Wiley Still, and Jimmy Larney. They were taken to Fort Smith to be charged with the murder of Moses McIntosh.

Wesley Barnett had gained such notoriety as a violator of the law that many suspected his involvement in every criminal act that occurred in the Creek Nation. For example, about a month after Wesley escaped the posse near Checotah, a young man carrying a rifle and keeping his hand on the butt of his holstered pistol walked into a store in Muskogee. He didn't speak, and after looking around, he left. The stranger entered other stores and preformed in a like manner. His ready weapons and lack of dialog prompted suspicion that he was Wesley Barnett, looking for another victim. Capt. Charles LaFlore of the Creek Lighthorsemen was in Muskogee at that time, and he was advised that "Barnett was stalking the town." Captain LaFlore, with three well-armed deputies, approached the suspect. The startled stranger quickly showed his badge and announced that his name was Childers. He promptly explained that he was a U.S. Indian police officer from Tulsa and named the man he was looking for.

In late December 1888, Col. C. M. McClellan's favorite saddle horse was stolen. McClellan was a prosperous stockman and prominent in the Creek tribe. He was renowned as being a fearless and honest citizen. Barnett's reputation immediately led him to become the prime suspect of this larceny. McClellan wrote to U.S. Marshal John Carroll at Fort Smith, requesting that a warrant for the arrest of Wesley Barnett be issued and sent to him. McClellan informed the marshal that if he received the warrant, he would soon have the return of his horse, or Wesley Barnett in custody, or both. Marshal Carroll issued and mailed the warrant.

In the early days of 1889, Deputy U.S. Marshal David V. Rusk was leading a posse in the central part of the Creek Nation, again attempting to apprehend Barnett. On Saturday evening, January 12, 1889, Rusk sent three members of his posse to spend the night at the home of John S. Porter, who lived five miles east of Okmulgee. About 10:00 P.M. the Porter household was alerted that riders were approaching. The three officers grabbed their weapons and rushed outside to hide in the shadows. Just as the deputies reached their chosen places of concealment, two riders leading a pair of horses arrived at the entrance to the homestead.

The two horsebackers paused at the gate and held a brief

conversation; then one of the riders continued toward the house while the other remained behind holding the two extra horses. When the mounted stranger approached close enough that Deputy U.S. Marshal Wallace McNac was able to confidently recognize him as Wesley Barnett, the hidden officer triggered his shouldered rifle. Barnett slid from the saddle, dead. The second rider, who was thought to be Willy Bear (Barnett's longtime ally), fired his pistol at the lawman, then spurred his mount and quickly rode away with the two unsaddled horses "trailing in his dust." The outlaw's death was reported on January 17, 1889, in the Creek Nation's major newspaper, the *Muskogee Phoenix,* which stated, "At last Wesley Barnett has been killed and we presume that the good people in Creek Nation will breathe easier. It looks a little hard to shoot a man down in cold blood, but, when one considers the numerous bloody crimes that Barnett has committed, and the fact that he could be taken no other way, we should, one and all, praise Deputy McNac for ridding the country of this desperado." And so while still a teenager, Wesley Barnett, the "Terror of the Creek Nation," met his doom.

CHAPTER 2

The Devious Outlaw Career of Bob Rogers

The last decade of the nineteenth century is frequently referred to as "the gay nineties." That implied carefree attitude might be an appropriate general image of that era, but it is not a fitting memory of the aura that existed in the Cherokee Nation at that time. A more somber mood prevailed, due in part to the high incidence of criminal activity that plagued the area during that period. As the nineteenth century approached its final years, native sons added to the problems of the bedeviled Cherokee Nation.

Among those who developed their own outlaw career in their homeland during that epoch were Bill Cook, Ned Christie, Henry Starr, and Crawford "Cherokee Bill" Goldsby. The Dalton brothers, who had lived in the region for some time while growing up, returned and demonstrated their expertise at robbing trains. This cast of local talent was augmented when Frank Rogers with his three sons moved into the Cherokee Nation.

The Rogers family had lived in Benton and Washington counties of Arkansas prior to settling on Big Creek, near Horseshoe Mound. Bob, the oldest of Frank's sons, is thought to have been born in 1873, followed by Sam about two years later, then Jim two years after Sam. Each of the Rogers boys was destined to try his hand in the outlaw world.

Shortly after Frank Rogers moved his family into the Cherokee Nation, Bob started working for ranchers in the vicinity of Nowata. The earliest record of Bob Rogers's "breaking the law" came on November 10, 1891, when he was arrested by Deputy U.S. Marshal Bynum Colbert. Deputy Colbert delivered young Rogers to Fort Smith, where he was charged with assault with intent to kill. Neither the intended victim nor the circumstance of the crime is now known. Bob was released on bond within a few days.

At that time, the Dalton gang was at the apex of their successful criminal activities and attracted the attention of Frank Rogers's oldest son. He developed an admiration for the gang's leader and seemed to consider that they had more in common than mere first names. The young ranch hand was greatly impressed with the Dalton gang's reputation and reports of their big-money train robberies.

Upon returning to the Cherokee Nation after being released from the assault charge at Fort Smith, Bob Rogers began to attract others of his age and disposition. Within a few months he had assembled a gang to follow him into his chosen career. Seeking a more exciting life than the one they could foresee in their present roles, Bob Stiteler, Willis Brown, "Dynamite Jack" Turner, and his brother "Kiowa" Turner joined Rogers. The quintet then set forth to seek their fortune on the foul side of the law. Bob's younger brother Sam and a Ralph Halleck later joined the outlaw band.

The Rogers gang's first encounter with the law was in the summer of 1892. The illegal act may have been committed to emulate one of the first crimes that Bob Dalton was charged with: larceny of horses. Rogers and his recruits were suspected of stealing some horses in the Cherokee Nation and selling them in Arkansas. Deputy U.S. Marshal Hickman "Heck" Bruner, with a posse, arrested the five young men and escorted them to Fort Smith. The Rogers gang was to be charged with the theft, but for some unknown reason, the case was dismissed.

Judge Isaac C. Parker gave the errant boys a stern lecture and strongly advised them to mend their ways. The judge warned Rogers, in particular, that death would result if he continued his current course.

Upon being released of the charges at Fort Smith, Bob Rogers again returned to the Cherokee Nation. He then went to work for Jim Dougherty on a ranch near Catoosa. Whatever deterrent from his past and inspiration to alter his future that Judge Parker might have instilled in the youth was apparently soon forgotten.

Deputy Constable Jess W. Elliott of the Cherokee Indian Police was a forty-year-old part-Cherokee from Vinita. He was also an attorney and had practiced law for ten years, in both the Cherokee and the U.S. courts. Deputy Elliott was dispatched on the morning of Tuesday, November 3, 1892, to serve some legal papers at Catoosa. After arriving at his destination in the afternoon, Elliott and Bob Rogers got into a confrontation in the town's pool hall.

It was reported that both men were drunk when they started to argue over some unknown point of conversation. Words soon escalated to violence, and Rogers knocked Elliott to the floor and began beating him unmercifully. Bystanders pulled the young ranch hand from Elliott and hustled him outside. Deputy Elliott was detained until he revived. When Elliott recovered and felt able, he got on his horse and rode out of town.

He had ridden only a short distance from Catoosa when Rogers jumped from his hiding place by the side of the road. Rogers grabbed the horse's reins, pulled the startled constable from the saddle, and wrestled the older man to the ground. Rogers pulled a knife and slit Elliott's throat, leaving the bleeding man by the side of the road. An approaching traveler saw Rogers leaving the scene. Arriving at the site, the witness saw Elliott in the throes of death. Unable to forestall the inevitable, the traveler watched Elliott die moments later.

A dispatch was sent to Deputy U.S. Marshal John Taylor, who was also a Cherokee police officer, requesting his presence. Dr. Warren and some of the neighbors planned to watch the body until Taylor arrived. Shortly after dark, Bob Rogers returned to the scene of the crime and rode amid the group. He jumped his horse over the fire and scared away those who were present. As the frightened attendants ran from the site, Rogers leaped from his mount and pounced upon the corpse.

Those who had fled and paused in the darkness to observe the spectacle of the morbid murderer witnessed the gruesome performance of an obvious maniac. Their eyes filled with disbelief as they watched Rogers kick and stomp his victim. He then put on Elliott's hat while searching the dead man's pockets and looking through the papers that he found. The demented killer left the constable's desecrated remains shortly before Deputy John Taylor arrived and took charge of the body.

Officers trailed Bob Rogers to Sapulpa, and learned at a blacksmith shop that he had ridden in Saturday morning and had his horse shod. Bob had tauntingly left word for his pursuers with the farrier "that he was going west." The mutilated body of Constable Elliott was returned to Vinita on Saturday. Those who saw his remains related that even more grotesque than the three grisly gashes that slit his throat, was the victim's disfigured head and torso. His swollen face was badly bruised and severely cut from Rogers's stomping boot heels and jutting spurs. Jess Elliott left a wife and children. He was laid to rest in a small cemetery a few miles south of Vinita, where several members of his family had been buried.

Bob Rogers kept a low profile until Friday, June 30, 1893. Shortly after J. F. Tibbs, the Frisco railway agent at Chelsea, returned to work his evening shift, the Rogers gang rode to the depot. A couple of the young renegades dismounted and entered the station, as the others remained with the horses and maintained surveillance of the area. The two well-armed

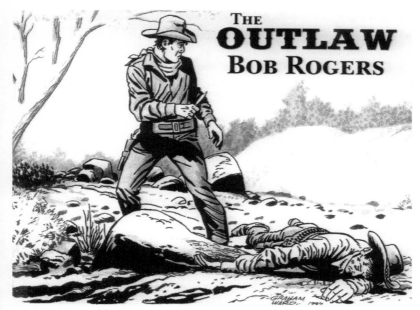

Rogers pulled a knife and slit Elliott's throat, leaving the bleeding man by the side of the road. (Illustration by permission of *True West* magazine)

bandits forced the agent to open the safe, making off with $418.

A few days later the gang hit the railroad depot at Bluejacket. Using the same plan as before, they encountered no problems in robbing the station safe. Within a few minutes, the gang escaped with the booty.

These successful robberies prompted Bob Rogers to seek a more ambitious goal. He led his renegades into southern Kansas where they robbed the bank at Mound Valley, on Thursday, July 13, 1893. Three members of the gang entered the bank at noon, when only cashier J. O. Wilson was present. The cashier was bound and gagged by the armed trio, who then removed some eight hundred dollars from the money drawer. After a quick, but unsuccessful search for more money the robbers left the bank. Wilson was unable to free himself for several minutes, which permitted the outlaw band to get well out of town by the time he could sound the alarm.

The bandits were last seen riding toward Indian Territory, only fourteen miles away. Henry Starr and his desperadoes were suspects in the Mound Valley Bank robbery as were the Rogers and Wooten gangs. Each of the three outlaw bands nested in the Cherokee Nation.

Following the heist of the Kansas bank, lawmen throughout the Cherokee Nation were on the lookout for the robbers. Deputy U.S. Marshal Heck Bruner and his brother Wood Bruner along with "Dink" Douthitt located a house on the George Harlan farm a few miles west of Vinita. They believed the outlaws had made their rendezvous at the location. On Saturday, July 29, Heck Bruner and his two deputies secreted themselves on the premises and waited for the suspects to return. Late in the evening, the gang began to converge on the area. The first to arrive were two young men who rode to the house. The officers stepped from hiding, identified themselves, and called for the suspects to surrender. When the young men ignored the officers' orders and attempted to use their rifles as they tried to get away, the posse opened fire.

Both of the suspects were shot and their horses killed by the lawmen. The other members of the gang fled the area, leaving their companions behind. Ralph Halleck had been shot through the breast and died within minutes. When notified of his death, the outlaw's wife declined to take any action for his burial. Halleck's companion, Sam Rogers, was badly wounded in the hip.

Sam was arrested and taken to Fort Smith. J. O. Wilson, the cashier from the recently robbed Kansas bank, could not identify Sam as one of the robbers. Sam was held on charges of stealing horses from two farmers near Lenapah on July 12. He was also charged with assault with intent to kill on the three lawmen in the altercation near Vinita. He was tried in August

1893 and found not guilty of the assault charge as it pertained to the Bruner brothers, but he was convicted of assault with intent to kill in regard to Dink Douthitt. Sam's hip wound was considered a permanent handicap, and he was released on bond in late August 1893 to await sentencing.

During the late afternoon of December 22, 1893, the Rogers gang attempted to rob a Missouri, Kansas & Texas train near Kelso, five miles north of Vinita. The five outlaws used an axe to cut the staple that secured the locking switch, then set the track to divert the train onto a siding. When the southbound train arrived a few minutes later, the engineer was greeted with gunshots as the train was sent down the alternate track.

Knowing that the junction was equipped with a "split switch" and that there were no cars on the railings, the engineer sped the train through the siding and returned to the main track. Despite the engineer's quick thinking and prompt reaction, the crew suffered one casualty during the gang's foiled attempt.

Charles Milne, the fireman, had been hit by one of the bandit's bullets. The projectile had struck him in the face and tore away part of his jaw. Milne was taken aboard the next train and returned to his home in Parsons, Kansas. In October 1894, Milne was sent to New York City, where his jaw was to be reconstructed.

As darkness closed in on Christmas Eve, the Rogers gang struck again. On this occasion they hit an Arkansas Valley passenger train at Seminole Switch, a few miles south of Coffeyville, Kansas. Having recently learned a lesson about train robbery, the outlaws chose a site that had railroad cars parked on the siding, then threw the switch.

Within a few minutes the expected southbound train arrived. As it braked to a stop, one of the bandits took charge of the engineer and fireman. The other four went through the train, and while keeping up a fusillade to intimidate the passengers and crew, stole everything of value. They commandeered the express money and mail, then robbed the passengers of money, jewelry, watches, overcoats, and pocketknives. After about an hour and a half, they permitted the train to resume its journey to Fort Smith.

Bob Rogers had refused to let his younger brother Jim ride with the gang. On December 30, 1893, Jim recruited an older neighbor boy, Carmie Riverburg, and they began their own careers of crime. With Jim as the leader, the two novices held up the post office and store at Hayden, ten miles east of Nowata. Postmaster Henry C. Hayden and customers Harry Still and Alanzo Mauley were robbed by the gun-wielding Jim Rogers and his cohort.

Later, Frank Rogers located his teenage son and Riverburg, then delivered the wayward pair to the officials at Fort Smith, where they were charged with the robbery. Each was tried and convicted in April 1894. Jim was sentenced to three years in a District of Columbia reform school, and Carmie Riverburg was to serve four years in prison.

Shortly before midnight on Monday, January 8, 1894, a posse led by Deputy U.S. Marshal William C. "Bill" Smith found Bob Rogers and Bob Stiteler at the home of Henry Daniels, Rogers's brother-in-law. The officers burst into the house and found the outlaw leader sitting alone, barefoot, in front of the fireplace. The officers learned that Stiteler was in an upstairs bedroom. Daniels was ordered to go and bring him down, which he did. When the "wanted men" were dressed, and the posse was preparing to take them away, Rogers knocked down one of the deputies, and the two outlaws attempted to make a break. Rogers escaped into the darkness, but Stiteler failed to get away. Deputy Smith transported Stiteler to the Fort Smith jail. Seven indictments were filed against Stiteler, and he went to trial in April 1894. He was convicted and sentenced to three years in prison, two of which were to be at hard labor.

Some two weeks after the encounter at the home of Henry

Daniels, Deputy Marshals Heck Bruner, Bill Smith, and Charley Copeland, a postal inspector and railroad detective, located Bob Rogers and the remaining three members of his gang. The Bruner posse found the outlaws at the home of Frank Rogers on Tuesday morning January 23, 1894. Frank advised the officers that Bob and his friends had been drinking heavily the night before and were soundly asleep. Thinking that they might disarm and secure the four young hellions before they awoke, the lawmen silently crept to the upstairs room with Bruner carrying the lantern, leading the way.

Kiowa Turner, who was sharing a bed with Willis Brown, had apparently been aroused by the commotion. He opened fire as the lawmen approached. The officers returned the fire at the pair, as Brown was attempting to bring his weapon into play when the lantern's flame flickered out. The posse's bullets struck Kiowa in the head and heart, killing him instantly. Brown was also hit twice, which rendered him unable to use his gun. The officers then arrested the wounded Willis Brown along with Bob Rogers and Dynamite Jack. Although the latter two were in the room where the shooting occurred, neither had fired a shot.

The posse took the dead outlaw and their three captives to Vinita, where the wounds of Willis Brown were tended. Brown responded well to the doctor's treatment and appeared to be strong enough to travel. A few hours after their arrival at Vinita, the three prisoners were put aboard a train destined for Fort Smith.

The body of Kiowa Turner was left at Vinita pending confirmation of identity and authority to release the body. His parents, who lived at Eureka, Kansas, were notified of his death. The Turners responded but did not come to claim their son's remains. The parents only requested that he be given decent burial. On Sunday, January 28, 1894, their request was carried out at Vinita.

Shortly after delivery to Fort Smith, the wounded Willis Brown took a turn for the worse. As death drew near, he confessed to his role in numerous crimes. Brown admitted participating in robbing the railroad stations at Chelsea and Bluejacket, the Mound Valley bank robbery, attacking the train at Kelso, and the train robbery at Seminole. Five days after the prisoner had been taken to Fort Smith, his body was released to his parents, who lived near Chelsea.

The same day that Kiowa Turner was buried, and the body of Willis Brown was returned, Bob Rogers also arrived at Vinita. Rogers had been bailed out of the Fort Smith jail on an eight-thousand-dollar bond, which was reported to have been provided by an uncle, Robert W. Rogers, who lived in Arkansas. Soon after Rogers came back from Fort Smith, a rumor circulated throughout the area that Bob's quick discharge from jail was only a part of a deal that the outlaw leader had negotiated. The common talk developed into a generally held opinion that Rogers had betrayed his confederates. In return, he was to receive a portion of the reward money and immunity from the charges pending against him.

The label of a traitor became firmly affixed to the name of Bob Rogers. Having never been popular in the Cherokee Nation, he was now considered to be the absolute scum of the earth. Although robbery was not condoned by the populace of Cherokee Nation, it was thought to be a noble deed when compared to the dastardly act of betraying one's own followers.

Dynamite Jack was being held in the Fort Smith jail when Bob Rogers was freed. He was indicted on seven counts of larceny and was tried in April 1894. Dynamite Jack Turner was found guilty as charged and was sentenced to fifteen years in prison, five of which were to be at hard labor.

For some time after his release, it appeared that Bob was no longer an active outlaw; instead he was living off his ill-gotten share of the bounties. In October 1894, it was reported that the charges pending against Rogers had been nullified by the attorney general at Fort Smith. It was then rumored that Rogers had been commissioned as a deputy.

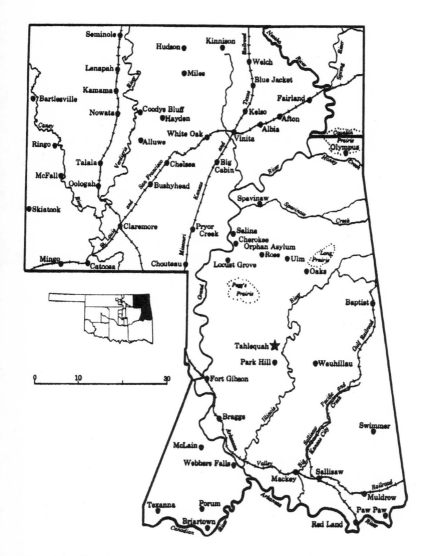

Map of the Cherokee Nation, Indian Territory, showing the major settlements, circa 1890. (Author's collection)

Within a few months it was believed that Bob had spent his portion of the reward money, and he became suspected of stealing cattle. This rumored cattle rustling operation, in the northern part of the Cherokee Nation, extended into Montgomery County of southern Kansas. It was thought that Rogers disposed of the stolen beef in the town of Edna.

In late February 1895, an arrest warrant was requested by Deputy U.S. Marshal "Ike" Rogers against Bob Rogers for introducing and selling whiskey in the Cherokee Nation. The deputy reported that Bob Rogers had sold six gallons of whiskey to a John Pascal and a Will Swain on February 17, 1895.

Deputy U.S. Marshal E. D. Jackson of Nowata requested a warrant from Marshal George J. Crump at Fort Smith, for the arrest of Bob Rogers and a Bill Elmore. The charge was robbery of C. W. Adams on February 27, 1895. The victim reported that the pair had held him up for four dollars.

A few days later, Deputy U.S. Marshal A. I. Laudis, at Bartlesville, requested a writ from Marshal Crump for Bob Rogers and an unknown accomplice. The charge was highway robbery of three dollars from a William Wiley on March 7, 1895. While these suspected crimes were being reported by the deputy marshals, there had been another raid on cattle in the area. Rogers was again the prime suspect.

The citizens of the community believed that Rogers had betrayed his own companions to gain favor for himself, and they became disgusted with the law and its lack of justice. They were gravely aware that three of the men who had ridden the outlaw trail with Bob Rogers had been killed by officers and two were doing time in prison. The other man, his brother Sam, was crippled for life. Only Bob Rogers, the perfidious leader of the gang, had escaped unblemished and unpunished.

The disdain that the people had developed for Rogers and their anger at the recent cattle thefts prompted the citizenry to take action. Deputy U.S. Marshal Jim Mayes was also a member of the local Anti-Horse Thief Association. He became the leader of a group of citizens intent on stopping Bob Rogers.

Members of the association watched Frank Rogers's place, hoping to spot the son returning home. On the evening of March 14, 1895, Bob was sighted near Horseshoe Mound, riding toward his father's house. The next morning, Deputy Mayes led a dozen men through the darkness toward the Rogers place. After placing several men around the home, Mayes knocked on the door and advised Frank that the place was surrounded.

Frank went upstairs to advise his son to surrender. As the elder Rogers returned to the lower floor, Bob defiantly opened fire from his position. In reply, the posse commenced shelling the upstairs. After some two hundred rounds had been fired, Deputy Mayes halted the shooting.

When they could get no response from Rogers, three of the posse volunteered to enter the house and investigate. W. D. McDaniel led the way, followed by Phil Williams and C. E. Smith. As the trio reached the top of the stairs, Bob Rogers, lying in wait, triggered his weapon. His first shot hit McDaniel in the heart, killing him instantly. Bob's second shot tore through Williams's right arm, knocking him and Smith down the stairwell. When Williams and Smith ran from the house and reported the fate of McDaniels, the posse unleashed another barrage on the house. This volley continued for several minutes, pumping hundreds of rounds into the structure. Mayes again halted the shooting and yelled to Bob to surrender. The lone gunman agreed to come out, if allowed to keep his rifle. Bob was advised that he could bring his rifle, if he kept the muzzle down.

Within a few moments Bob Rogers emerged through the doorway, carrying the lowered rifle. Standing on the porch in the semidarkness, he appeared to be unscathed in contrast to the splintered house. With but slight hesitation and seemingly undaunted Bob began walking slowly into the yard toward Jim Mayes. As he approached, brief words were exchanged between Rogers and Mayes. Suddenly, the rising movement of Bob's rifle was detected in the dawn's dim light of Friday, March 15, 1895. Immediately, several bullets struck Bob Rogers, and he fell upon the ground, dead.

A March 21, 1895, article in *The Indian Chieftain,* Vinita's newspaper, reported: "There may be regrets among the officers of the government at Ft. Smith and also in the post office inspector's office at St. Louis, because of the killing of this miscreant, but the good people of the territory will say 'amen'. Rogers was the leader and organizer of as blood-thirsty lot of cut-throats as were ever banded together in this country and in compromising with him, permitting him to betray them into the officers hands in exchange for immunity, the authorities were guilty of one of the most reprehensible acts ever perpetrated upon a decent community."

Bob Rogers' tombstone. (Author's collection)

During the last four years, Bob Rogers had been accused of murder, train robbery, bank robbery, assault with intent to kill, horse theft, cattle rustling, and numerous other felonious acts. In spite of being arrested and jailed several times for many violations of the law, there is no record that he was ever tried or convicted on any charge. Bob's sway with the officials had set him apart from all others. The outlaw leader had manipulated and had never been held accountable for his crimes. The source that provided the series of elusive events that had prolonged his life as an outlaw had also instilled the wrath that caused his death.

The posse that did away with Bob Rogers had no warrant for his arrest, nor is there any evidence that they requested one. The demise of the devious outlaw came at the hands of a group of dedicated men who responded to the situation to see that justice prevailed.

CHAPTER 3

"No Heroes Were There"

Everyone has heard the statement, "Truth is often stranger than fiction." Sometimes actual history reveals more colorful names, places, and sordid events than an author of a novel could realistically expect his readers to accept. I believe that the following true story is an example of such paradoxes.

During the twenty years following the Civil War, millions of longhorn cattle were driven from Texas, across Indian Territory, into Kansas. As the cattle drives became impeded by an increasing number of settlers along the trail, the railroads extended their lines to other locations, and new trails were established. Some of these Kansas cow towns like Abilene, Ellsworth, Newton, and Wichita lasted only one year as the destination of the many large herds.

The citizens of these towns did not expect cowboys after long cattle drives to be exactly mild-mannered guests, and they proved to be neither mild nor mannered. The towns soon realized that even a worse problem was the saloons, gambling halls, and brothels that were established to cater to and take advantage of the cattlemen during their few days in town. After one or two years, the townspeople were glad to see these businesses move on. Those who profited by offering whatever they had found to attract the cowboys moved to each new cow town in order to continue operating.

Dodge City was the last of these so-called Kansas cow towns. It remained the shipping point of the Texas longhorns—longer than any previous sites. Perhaps this was partly because Dodge had been founded as a buffalo hunters' supply post. The coming of trail drives at the time that buffalo hunting faded out caused no major change in the local environment. Dodge continued to be the "Cowboy Capital" until it became more feasible to ship the cattle from Texas than to push them through the trail to Kansas.

Another factor appeared at about this same time. Due to the new restrictions on prostitution and enforcement of the state prohibition laws, many of the denizens found that Dodge no longer provided for their livelihood or catered to their desired lifestyle. As law enforcement and respectability began to prevail in each of the previous places, moving on had become a way of life for the gamblers, con artists, booze bums, and wild women. But after Dodge there was no new cow town to move to. Civilization had crowded them out of their way of life. What could this covey of rowdies do to continue their desired constant wild party? The solution was simple—they would build their own town, some place where the law would not interfere.

South of western Kansas was the ideal location, in what was then known as "No Man's Land." For forty years this five-thousand-square-mile area (that is now the Oklahoma Panhandle) was not attached to any state or territory. Therefore, there had been no attempt by anyone to enforce any law. The riffraff of Dodge congregated at their selected site to build their new "Sin Capital."

This "Paradise of the Promiscuous" was first known as White City, since it was built entirely of tents. Later, as some frame structures were built, it became known as Beer City because of the huge stacks of empty beer kegs behind each of the saloons. Two of the more prominent saloons were the Pink Elephant and the Yellow Snake. Beer City soon became the headquarters of a few hundred lazy cowboys, bartenders, gamblers, shady ladies, and other misfits who were attracted to an environment completely devoid of law. The town had no school, church, or even a post office, but it is doubtful that anyone noticed, as there were few if any children, a church would have been unused, and most of the town's citizens had long before lost contact with anyone in the outside world.

Lewis "Brushy" Bush, a local cowboy who frequently bragged of being a cattle rustler and man-killer, was an enthusiastic customer of this oasis on the prairie. He was accepted as a man ready, willing, and able to fight with gun or knife, anyone at any time for any reason. Brushy Bush was smitten with the fast life offered at Beer City; however, he could not finance total devotion to his pleasure. He fancied himself capable of being more than a small-time cattle thief, and saw the opportunity to do so at this "Sin City." To afford his desire for continuous carousal, he decided to establish himself as city marshal. Knowing there were legal bases for the position, and no salary, he schemed that he would just assess each business a fee, and was willing to accept most of the remuneration in commodities and trade.

Beer City, No Man's Land. This prairie haven of rest and relaxation for the cowboys of the Oklahoma and Texas Panhandles was called "The Sodom and Gommorah of the Plains." Lew Bush, the town marshal, who was later shotgunned to death by Madam Pussy Cat Nell, sits next to the standing fiddler. Photo taken in front of The Elephant Saloon on June 25, 1888. (Photo courtesy of Western History Collections, University of Oklahoma Libraries)

Another of the industrious residents of Beer City was "Pussy Cat Nell." The proper name for this "lady of the evening" has been lost to history. Only her moniker has been retained. It is assumed that she was a veteran of other cow town entertainment centers and had reached the position of "Madam" through in-house promotion.

When Brushy Bush pinned on his fake tin star, the booze business was booming, and the barkeepers did not object to passing him a few free beers. Meals were obtained with similar apathy. That was not the reception that he received at Pussy's Cat House, when he demanded his desired recompense. In Nell's parlor, where time was money, and patrons were waiting, his gratuity was granted, but not graciously.

That was the initial conflict between the pretend marshal and the perky madam, but it was not to be the last. The self-appointed officer very quickly wore out the reluctant, slight welcome that he had originally received from his other prey. His victims wanted to stop his shakedown operation, but no one was willing to chance the result by refusing his demands.

When Brushy Bush started collecting his booty, many of the people were excitedly looking forward to the upcoming celebration that they had planned for the Fourth of July. They had arranged for a "Prize Fight" to be held in Beer City on that date. In anticipation of the big event, many of the locals were placing bets on which of the combatants would win.

Pussy Cat Nell placed a large wager on her choice and deposited the money with one of the local bartenders who were acting in that capacity. During the morning of the big day, Brushy decided that in his official position he was the proper authority to hold the stakes, which would entitle him to a percentage of all bets.

Needless to say, this new service of Bush's was not appreciated by Pussy Cat Nell. When she found out about it, after the fight, she sallied forth and confronted her antagonist. Her tirade was unwelcome by the man wearing the "star." He answered her rage by a blow across her face with his pistol, then reminded her that he was "Boss of Beer City." The shocked and stunned woman scurried to her boudoir above the Yellow Snake Saloon. A cold and calculating vengeance consumed her as she noted her reflection in the mirror. The toil and torment of her trade had deteriorated her never very attractive face that was now bashed and bloody. Through the window she saw the despised man in the street below, facing another direction. In her fury, she grabbed a double-barreled shotgun, pointed it out the window, and pulled both triggers.

The recoil of the dual blasts knocked the mad madam from her feet, and she did not see the result. As she tried to regain her posture and wits, to comprehend the situation, she heard shots being fired in the street. Fearing that she had missed, she assumed that Bush was shooting at her. When she realized that there were no bullets hitting her room, she bravely raised her body. A sneak peak at the window's edge revealed that several of the local gents were standing around the downed "marshal" firing point-blank into his helpless body. Many of the cowards, now anxious and ruthless, stepped forward and "shot it out" with the dead Bush.

The bullet-riddled remnants of Lewis Bush were buried at the end of one of the town's unnamed streets. His short tenure as the self-appointed city marshal was over. And, soon thereafter, Beer City wallowed itself into oblivion, leaving only sad stories and piles of rubbish.

There are now several fine homes just south of Liberal, Kansas, where once stood the Pink Elephant, the Yellow Snake, and other thriving enterprises, but there is no marker to the memory of the "Sin Capital of the High Plains," nor to its make-believe marshal.

It was a large crowd of men that gathered at Beer City on July 4, 1888, and surely it would be unfair to say that none of them was without some merit, but it does seem fair to say, "No heroes were there."

CHAPTER 4

Massacre at Wild Horse Lake

When the West was being settled, there were many personal conflicts and acts of mob violence. Some of these disputes were caused by occupational discord such as occurred between cattle ranchers and sheep men. Others were family feuds that were brought on by actual misdeeds, or sometimes ignited by mere fancied insults. None of these disagreements were more divisive or intensely fought than the so-called county seat wars. One such tragic conflict was the Stevens County Seat War, which erupted in southwestern Kansas but spread outside of the state into what is now Oklahoma.

By 1885, several hardy families had taken land in this plain, semiarid region, and many of them desired to organize the area into a county. Some of these early settlers had previously known each other when they resided in the vicinity of McPhearson, Kansas. These former acquaintances became the core of the initial group to promote county status. The Cook brothers, C. E. and Orin, were the leaders of these enthusiastic citizens, and the Cooks had established a small town in the midst of their claims, which they called Hugoton. At the time that these former friends from McPhearson started the campaign to be designated as a county, Hugoton was the only town in the area, and it was assumed that the little settlement would become the county seat.

While the Cook brothers and their followers were maneuvering (including taking a census) to get Stevens authorized as a county and Hugoton named as the county seat, another faction of settlers began a competitive course. Samuel "Sam" N. Wood and I. C. Price of Meade, Kansas, started another town, Woodsdale, eight miles northeast of Hugoton. Wood and Price aspired that their new town could overtake Hugoton, and they could get it named as the county seat. A third village, Vorhees, emerged south of Hugoton, but it was never considered to be a contender for the county seat.

To overcome the edge that Hugoton held from its earlier inception, the founders of Woodsdale offered "free city lots" to anyone who would build immediately. This enticement started a boom in Woodsdale and prompted a very heated contest between the two towns to be selected as the county seat. However; when Stevens County was established in 1886, Hugoton was named the interim county seat.

Following that announcement, conflict between the two towns escalated, as each sought to become the permanent county seat. Sam Wood had served as a colonel in a Kansas regiment during the Civil War, and later he was still being referred to by that title. In the spring of 1887, while Colonel Wood and I. C. Price were traveling to Topeka to file a protest over the census figures that had been submitted for the county, they were taken into custody by a group of men from Hugoton.

The two prisoners were brought back to the interim Stevens County seat and placed on trial. Wood and Price were found guilty and were sentenced to accompany the posse on a buffalo hunt into "No Man's Land" (a tract of more than five thousand square miles of land that lay just south of Stevens County and which was not assigned to any state or territory. The area is presently known as the Oklahoma Panhandle).

The sentences imposed on the Woodsdale men appeared to be strange, and the purpose of the hunt raised suspicions, as there had been no buffalo herds found in that area in recent

Col. Sam Wood. (Author's collection)

years. When the Woodsdale people became aware that their two leading citizens had been taken away under such pretenses, they assumed that Wood and Price were destined to become victims of an intentional hunting accident.

S. O. Aubrey, a veteran Indian scout, took charge of the twenty-four Woodsdale men who volunteered to go into No Man's Land (aka The Neutral Strip) and rescue Wood and Price. Aubrey and his men not only succeeded in recovering their leaders, they also forced the Hugoton men to accompany them to Garden City, Kansas. At Garden City, Aubrey had the Hugoton party charged with kidnapping. These charges were later transferred to the new Stevens County, and the trial was scheduled to be held in a Hugoton church, which also served as the first county courthouse. The trial was held in the fall of 1887. As expected, those tried (all were from Hugoton) were found not guilty.

One of the main leaders in Hugoton during that period was a Sam Robinson, who was reported to be an experienced troublemaker from Kentucky. He had previously been attracted to Woodsdale because of the offer of "free city lots," and he had built a hotel there. Robinson had hopes of becoming the Stevens County sheriff, but when Sam Wood refused to endorse him for that position, he become irate at the founder and his town. Robinson sold his hotel and moved to Hugoton. Colonel Wood and Woodsdale strongly supported J. M. Cross for county sheriff, and he was elected. Cross maintained his county sheriff's office in Woodsdale, in defiance of Hugoton's having been named the interim county seat.

Sam Robinson's animosity toward Woodsdale immediately made him a popular figure in Hugoton, and he was elected to be the city marshal of the county seat. The intense bitterness that had been displayed in the county sheriff's race had set the stage for further troubles to develop between these two officers of the law.

Early in 1888, Stevens County issued bonds to attract rail-

Sam Robinson. (Author's collection)

road development in the area. Robinson was accused of over-stepping his authority in processing the county certificates, and a warrant was issued for his arrest. When Sheriff Cross (along with others, including Ed Short, city marshal of Woodsdale) attempted to serve that warrant in Hugoton, some shots were fired. Several of Robinson's supporters joined him in defiance of the order, and their interference prevented his arrest. After this foiled attempt to arrest their city marshal, the citizens of Hugoton prepared for an assault on their town. They dug trenches and erected barricades at the approaches where they expected the Woodsdale men to attack. Anxiety ran high as each side anticipated a showdown, but no further attempt was made to arrest Robinson for some time.

In July 1888, it was learned that Robinson, with his family and some friends, had gone into The Neutral Strip for an extended trip to camp out, fish, and pick wild plums. Woodsdale City Marshal Ed Short was selected to lead a posse and arrest Robinson while he was without the alliance of his Hugoton supporters. When Short and his posse located the picnicking party, Robinson was not with the others. Ed Short then sent word back to Woodsdale that he would continue the search for Robinson, but he needed more men.

Robinson had become aware of Short's approaching posse, and to preclude an inevitable gunfight in which women and children would be in danger, he had decided to leave his family with their friends where they had set up camp on Goff Creek. He headed for Hugoton, and was making good time, because he was aware that Short and his men were on his trail.

Upon receiving the message from Ed Short, Stevens County sheriff Cross recruited Ted Eaton, Bob Hubbard, Roland Wilcox, and Herbert Tooney to assist him. The sheriff and the four young men departed from Woodsdale to join City Marshal Short and his posse in their quest to locate and arrest Robinson. Sheriff Cross and his men traveled south to Reed's camp on Goff Creek, from where Short had sent his dispatch requesting assistance. When Cross and his men arrived, Reed told them that Short had departed and had left word with him to advise the posse to return to Woodsdale.

As Robinson (being trailed by Ed Short and his squad) neared the Stevens County seat, he met a band of Hugoton men who were headed south to locate and help their city marshal, after learning that Short and posse had been sent from Woodsdale to arrest him. Shortly after Robinson met this group of supporters, they took chase following Short and his posse. During the ensuing running gun battle in which no one was injured, the Hugoton posse chased Short and his men back to Woodsdale, where the shooting ceased and the chase ended.

Some of the Hugoton men were aware that Sheriff Cross had left Woodsdale and was leading a posse into No Man's Land to join Short and his men. With Robinson now leading the posse that had just chased Ed Short and his men back to Woodsdale (a rather cowardly appearing retreat), the Hugoton squad quickly decided to proceed south and try to locate Sheriff Cross's posse and attack them while they were outside of Stevens County. Some of the men in the Hugoton posse obtained fresh mounts for the journey, but others continued on, riding their somewhat jaded horses.

After Sheriff Cross and his posse had rested a while at Reed's camp, they started the return trip to Woodsdale. In the evening, they came upon a work crew, consisting of A. B. Haas, his two sons, and a friend named Dave Scott. Haas and his men were gathering hay and had setup camp at a site that was locally known as Wild Horse Lake (reported to be twelve miles west of present-day Hooker, Oklahoma). The name had originated from the wild horses that had previously roamed the area and the water that had gathered in the low-lying site during the rainy season. As the typical summer would progress, the so-called lake would dry up, leaving the locale covered with lush grass that grew from the well-watered sod. The site that had been known as "Wild Horse Lake" in the spring and early summer became

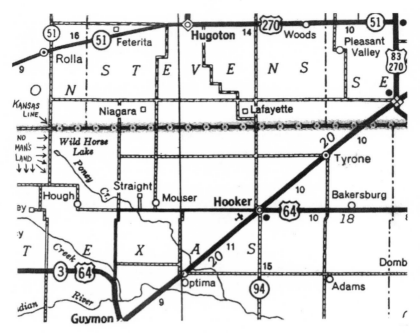

Map of Texas County, Oklahoma, and the Neutral Strip, or "No Man's Land." (Author's collection)

commonly refereed to as "the hay meadow" as the hay was reaped during the hot dry summer months. The Cross posse decided to spend the night in camp with the Haas haying crew and would continue their return trip to Woodsdale come morning.

Not long after Cross and his men had settled in for the night, Robinson and his band of men arrived at the Haas camp and abruptly awakened the lot. The Cross posse had not expected any trouble during the night, and only one or two of the men were able to reach a gun, but seeing that they were outnumbered they did not fire. All weapons were taken from Sheriff Cross and his men, as they were brought forth and assembled before Sam Robinson. The Hugoton city marshal and his posse held the five disarmed men from Woodsdale at gunpoint, near two of the haystacks in the meadow.

It is reported that as Robinson slowly raised his rifle he said, "Sheriff Cross, you are my first man," and coldly pulled the trigger. After killing the sheriff, Robinson and his men fired their guns point-blank into each of the unarmed Woodsdale posse. Hubbard was the second of the men to be executed, then Tooney, followed by Eaton and Wilcox. After the men had been gunned down, matches were lit and held to their faces to confirm their death. Some of the victims were shot a second time. When confident that all of the Woodsdale men were dead, Robinson and his posse escorted the Haas haying crew away, leaving only the bodies of Sheriff Cross and his four men as they had fallen.

Tooney had been shot through the neck but was still alive. He had feigned death so well that he had not been shot again. After he was confident that all had left, he began to move about and check his companions, but found no sign of life. Tooney slowly made his way to his staked horse and with great effort mounted the animal.

After riding a few miles, the wounded man came upon an old "buffalo wallow." His desperate condition prompted him to dismount and lie down in the muck. A few minutes in the sludge renewed his hope to survive. Tooney got back on his horse and continued riding north.

Shortly after daylight the next morning, the wounded man met a rider on the trail. The man was Herman Cann, a constable from Vorhees, Kansas. Cann had been advised by Haas about the killings and was on his way to "the hay meadow" to check it out. Cann delivered Tooney to a local doctor, who tended the wounded man. The next day he was taken by wagon back home to Woodsdale, and in time nineteen-year-old Herbert Tooney recovered.

The bodies of the four slain men were brought back to Woodsdale and returned to their families The Stevens County

Seat War had reached its climax about 11:30 P.M. on July 25, 1888, in a hay meadow, beyond the boundaries of Kansas.

Without hesitation, upon returning to Hugoton, Robinson quickly left the much-troubled county. Tooney reported the massacre and the attempt on his life. When word of the murderous encounter reached the governor's office, he sent the military to set up camp between Hugoton and Woodsdale and disarm everyone.

Colonel Wood had "practiced law" and had served in the Kansas legislature, before settling in Stevens County. He was adept at legal procedures, and he initiated action to bring criminal charges against the Hugoton men. Wood's intense pursuit of this matter culminated in a hearing in Federal court during October 1889, at Paris, Texas, which was more than five hundred miles from where the murders had been committed. As a result of that hearing, six men were indicted for the crimes: Cyrus E. Cook, O. J. Cook, J. B. Chamberlain, Cyrus Freese, J. J. Jackson, and Jack Lawrence.

The name of the posse leader who carried out this atrocity, Sam Robinson, was not listed among those indicted, and it appears that he was not present at the hearing. After leaving Stevens County (before the military arrived) Robinson had gone to Colorado. Most of his activities in the Centennial State are not now known, but it is known that in May 1889 he held up a combination store and post office at Florissant, Colorado, and was captured. Sam Robinson was convicted of the robbery and was sentenced to serve fourteen years in the Canyon City prison. His incarceration in the Colorado State Penitentiary permitted Robinson to be bypassed in the legal action that transpired in the Federal court at Paris, Texas.

In July 1890, the six men who had been indicted for the murders were brought to trial at Paris for what was commonly being referred to as the "Hay Meadow Massacre." Col. Sam Wood highlighted the prosecution's case with an eight-hour presentation. So well did he acquaint the jury with the evidence of the crime, while using the star witness Herbert Tooney for maximum benefit, that all six men were found guilty. A few days later, the court sentenced the six convicted men to be hanged on December 19, 1890.

The case was appealed to the U.S. Supreme Court, and the executions were put on hold. The case was argued before the nation's highest court on December 11–12, 1890. That tribunal announced its decision on January 26, 1891. It determined that neither the Paris court (nor any other court) had jurisdiction over the site (in No Man's Land) at the time that the crimes had been committed. The convictions were voided.

Four men had been disarmed and murdered. Witnesses, including a fifth man who had been left for dead, had identified the killers, but no one was ever punished for the crime. Lack of legal jurisdiction for this strip of land at the time of the criminal act precluded any state or territory from exercising any authority over it. As the case was being processed, the track of "orphan land" was assigned to Oklahoma Territory.

The fires of "hate and hell" were still ablaze in Stevens County. On June 23, 1891, Sam Wood had gone to Hugoton to answer a bribery charge that had been filed against him. Shortly after arriving in the county seat, Wood entered the courthouse (church), and as he did, James Brennan approached him from behind and shot him in the back. After being hit, the colonel tried to run, but Brennan fired twice more, hitting him once in the head. Mere moments later, Sam Wood lay dead.

It was thought that the murder of Sam Wood had resulted from hard feelings that had been generated and carried over from the trial at Paris, Texas. At that litigation, Brennan was a witness for the defense, and Colonel Wood had aggressively attacked his testimony. After killing Wood, Brennan was arrested and charged with the murder. The following November he was presented for trial at Hugoton. After examining nearly every qualified elector in Stevens County, it was decided that an unbiased jury could not be assembled, which prevented the accused man from being tried.

Under Kansas law at that time only the defense was permitted to request a change of venue. Meanwhile Brennan was being held in county jail without bail. Another state law provided that if an accused man was being held without bond and had not been tried during two regular sessions of court, he should be released.

Charles Curtis, one of the lead attorneys representing the state, was involved in the peculiarities of the Brennan case. Curtis later served as vice president of the United States (1929–33).

Due to these oddities of the Kansas laws, James Brennan was never tried for having murdered Col. Samuel N. Wood. After becoming a "free man," Brennan moved into the newly opened Oklahoma Territory, where he became a prominent and prosperous rancher. One unconfirmed account reports that James Brennan was elected and honorably served as sheriff of Kiowa County in southwestern Oklahoma. In November 1916, while Brennan was living in Gotebo, Oklahoma, he passed away and was buried in a cemetery north of Enid.

Another key figure in the Stevens County Seat War also moved to Oklahoma. Ed Short had become rather unpopular among his clients after the Hugoton posse chased him and his men back to Woodsdale. The murder of Sheriff Cross and his men also reflected badly on Short and raised questions about the role he had played in the affair. After moving into Oklahoma Territory, Short became a deputy U.S. marshal and at the sane time served as city marshal at Hennessey, O.T.

While performing this dual role, Officer Short became aware that an ailing man who was being treated by a local doctor and staying in a hotel at Hennessey was actually "Black-faced" Charley Bryant, who was a member of the Dalton gang. Marshal Short arrested the "wanted man" and made plans to take him by train to the Federal jail at Wichita, Kansas.

Ed Short's prisoner was being held in the baggage car

James Brennan is buried at Enid, Oklahoma. (Author's collection)

aboard the Rock Island train when he managed to get hold of a pistol. Moments later, as the newly armed Bryant opened the door to the platform at the end of the rail coach, he met the rifle-toting marshal, and each man started shooting. Both men were fatally wounded in the exchange. They were still aboard the northbound train when it pulled into Waukomis, O.T., on the evening of August 23, 1891. "Black-faced" Charley Bryant was dead, and Deputy U.S Marshal Ed Short was dying. Each man had killed the other, with the victim's own gun.

Following the Stevens County Seat War, several of Colonel Wood's supporters settled in a section of northwestern Oklahoma Territory. At their insistence, when the counties began to be named in lieu of being designated merely by single letters of the alphabet, "M" County became Woods County and remains so today.

In 1887, Hugoton had been designated as the permanent county seat of Stevens County, Kansas. That announcement did not settle the issue, but seemed to have intensified the ongoing county seat war. Following the death of Colonel Wood, his town began to wind down. During the twentieth century, Woodsdale withered away as did Vorhees and many other small towns in the Midwest. Hugoton, Kansas, has survived and still serves as the seat of Stevens County.

CHAPTER 5

"Black-faced" Charley Bryant's Blazing Moment of Glory

Charles Bryant inherited the moniker "Black-faced Charley" because of powder burns from a gun that was fired too close to his face, causing permanent darkened and irregular spots on his otherwise grizzled countenance. He had left Wise County, Texas, in the late 1880s to keep from answering to the law for some troubles of his creation.

After drifting into "The Territory," Charley got a job working for the Turkey Track Ranch, which was located in "Cowboy Flats" (an area east of Guthrie). While riding for the Turkey Track, Bryant became acquainted with Emmett Dalton, Bill Doolin, George "Bitter Creek" Newcomb, and others, who were then working on cattle ranches in that area but would later "take the outlaw trail."

Charley Bryant was regarded as a restless and reckless individual. He suffered from occasional dysfunctional episodes, resulting in violent seizures and momentary blackouts. After those intense attacks subsided, he would often announce, "This is the way that I want to go," draw his pistol and fire away, then add, "in one blazing moment of glory." When not plagued by these fits, his disposition was not particularly unusual.

Bob Dalton was a former deputy U.S. marshal, who decided that the "grass was greener on the other side of the fence." He, with his brothers Grat and Emmett (both of whom had worked in law enforcement), began to steal horses in the summer 1890. The three Dalton brothers soon became suspects of their misdeeds. To elude their former comrades, they went to California where an older brother, Bill, lived.

In February 1891, a train was held up and the engineer was killed near Alila, California. Each of the four Dalton brothers (then in the area) became suspect of that robbery and murder. Bob and Emmett escaped before being arrested and headed back to Oklahoma Territory, but Bill and Grat were caught and charged with the crime.

Upon returning home, Bob and Emmett anxiously set about to renew their criminal careers. They began to recruit men who were interested in activities on the foul side of the law. The newly formed Dalton gang was waiting near the water tower at Wharton (now Perry, Oklahoma) when the Texas Express arrived on Saturday night, May 9, 1891. Bob Dalton was the leader of this train-robbing brigade, and his supporting cast consisted of his brother Emmett, "Bitter Creek" Newcomb, and "Black-faced" Charley Bryant.

When the train stopped to take on water before it reached the depot, two of the bandits "jumped" the engineer and fireman, then marched them back to the express car. Emmett and Charley covered the two railroad men at that point and watched the outside of the train. Bob and Bitter Creek gained entry into the express car where they displayed their guns and ordered the messenger to open the safes. He did unlock the smaller of the vaults and handed over the meager contents. The messenger insisted that the combination to the "big safe" had been wired to its destination (in Texas) and that he was not privy to that information. Bob Dalton did not believe the man's story and fired two shots impressively close to his shuffling feet. This proved to be a good remedy for the messenger's faulty memory as it enabled him to recall the combination, manipulate the dial, and open the safe. The robbers stuffed their ill-gotten gains into a gunnysack, mounted their horses, and rode west.

Posses searched for miles around trying to find the four culprits who had held up the train, but they were "long gone." The bandits had worn bandanas over the lower part of their faces, though a portion of Bryant's blackened cheek was still visible. Based on the limited descriptions provided by the train crew, wanted posters were prepared and distributed throughout the area.

The train-robbing quartet made their way to Jim Riley's ranch on the Canadian River (close to present-day Taloga), a hundred miles west of the hold-up site. The ranch was considered to be "a safe haven" and was frequently used by outlaws. The Dalton gang enjoyed the hospitality provided by Riley and his crew. The robbers were welcome at the ranch as they mingled along with Jim's hired hands, helping build fences, work cattle, and do other chores.

After "laying low" for a couple of months the outlaw band became restless, and Bob began plotting another heist. The bandit leader decided that Wagoner, in Indian Territory (Wagoner County) would be their destination, where they would hit a "Katy" (MK&T) train. To avoid the more populated areas, they planned to circle north while leisurely riding to the targeted site.

A few days after leaving the Riley ranch, the four companions met up with some riders who had set up a cow camp at Buffalo Springs. While visiting with these friendly cowboys, Black-faced Charley had a severe attack. He was not able to continue the journey when his comrades were ready to proceed. The trio left their sick ally at the cow camp and rode away to their next job.

Bryant's condition lingered on, and the cowboys prevailed upon him to seek medical help. They took the ailing man to see a doctor in Hennessey (Kingfisher County) who advised him to rent a room at the local hotel, so he could receive daily treatments. When Black-faced Charley learned that Jean (the younger sister of Ben Thorne, who owned the hotel) would bring his meals, he decided to accept the doctor's advice and arrange for the hotel's services.

Ed Short, a deputy U.S. marshal and Hennessey's city marshal, happened to be out of town when Bryant visited the doctor and checked into the hotel. Short was a native of Indiana and had served as a lawman in southwestern Kansas during the final years of the big cattle drives from Texas. He had been an active participant in the Stevens County War, an armed encounter that grew out of a conflict over the selection of a county seat. With the taming of the cow towns and the calming of the county seat issues, his gun-toting talents no longer carried a priority in Kansas. In 1889 he moved into Oklahoma Territory, where his expertise with weapons was an asset.

When Ed Short returned to Hennessey, he was informed of the doctor's new patient who was staying at the local hotel. The deputy was also apprised that the man's appearance matched the description that had been reported to fit one of the Wharton train robbers. Upon learning of this suspicion, the officer maneuvered an opportunity to observe the hotel guest. After seeing the newcomer, Short felt confident that he was one of the "wanted men."

Deputy Short discussed with Ben Thorne his intent to arrest his upstairs guest. With the cooperation of the hotel owner, Short set forth to nab the roomer. Taking advantage of a moment when Bryant thought that Jean was entering his room alone, the deputy moved in on the unsuspecting tenant and took him into custody without difficulty. By the time Bryant realized that another party was in his room, Officer Short had him covered, and the suspect couldn't grab either of his guns that he had placed to be handy. Black-faced Charley had been captured without a shot being fired. He had been denied his real "blazing moment of glory."

Following Bryant's arrest, Ed Short faced a new problem: how

Ed Short, Deputy U.S. Marshal, died in a shoot-out with his prisoner "Black-faced Charley" Bryant. (Author's collection)

to get his prisoner safely behind bars. The closest jail was at Guthrie, some forty miles away. The deputy considered it risky to ride alone to the capital city through the heart of Dalton country with one of their gang as his prisoner. Rumors were already being reported that "Bob and his boys" intended to rescue their cohort. Deputy Short decided that the best way to get his prisoner safely incarcerated was to take him by train to the Federal jail at Wichita, Kansas.

When the northbound Rock Island train departed Hennessey, at five o'clock the next evening (Sunday), Deputy Short and his prisoner were aboard. Wishing not to expose innocent people to the shooting if the Daltons did attack, the lawman had placed Bryant in the baggage car. Soon after Short heard the "all aboard" and felt the car start rolling, he rearranged his prisoner's manacles. The deputy removed the handcuffs from behind Bryant's back and recoupled them in front, so the ailing man could be more comfortable.

As the passenger train pulled out of Hennessey, Ed felt some relief. Mindful that each turn of the wheels would take him closer to the Federal jail, the law officer remained alert but less apprehensive as the locomotive chugged on. Black-faced Charley appeared too ill to fret about his circumstance or be concerned about his future.

Deputy Short surmised that if the Daltons did plan to rescue their charter member, they would most likely attack at the first station, Waukomis, thirteen miles north of Hennessey. When the train began slowing for that scheduled stop, Ed asked the mail clerk to watch his prisoner while he stepped out on the platform between the baggage car and the smoker for "a look around." The reclining, moaning figure would require no attention, thought the clerk as he nodded accord. Short laid his pistol on the desk where the clerk was working; then carrying a rifle that he had taken from Bryant after his arrest, he stepped to the end of the car and out the door.

The clerk was not particularly impressed with his additional assignment. He merely pushed the pistol aside and continued his mail-sorting duties. Seeing this unexpected opportunity inspired Black-faced Charley to make a break for freedom. Contrary to his apparent condition, with great gusto Bryant abruptly sprang forth and grabbed the unattended revolver. Clasping the pistol, the desperate man's physical posture and mental awareness appeared to soar.

Pushing past the cowed clerk, Black-faced Charley rushed to the exit. As he opened the door he saw his target, the back of his captor. When Deputy Short realized that the door was opening, he instinctively turned with rifle in hand and saw his pistol being raised in the cuffed grasp of his prisoner.

The six-gun fired, then the rifle spoke. Both hit their mark. Each man triggered his weapon until the outlaw fell and began sliding off the railroad car. Even though Ed Short was mortally wounded, he grabbed his dying prisoner and pulled him back on the platform.

When the northbound steam engine pulled into Waukomis, O.T., on the evening of August 23, 1891, the prisoner was dead and Deputy Short was dying. Due to the course of events that set up this shoot-out, each man had been killed by his own weapon, while in the hands of and being fired by his opponent. Without pretense but in vivid reality, Black-faced Charley Bryant's concluding "blazing moment of glory" had come to pass.

CHAPTER 6

Clyde Mattox, an Oklahoma Hellion

A son was born to Dr. Charles W. and Sadie (Fairchild) Mattox, whom they named Henry Clyde. The date of his birth has been variously reported from 1868 through 1872. His place of birth has been disparately recorded as Huntsville, Arkansas, and Springfield, Missouri, as well as Kentucky. While growing up, the boy's first name was seldom used, and he became known as Clyde Mattox (also spelled Maddox).

Doctor Mattox died a few years after Clyde was born. The 1880 census lists Sadie (head of house) as a dressmaker, then living in Whitesborro, Texas. At that time, her last name was recorded as Darnell, and her two sons, who were living with her, were listed with Mattox being their surname. Later, Sadie married a M. W. Hatch, who was a prominent merchant in Whitesborro. Mr. Hatch passed away in 1887.

Little is known about Clyde before he and his mother arrived at Oklahoma Station (which later became Oklahoma City), shortly after "the opening," meaning the Oklahoma Land Run of 1889. One account reports that Clyde made the run and raced directly to the settlement, which was then known simply as "Oklahoma." Soon after Clyde arrived in the territory, he became a deputy marshal in South Oklahoma (City), and his mother operated a boarding house on Reno Avenue.

Some two months after the April 22, "89er run," on June 13,

Mattox and his friend Bill Hart were fired from the city police force. One would assume that Clyde's employment was terminated because his many bad habits (which included excessive drinking and a violent temper) had been recognized as unacceptable traits for that profession. The next afternoon following their dismissal, Clyde was informed that Bill Hart had been arrested. Upon being advised that his friend was in custody, Mattox gulped down another shot of booze, grabbed his Winchester, and headed up the street.

Upon reaching Reno Avenue, Mattox stopped in front of Judge Enoch Fagan's office and fired his rifle. Deputy Marshals Howard and McKay (both of whom had been hired the evening before, to replace Mattox and Hart) stepped from the judge's chamber. With drawn pistols, the new officers confronted the irate ex-officer. Mere moments later, the three men began shooting as rapidly as they could trigger their weapons.

Shoot-out on Reno Street in Oklahoma City on June 13, 1889, between Deputies Howard and McKay and the inebriated Clyde Mattox. (Illustration courtesy of Al Napoletano)

When the smoke cleared, Deputy Howard was lying in the street mortally wounded, having been shot through the breast and abdomen. Deputy McKay had also been struck by a bullet and was sprawled on the sidewalk, but had not been seriously injured. The hostile former officer, who had instigated the gunfight, had been hit three times but was not critically wounded. Mattox had fired his rifle until empty, then with three flesh wounds he ran from the scene of the shooting.

After escaping from this armed conflict with two officers, Mattox holed up in a stable on Washington Street. In the process of being dislodged and arrested, Clyde was shot in the chest. He was taken to his mother's boarding house, and a doctor was summoned to treat him. One bullet had passed through Clyde's right lung, inflicting what was thought to be a fatal wound.

The next day, Dr. Howard of Sanger, Texas, arrived in Oklahoma to receive the body of his thirty-five-year-old son, John. Deputy Marshal Daniel F. McKay returned to work with hardly any ill effects from the previous day's shoot-out, and Mattox showed slight signs of improvement.

A local newspaper article described Clyde as handsome, smooth shaven, about twenty-one years old, slight of built, and mild mannered until he started drinking. Those who knew Mattox realized that whiskey instilled the depravity and anguish of a killer in the otherwise rather meek young man.

Clyde Mattox was charged with the murder of Deputy Marshal John S. Howard, who was the first police officer killed in Oklahoma (City). Not only did Clyde recover from his severe wound, but somehow he evaded punishment for his crime.

It was reported that Clyde's mother had assets in excess of twenty thousand dollars and that Sadie was known to do everything possible in behalf of her son. The particulars of the trial and disposition of the case have not been found. Obviously, the legal system in the new territory was not yet rendering justice, because Clyde Mattox beat the charge and was not convicted of murdering Deputy John Howard.

Six months after this three-man shoot-out on Reno Avenue, John Mullins (some accounts list his name as Mullen and Mullens) was killed in Oklahoma City. Witnesses identified Clyde Mattox as the party who fired the three fatal pistol shots into Mullins, a black man, as the victim stood in the doorway of Laura Walker's home, on Choctaw Street. The shooting occurred during the evening of December 12, 1889, and Mattox was arrested a few hours later. He was subsequently charged with the murder..

This murder case against Clyde Mattox was processed through the Federal court system, and he was tried at Wichita, Kansas. On October 5, 1891, he was found guilty and was sentenced to be hanged for the murder of John Mullins. Clyde's attorney appealed the court's action. While he was being held in the Wichita jail, a kerosene lamp in Clyde's cell exploded, and his hands were severely burned. Had not the floor been constructed of steel, extensive damage to the structure and severe harm to the inmates might have resulted from this unexplained accident.

Ultimately, Clyde's appeal prevailed, and his conviction was voided. During his second trial, a disagreement developed within the jury that resulted in that panel taking improper action, and a mistrial was declared. While Mattox was waiting to be retried, he was permitted to bail out of jail.

Tom Whitman, another black man, was one of the witnesses whose testimony had been most damaging to Clyde's case. Whitman was killed with a shotgun blast, at the corner of Washington and Hudson, in Oklahoma City. Tom's frozen body was found in that intersection the next morning, Monday, January 16, 1893.

Doc East, a former associate of Mattox's, became the major suspect in the killing of Whitman. A few days after the murder, a preliminary hearing was held to determine the evidence against East. One witness claimed that he had overheard the suspect remark during the trial at Wichita, that if Whitman testified against Mattox, he would kill him. A mulatto boy swore that he had taken a message to Whitman late Sunday, asking him to come to Sadie Hatch's place. Another witness claimed that he had observed Doc East visiting with Sadie Hatch the evening before the murder and had heard East say, "Five dollars is enough."

The suspect produced witnesses who vouched that he was elsewhere when Whitman was killed. The evidence against Doc East was determined to be insufficient, and he was released on January 27, 1893. There was a great deal of speculation that Clyde Mattox had killed Tom Whitman, whose murder was never solved.

Another account relates that while free on bond, Mattox went on a hunting trip into the Seminole Nation, with a white man who had also witnessed the murder of Mullins. It was reported that the gentleman did not come back from that adventure.

Clyde never returned to Wichita to honor the schedule of his bond. It became known thoughout the territory that Clyde Mattox had "jumped bail."

Mattox was seen entering Pat Haggerty's saloon in Enid, on Saturday afternoon, December 9, 1893. According to the local newspaper article that reported the incident, two deputy marshals who observed his entrance hesitated to go in and arrest him. J. D. Clark, a city policeman, told them that he had the "nerve" to arrest the wanted man, which they gladly gave him the chance to demonstrate. When the policeman stepped inside the saloon, the officers were heard to comment that "they did not expect to see Clark come out alive." Much to their surprise, a few moments later Mattox was in custody and was heard remarking to Clark, "Partner, you are the first man who ever had grit enough to try to arrest me without a gun." Mattox was taken to Guthrie under heavy guard and was later returned to Wichita.

Four years had passed since John Mullins had been killed in Oklahoma, when Clyde Mattox was tried the third time at

Wichita. Even though the two major witnesses had expired since Mattox had been convicted at his first trial, he was found guilty again, in mid-January 1894.

Within an hour after the jury brought in this last conviction, Mattox escaped from the Wichita jail. He got away by slithering through a small hole (he weighed only 110 pounds) in his second-floor cell. The next day, Clyde was recognized on a train and was recaptured at Yates Center, Kansas. The elusive young man was then taken back to Wichita.

Clyde Mattox was again sentenced to the gallows. One of the newspapers in reporting his recent trial referred to Mattox as having killed four men (Howard, Mullins, and the two deceased witnesses), "but will at last, face the hangman." Mattox was delivered to the Federal penitentiary at Fort Leavenworth, Kansas. He was scheduled to be executed on October 11, 1895.

There are numerous accounts of Clyde's mother working incessantly to relieve her son's death sentence. Years later one editor wrote (in part): "It was because Mattox had a guardian angel in the person of his mother, Mrs. Sadie W. Hatch of Ponca City that he was not hanged during the early days of Oklahoma. She was a winsome woman, gray haired, motherly, who could plead unceasingly for her wayward son, and it was a difficult matter for any official to gainsay her."

The editor's comments were based on Mrs. Hatch's successful plea in getting Pres. Grover Cleveland to commute her son's death sentence to life imprisonment, on September 29, 1895, twelve days before he was to be hanged. After President Cleveland issued the commutation, some concern developed over the safe custody of Clyde Mattox. In May 1897, to confirm a safe environment for the prisoner, the U.S. attorney general ordered that Mattox be transferred from Fort Leavenworth Prison to the Kansas State Penitentiary at Lansing.

In January 1898, Sadie influenced Pres. William McKinley to pardon her son. Benefiting from the persuasive talents of his devoted mother, less than four years after Clyde Mattox had been sentenced to be hanged (the second time), he received a presidential pardon and was released from prison.

Upon being freed, Clyde went to Ponca City to visit his aging, ever-loving, mountain-moving mother. Mrs. Hatch was not then considered to be a wealthy woman, having long before expended most of her resources in garnering favor for her son. After spending a few days with his guardian angel, Mattox got a job on a ranch in the Osage Reservation.

At various times over the years while being interviewed by reporters, Clyde and his mother each stated that he was her only living child. Conflicting with those statements are census records that show Sadie had another son, Charles Edward three years older than Clyde and still living in 1920. In March 1898, one local newspaper reported that a well-dressed Clyde Mattox (wearing a suit that had been tailored by Emmett Dalton while in prison) had passed through Guthrie en route to visit his brother Charles, in Mexico City. There are also some stories (unconfirmed) which relate that during this period, Clyde joined Teddy Roosevelt's Rough Riders and went to Cuba during the Spanish-American War.

For more than a year Mattox managed to keep out of trouble. By mid-March 1899, he was back in Ponca City living with his mother. While residing in Ponca City, Clyde began to frequent the local saloons and partake heavily of the demon rum. Sadie's son usually carried a pistol or a knife while on these sprees and often displayed these weapons as he caroused about.

On Monday evening, April 3, 1899, Lincoln Swinney, a rancher from the Osage Reservation, became intoxicated in Ponca City's White House Saloon. Swinney was a large man and displayed a mean disposition when drinking. While in this obnoxious condition he had troubles with two patrons of the Ponca City tavern, before he engaged Mattox.

Swinney threw his coat on the floor and dared anyone to walk on it. The drunken rancher then made a personal remark to Mattox, who also had been swigging heartily from the whiskey bottle. The former felon replied that he could walk on it, and on Swinney's carcass too; whereupon, the rancher struck the smaller man and knocked him against the bar. With raging fury, Clyde flew into Swinney like a wildcat. He managed to pull his knife and cut the bigger man on the hand, face, and neck. Mattox then slashed a long, four-inch deep gash into Swinney's side, just above his hip bone, from which the rancher's entrails protruded.

Prior to the arrival of the police, the victor of this gory brawl left the saloon. Mattox got out of Ponca City before officers could find him. Doctors were not successful in their efforts to remedy Swinney's extensive wounds, and he died a few hours later. When interviewed by a reporter the next day, Mrs. Hatch professed her support for her son and defended his actions.

A coroner's jury issued a verdict stating: "Lincoln Swinney came to his death from wounds caused by a knife in the hands of Clyde Mattox, with felonious intent." The local newspaper commented in its report of the incident: "Public sentiment is strongly against him [Mattox] in this killing, although sympathy for Swinney is not generally entertained."

Officers could not locate Clyde Mattox, but rumors circulated that he would surrender to the Kay County sheriff at Newkirk. There was speculation that Federal agents would join the search for Mattox because of his recent pardon. Within a few days, it became obvious that the wanted man was well hidden or out of the area. The local officials also became aware that Clyde's presidential pardon was "unconditional" and that the Swinney case was the only charge pending against the missing man.

One source relates that after Clyde killed Swinney, he hid out in the Osage Reservation. More than three months had passed since Lincoln Swinney had been slashed to death by the knife-wielding ex-convict, who after committing the crime had merely walked away and was still at large. Lawmen had no leads as to the whereabouts of Clyde Mattox and were at a loss in trying to locate the known killer.

LINCOLN SWINNEY CUT TO DEATH.

CLYDE MATTOX HIS SLAYER.

Mattox has Escaped and is Still at Large.

(From Tuesday's Daily.)

Clyde Mattox has added another killing to his list of victims. Lincoln Swinney, an Osage ranchman, was cut to death last night by Mattox in a quarrel in the White House Club saloon in this city. Immediately after the cutting Mattox disappeared and was not seen until this morning when he met friends near this city who advised him to go to Newkirk to give himself up to the officers. He was seen at Kildare driving a black horse on his way toward

Newspaper clipping about the killing of Lincoln Swinney by Clyde Mattox. (from the Ponca City Daily Courier, April 4, 1899)

In mid-July, Kay County sheriff Frank Pierce learned that Clyde's mother had expressed a valise to a Frank Jones at Los Angeles. Sheriff Pierce dispatched Deputy Ward to Los Angeles. A man claiming to be Frank Jones called for the valise and was arrested by waiting officers. When questioned by officials, the young man readily admitted that he was Clyde Mattox. The sheriff then went to Los Angeles and joined his deputy in bringing the notorious murderer back to Oklahoma Territory.

When the Kay County officers and their prisoner passed through Ponca City on the last leg of their trip from California, Matt Fortner boarded the train. The rail car was filled, and Mattox had his feet propped in the only vacant seat that the boarding passenger could find. Fortner, a black man, asked Mattox to move his feet so that he could sit. This request prompted the prisoner, who was handcuffed and chained with a ball, to unleash a volley of oaths upon Fortner. The guards tried to quiet Mattox and get him to refrain from such profanity. He retorted that they could stop him when he was in his grave. Mattox was booked into the Kay County jail on August 10, 1899.

Temple Houston, son of the noted Sam Houston, was a leading attorney in Oklahoma Territory. Mrs. Hatch hired Houston, who was then living at Woodward, to defend her son. On September 18, Mattox was indicted for the murder of Lincoln Swinney. Less than three months later, Clyde was tried at Newkirk, O.T., and on December 7, 1899, he was found guilty of manslaughter. Judge Benjamin F. Burwell sentenced him to twelve years in prison.

Clyde Mattox was received in the Kansas State Prison, on January 8, 1900. The Kay County census taken on June 12, 1900, lists fifty-five-year-old Sadie W. Hatch (head of house) and her son Clyde, as living together in Ponca City, even though prison records show that he was incarcerated at that time. The enumerator, who recorded the census in Leavenworth County, Kansas, on June 28, 1900, listed Clyde Mattox, age twenty-eight, among the inmates in the Lansing prison.

As a prisoner of Oklahoma Territory, Mattox was confined in the same penal institution in which he had been celled the last months of his Federal sentence (for the murder of John Mullins). After he had served approximately eight years for having killed Lincoln Swinney, Sadie again swayed an official to bestow a kindly act upon her perverted offspring. On March 12, 1908, with Mrs. Hatch as a guest in his office, Oklahoma Governor Charles Haskell issued a parole for Sadie's son, Clyde Mattox.

Following his release from the penitentiary, Clyde continued his irresponsible conduct, which did not conform to the terms of his parole. Some twenty-two months after letting Mattox out of prison, Governor Haskell revoked his parole. Clyde's release was rescinded on January 11, 1910, because "the said Clyde Mattox has violated the terms of his parole in every particular."

Clyde was then sent to the penitentiary at McAlester. Eighteen months later, his mother worked her magic once again. On July 12, 1911, Sadie persuaded Oklahoma Governor Lee Cruce to grant a full pardon to her vagarious son.

In commenting about Mrs. Hatch's recent success in getting her son freed once again, two weeks after Clyde was released by Governor Cruce, one newspaper reported: "Mattox was arrested in Oklahoma City on a charge of drunk and disorderly. It begins to look as though the people who are always working to get Clyde out of prison are doing him an injury instead of a benefit. He is said to make a model prisoner, and that can hardly be said of him as a citizen."

For the past several years, Mrs. Hatch had been a special friend of John E. "Jack" Love, who was chairman of the Oklahoma State Corporation Commission. Love, the former sheriff of Woodward County, was a friend of Temple Houston. During the evening of October 8, 1895, Houston and Love were involved in a gunfight with Ed and John Jennings in a Woodward saloon. Ed was killed in this encounter, and John was severely wounded. Neither Houston nor Love was hit. They were later tried for manslaughter and were acquitted.

After statehood, Love became a popular state official and was Mrs. Hatch's most loyal and influential supporter in gaining favor for her errant son. In behalf of Sadie, Jack Love had been instrumental in getting the state's first governor to parole Clyde Mattox. After that parole was revoked, the chairman of the Corporation Commission exerted his influence in swaying Oklahoma's second governor to issue Sadie's son a pardon.

When Mattox was released from prison in 1911, Love persuaded Jake Hamon, railroad builder and politician, to put Clyde on the payroll of his Oklahoma, New Mexico and Pacific Railroad Company. This arrangement created frequent problems for Hamon, as Mattox reverted to drinking, and often his performances brought embarrassment to his employer. Jake Hamon kept Sadie's son on the payroll for some time but finally terminated this relationship, because of Clyde's drunken shenanigans.

Ben Cravens (aka Charles Maust) was a notorious outlaw in the early years of Oklahoma. In January 1912, he was being tried in Guthrie for murder. One of the major complications that developed during his trial was the prosecution's case to prove that Ben Cravens and Charles Maust were the same man.

At the height of this identity controversy, Clyde Mattox was called as a witness by the defense. Mattox had known Cravens some fifteen years earlier, when they were in the penitentiary. The witness had worked with the prison photographer and had taken pictures of Cravens, while both were confined. At Guthrie, Mattox testified that he could not recognize the man who was on trial as the person he had known in prison.

Assistant Chief Joe Burnett was acting as Oklahoma City police chief in mid-March 1912. The name Joe Burnett may appear familiar because on January 13, 1904, while patrolling his beat in Oklahoma City, Burnett fought and killed Ed O. Kelly. Ed Kelly had killed Bob Ford at Creede, Colorado, on June 8, 1892. Bob Ford had become known as "the dirty little coward that shot Mr. Howard," an allusion to Ford's having killed Jesse James on April 3, 1882, in St. Joseph, Missouri.

Joe Burnett received a request on Wednesday afternoon, March 13, 1912, from the Creek County sheriff's office to arrest Clyde Mattox. Creek County officers wanted to question Mattox as a suspect in the recent robbery of the Guarantee State Bank at Keifer. Acting Chief Burnett ordered that Clyde be picked up. Mattox was located in the Capital City and was arrested Wednesday evening. Creek County deputy sheriff Hemphill departed from Oklahoma City on the train Thursday morning with Mattox as prisoner and delivered him to Sapulpa, Oklahoma.

As soon as Sadie learned that Clyde had been arrested and was again facing criminal charges, she hired Al Jennings to defend her troublesome boy. Al had drifted into outlawry after his brothers' disastrous gunfight with Houston and Love at Woodward. Al's efforts as a train robber were inept, and his outlaw career was short-lived. He had been arrested, tried, convicted, and sentenced to serve life in prison. While in the penitentiary, Al had got his sentence reduced and after gaining parole (later, a pardon from Pres. Theodore Roosevelt), he had returned to Oklahoma and was again practicing law.

Mattox had been identified as one of the two men who had robbed the Kiefer bank, on February 26, 1912. He was arraigned at Sapulpa, on March 25, and his trial was scheduled for April. Shortly after the arraignment, Judge Elihu Root received an affidavit from Oklahoma City Chief of Police Bill Tilghman. This document from the noted lawman stated that three men from Texas had come to Oklahoma City and had sworn that Mattox was in El Paso the night that the safe was blown in Kiefer. The Creek County judge considered that this affidavit from Bill Tilghman was sufficient evidence to drop the charges against Clyde Mattox, and he was released from the Sapulpa jail. Two years later, Clyde's attorney Al Jennings was an unsuccessful candidate for governor of Oklahoma.

Most of Mattox's troubles with the law had stemmed from his yen for whiskey and the killer instincts that it induced. Apparently Clyde finally learned to control his alcoholic binges and violent temper, at least well enough not to murder again. Obviously his activities mellowed after 1912. In the years that followed, his conduct was sufficiently orderly that it did not make the newspapers, and his whereabouts during that period is not now known.

The next confirmed activity of Clyde Mattox occurred on October 15, 1921. On that date, Clyde fell from a bridge, which spanned Salt Creek, east of Burbank in Osage County. Three boys, who were playing nearby, saw Mattox walk to the railing and sit down. Moments later as they watched, he toppled headfirst some twenty feet below and lay motionless. The children reported the accident, and men soon arrived at the site. They found Mattox dead. In falling from the bridge, Clyde had broken his neck.

A death certificate for Clyde Mattox, which was not signed by a doctor, is on file. It shows that Clyde was an artist by trade and merely states that his death was accidental. At the time that Clyde was killed, his doting, ever-loving mother was living in Oklahoma City. At that late date, Sadie's means must have been exceedingly meager, as Clyde was buried in an unmarked grave in the cemetery at Fairfax, Oklahoma.

The newspaper articles written in 1921 about the demise of Clyde Mattox give but few details about his accidental death and provide no insight into his activities of recent years. Most of the articles that were written at the time he fell from the bridge and broke his neck did relate numerous accounts of Clyde's wild escapades of years past and recapped his earlier life as an Oklahoma Hellion.

CHAPTER 7

The Passing of the Oklahoma Outlaws

A rather strange title for a subject, and it is not the author's creation. The Eagle Film Company selected that title, in 1915, for their only motion picture production. Who were the men who formed the Eagle Film Company? They were William "Bill" Tilghman, E. D. Nix, and Chris Madsen. They had only one thing in common; each had been a law officer during the years Oklahoma was still a territory. Why would these old-time law officers, with no motion picture industry experience, decide to form a company for the sole purpose of producing one movie, *The Passing of the Oklahoma Outlaws*?

To understand the reason for this endeavor, we must backtrack twenty years. In 1897, Al Jennings, thirty-three years old and a failure in his reelection bid as county attorney, decided to jump to the other side of the law, and became an outlaw. Al's efforts at bank and train robbery were total failures monetarily. He succeeded in getting caught, convicted, and sentenced to a five-year and a life prison term. In 1902, with the help of many friends (including Tilghman, Madsen, and Nix), Al obtained a parole and later a pardon. After release from prison, Al returned to Oklahoma Territory and law practice. In 1912, he unsuccessfully ran for Oklahoma County district attorney.

In 1913, he and Will Irwin wrote a book titled *Beating Back*, which was presented as the true-life story of Al Jennings. The book was more fable than fact, but it was published as a serial in the *Saturday Evening Post*. Soon it caught the motion picture industry's eye and, with Al's promotion, was put on the silver screen, glorifying Al's outlaw career while showing the law officers as blundering idiots. The movie portrayed Al as a gallant, fast-draw leader of a notorious gang of horseback outlaws. His ego overflowed during his campaign bid for Oklahoma governor in 1914, but again he failed to win the election.

While Al's feeble train and bank robbery attempts hardly caused a sweat among the lawmen, his movie portrayal of the lawmen as dim-witted cowards really raised their hackles. They felt that Al had intentionally misrepresented his role and their character, belittling them through a media with which they were not acquainted. Bud Ledbetter and several of the old-time peace officers approached Tilghman, bemoaning the way Jennings had depicted them. Tilghman, always alert and willing for a new challenge, decided that the best means to combat this propaganda was to use the same media and tell the true story. He discussed this idea with Nix and Madsen, and each agreed; so the Eagle Film Company was born. E. D. Nix, president, would finance the enterprise. Bill Tilghman, vice-president, would get the picture made. Chris Madsen, secretary, would maintain records and help in any other manner.

Now let's take a closer look at these men, who were so offended by the Al Jennings movie, *Beating Back,* that they undertook a totally new venture to get the truth out.

E. D. Nix emigrated from Kentucky to Guthrie, Oklahoma Territory, in October 1889. He opened a general mercantile store. He was such a successful businessman that in 1893 he was appointed a U.S. marshal, even though he had no law enforcement experience. He was an administrator and knew how to pick good men and get the best out of them. He managed a very efficient law enforcement agency during the most difficult times, until he was relieved of duty in 1896. Two years later, he moved to Missouri, with continued success in grocery,

Alphonso Jackson "Al" Jennings, lawyer/politician/outlaw. (Photo courtesy of the Archives & Manuscripts Division of the Oklahoma Historical Society)

banking, and real estate businesses, in Joplin and Kansas City. He retained many friends and an interest in Oklahoma, as is demonstrated in his becoming the president and financier of the Eagle Film Company.

Several books and dozens of magazine articles have been written about Bill Tilghman's life and experiences. Some historians proclaim him as the most efficient lawman of the Old West. He had been an army scout, buffalo hunter, and city marshal of Dodge City, Kansas, during its heyday. He came to Oklahoma during the 1889 land run. Tilghman and other lawmen, such as Ed Short and Jim Masterson, realizing that their days in Kansas were through, moved to the newly opened territory where their experience was needed and welcomed. After arriving in Oklahoma Territory, Bill continued in law enforcement, serving as a deputy U.S. marshal, county sheriff, chief of the Oklahoma City Police Department, and special officer for several Oklahoma governors and Pres. Teddy Roosevelt. Tilghman also served as state senator and built up a fine breeding farm and a stable of top racehorses. The sixty-year-old, who was always able to cope with the situation at hand, had no hesitancy in undertaking the motion picture production.

Chris Madsen was born in Denmark. He had served in the Danish Army and French Foreign Legion prior to arriving in the United States in 1875. He was immediately accepted into the U.S. Cavalry and soon became quartermaster-sergeant. Madsen was stationed at Fort Reno in 1889, and obtained a land claim. In 1890, U.S. Marshal William C. Grimes appointed Madsen as deputy, a position that he held almost continuously for the next thirty years.

The intentions of these three men were to present a factual film of the "Passing of the Oklahoma Outlaws." They planned to use the real people, as much as possible, reenacting the original scenes at the actual locations of the incidents. Their initial goal was to record the true account of the Jennings gang. But since this material alone would hardly make a full-length

Deputy U.S. Marshal Bill Tilghman. (Photo courtesy of the Archives & Manuscripts Division of the Oklahoma Historical Society)

movie, they decided to include the activities of the Doolin gang; some of the men had ridden with both outlaw gangs. Following is a brief record of the men, deeds, and misdeeds of the Doolin and Jennings gangs:

Bill Doolin had "ridden the outlaw trail" with the Dalton gang, but was not with them during the double bank robbery attempt at Coffeyville, Kansas. on October 5, 1892. Just over a week after the Daltons fell during that failed effort, on October 13, 1892, Doolin and his gang robbed a train near Caney, Kansas, only twenty miles from Coffeyville. Less than three weeks later, on November 1, 1892, three hundred miles from Caney, they robbed a bank at Spearville, Kansas. Through the efforts of Ford County sheriff Chalk Beeson, assisted by Tom and Ham Hueston and George Cox of Stillwater, Oklahoma Territory, the first of the Doolin gang fell. Oliver "Ol" Yantis had been identified; when this four-man posse found him near Orlando, Oklahoma Territory, on November 30, 1892, he attempted to shoot it out and was killed. By the spring of 1893, the Doolin gang included Bill Dalton, brother of Bob, Grat, and Emmett. The Doolin gang held up a train near Cimarron, Kansas, on June 11, 1893.

Soon after the Cimarron train robbery, the marshal's office at Guthrie, Oklahoma Territory, became aware that the Doolin gang was frequently visiting the little town of Ingalls. Deputies Red Lucas and Doc Roberts were assigned to work undercover in that area and verify the report. Being unknown in Ingalls, they were able to move in and learn that the gang members were openly spending time there. Upon receiving confirmation of the gang's activities from Lucas and Roberts, Nix assigned Deputy John Hixon to raise a posse and capture the men at Ingalls. In addition to Lucas and Roberts, the posse consisted of Hixon, Jim Masterson, Ike Steele, Steve Burke, Lafe Shadley, Tom and Ham Hueston, Dick Speed, George Cox, and Hi Thompson.

During the morning of September 1, 1893, two covered

wagons with the thirteen-man posse entered the little town of Ingalls. As the deputies dropped from the moving wagons to get into position for the attack, five of the outlaws were in Ransom's saloon, George "Bitter Creek" Newcomb was on his horse in the street, and Roy Daugherty (aka Arkansas Tom) was in the upstairs of the hotel. When one of the wagons reached its position, the driver inquired of a local citizen the identity of the man on horseback. Learning that the man was Bitter Creek Newcomb, Dick Speed fired at the outlaw. This first shot of the gun battle knocked the magazine from the outlaw's rifle and seriously wounded him. Newcomb fired once at Speed, missing his target. Unable to get the damaged rifle to fire again, the injured Newcomb turned his horse and rode from Ingalls. While the deputies were closing in on the saloon, a shot from the hotel fatally hit Dick Speed. Seconds later,

Murray's Saloon, one of several businesses at Ingalls, Oklahoma Territory, where one of the most violent shoot-outs between outlaws and lawmen ever occurred in the history of the Old West. (Photo courtesy of the Archives & Manuscripts Division of the Oklahoma Historical Society)

Arkansas Tom got a glimpse of another man in motion; this shot was also fatal, but the victim was not a law officer, but a local youth, Del Simmons. The barrage of shots pumped into the saloon fatally wounded N. A. Walker, a customer, and injured Ransom, the saloon owner, and Murray, the bartender.

The outlaws had not been hit, but the shots coming thick and fast convinced them to make a run for it to the stable. Reaching the barn safely, they alternated, saddling horses and shooting at the officers. Arkansas Tom had not yet been discovered in the hotel and fatally brought down another deputy, Tom Hueston (one of the Yantis posse members). As soon as the outlaws had their horses ready to mount, they made a break for it. Bill Doolin and Charles "Dan" Clifton (aka Dynamite Dick) rode from the rear of the stable, as Bill Dalton, George "Red Buck" Waightman, and William "Tulsa Jack" Blake dashed from the front. Dalton's horse was hit and went down. Lafe Shadley ran to a position that would offer a better shot at the dismounted outlaw, but his movements were noticed by the observing eyes in the window of the upstairs room of the hotel. Arkansas Tom scored again, killing Shadley.

As the outlaws broke through the last line of fire, Dynamite Dick was hit, but with the help of Bill Doolin stayed in the saddle as the five men rode to safety. Arkansas Tom, who had been so successful in shooting the lawmen while his friends escaped, now found himself alone. Realizing that he could not get away, he surrendered. The Ingalls gun battle was over. Three of the law officers would die from their wounds, as would two of the local citizens. Two outlaws and two townspeople would recover from their gunshots. Only one of the outlaw gang was captured, Arkansas Tom.

Never again would Doolin and his gang enjoy the open hospitality of Ingalls. Their next raid was four months later, on January 23, 1894. They robbed a Pawnee, Oklahoma Territory, bank, escaping without any problem. Bill Doolin and Bill Dalton robbed the railroad station at Woodward, Oklahoma

Roy "Arkansas Tom" Daugherty, outlaw at the Ingalls, Oklahoma Territory, shoot-out. (Author's collection)

Territory, on March 13, 1894. They took the agent hostage and forced him to hand over the army payroll. Getting out of town without incident, they joined the other six members of the gang. Two weeks later, on April 1, 1894, Bill Dalton and Bitter Creek Newcomb attempted to rob a store at Sacred Heart. The store operator was Deputy Marshal Bill Carr, who recognized the pair when they entered. He not only defended the store, but also shot Bitter Creek as the two robbers ran to their horses. Bill Dalton left the Doolin gang at this time, but the wounded Bitter Creek returned to his old comrades. Bill Doolin led his men into Southwest City, Missouri, on May 10, 1894. They robbed a bank, and during the getaway J. C. Seaborn, a prominent citizen, was hit by the gunfire; Seaborn died a few days later.

In mid-May 1894, Arkansas Tom was tried for his participation in the Ingalls gunfight. He was convicted of first-degree manslaughter and was sentenced to fifty years imprisonment. On May 23, 1894, two weeks after Doolin hit the Southwest City bank, Bill Dalton and his new recruits robbed the bank at Longview, Texas. The Dalton gang encountered heavy gunfire when leaving the bank. One citizen, George Buckingham, and one robber, George Bennett, were killed in the exchange. The other outlaws escaped.

One reason the Doolin gang had been so successful in evading the law officers could be credited to their informant network. Two of these most dedicated sources were Annie McDoulet (or McDougal, known as Cattle Annie) and Jennie Stevens (or Stevenson) Midkiff (known as Little Britches). Law officers Steve Burke, Frank Canton, M. Zuckerman, and Gnat Owens approached these teenage girls, on August 19, 1895, near Pawnee. The girls fired several shots at the officers, as they attempted to get away, but were finally subdued. They were convicted of selling whiskey to the Indians and sentenced to two years in a reform school. Three weeks after Cattle Annie and Little Britches were caught, "Little Bill" Raidler, a member of the Doolin gang, was captured. Bill Tilghman with possemen

W. C. Smith and Cyrus Longbone found Raidler near Pawhuska, on September 6, 1895. When the outlaw saw the officers, he went for his gun. He was shot, seriously wounded, and captured. He was tried and convicted of robbing the U.S. mail and sentenced to a ten-year prison term.

Bill Tilghman received a tip that Bill Doolin was in Eureka Springs, Arkansas. Tilghman proceeded to this health resort city and shortly after arriving, on January 15, 1896, spotted the outlaw leader. Tilghman got the drop on Doolin and, after a brief struggle, made Doolin submit. The deputy delivered the outlaw leader to the Federal jail at Guthrie, Oklahoma Territory. After Red Buck Waightman departed from the Doolin gang, he mustered a few men of his own. They robbed a store at Arapaho and another in Taloga. He was suspected of being involved with a Wichita Falls, Texas, bank robbery and an attempted Canadian, Texas, railroad station robbery. In January 1896, Red Buck was injured in a gunfight with the Texas Rangers. On February 14, 1896, near Arapaho, he escaped another posse and killed W. W. Glover, who had tipped off the law officers where he could be found. On March 4, 1896, a posse composed of Bill Quillen, Joe Ventioner, Bill Holcomb, T. L. Shanan, J. T. Duckworth, and L. N. Williams found Red Buck in a half dugout near Arapaho. A gunfight ensued in which Red Buck was killed and one officer and Red Buck's partner, George Miller, were wounded. Dynamite Dick was arrested in Texas and turned over to the Oklahoma Territory authorities, then taken to the Guthrie jail on June 2, 1896.

On July 5, 1896, Bill Doolin and Dynamite Dick led a breakout of the Guthrie Federal jail. About six weeks later, a posse led by Henry A. "Heck" Thomas, with his son Albert, Rufus Cannon, Tom and Charlie Nobles, Bill Dal, and George and John Dunn learned that Doolin was visiting his wife at Lawson. During the evening of August 24, 1896, they set a trap for the outlaw leader. Doolin walked into the nest of hidden lawmen. When the surrender order was shouted to him, he fired in the direction of the voice. A shotgun in Heck Thomas's hands killed him.

Six members of the Doolin gang had been killed by law officers prior to the fall of their leader. Arkansas Tom and Little Bill Raidler were in prison. Only two members, Dynamite Dick Clifton and Richard "Little Dick" West were still at large. When Al Jennings decided to become a bank and train robber, he contacted these two men. Al brought along his brother Frank and the O'Malley brothers, Morris and Pat. The first robbery attributed to this newly created gang was a store at Violet Springs, on June 6, 1897. The following night they robbed a nearby railroad saloon. The minor jobs had gone easy, so they were ready for bigger game. On August 16, 1897, they stopped a train near Edmond, but were unable to blow open the safe, so their take was little, if any, money. Two weeks later they attempted to rob a train at Bond's Switch. They piled ties on the track to force the train to stop. But instead of slowing for the barricade, the engineer opened the throttle. Railroad ties flew in all directions as the train sped through, leaving the would-be robbers without a train to rob.

After being denied by the train that would not stop, they decided to burglarize a railroad station. For this hit, they selected Purcell, an express transfer-point station. While hiding in the rail yard, they observed a law officer nearby. Becoming concerned that their plan was known, they aborted the attempt. A few days later they planned to rob the bank at Minco. Scouting the target, they suspected that the bank officials had been tipped off and were prepared, awaiting their arrival. Again, they dropped the plan. They were desperate for money, so they planned to rob the train at Pocasset. On October 1, 1897 (one month after the Bond Switch failure), they took the railroad section gang hostage and forced them to wave the train to a stop. Again they failed to blow open the safes, but did pick up some money and valuables from the passengers. Posses were dispatched, but the six outlaws escaped.

At that point, Dynamite Dick Clifton and Little Dick West rode off, realizing that the Jennings and O'Malley brothers were a lost cause as bank and train robbers.

The Jennings and O'Malley brothers robbed a store at Cushing on the night of October 29, 1897, to get desperately needed groceries, ammunition, and clothing. They obtained the necessities plus a gallon of whiskey and a stalk of bananas. With their bonus, and no posse in immediate pursuit, they rode merrily away. Dynamite Dick who had evaded the officers for fifteen months after the Guthrie jailbreak, was located near Checotah in Indian Territory. Deputy Marshals Hess Bussey and George Lawson trailed the outlaw to a cabin. A gunfight followed. Dynamite Dick was killed as he raced from the burning cabin, on November 6, 1897. Al and Frank Jennings, with Morris and Pat O'Malley, hid out at the Spike S Ranch. When they awoke on November 30, 1897, they also found Deputy Marshal Bud Ledbetter and posse at the ranch. Morris O'Malley was captured. Al, Frank, and Pat O'Malley were wounded but escaped during a lull in the fighting. One week later, on December 6, 1897, Bud Ledbetter, with a rifle in hand, stopped the wagon carrying the three outlaws. Upon his surrender order, they raised their hands.

Only one member of the Doolin-Jennings gang was still at large, after the surrender of Al, Frank, and Pat O'Malley. The officers had been unable to locate the elusive Little Dick West. They had little confidence in a tip that he was hiding at a farm near Guthrie. More sense of duty than any hope of success prompted Chief Deputy Bill Fossett to lead a posse composed of Heck and Albert Thomas, Bill Tilghman, Ben Miller, and Frank Rinehart to the Arnett farm, on April 8, 1898. While firing at the approaching officers, Little Dick West was killed. This completes a brief account gleaned from the newspaper articles of the activities and demise of the Doolin and Jennings gangs.

These were the events that the Eagle Film Company

planned to put on the movie screen, as they launched into the project. They hired J. B. Kent for the camera work, as he had movie cameraman experience. Lute Stover, a magazine writer, with little, if any, motion picture business experience, was hired to direct the filming. As Stover prepared scenes to develop the film story, they decided to write a book providing a written account, to be sold at the theaters. A paperback titled *Oklahoma Outlaws,* with Richard S. Graves as the author, was prepared and published. This booklet was the first compiled account of these men and the events. The movie and booklet included two stories that had not been reported in the newspapers of the day. Since the first record of these events was twenty years after they occurred, they have always been controversial.

The first of the stories was about Bill Tilghman's accidentally entering a dugout where Doolin and his gang were hiding. When Tilghman's eyes adjusted to the semidarkness, he saw the outlaws hidden behind blankets with guns aimed at him. He maintained his calm manner and left the dugout without incident, even though one of the outlaws had to be restrained by the other desperadoes from shooting Tilghman in the back.

The second of these previously unreported stories is about the Rose of the Cimarron. The beautiful young lady, known only by that title, was in love with Bitter Creek Newcomb. She was visiting with a Mrs. Pierce, who operated the hotel at Ingalls, when the law officers opened fire on the Doolin gang, on September 1, 1893. She saw her sweetheart fall from the saddle when Deputy Dick Speed shot him. Seeing her wounded, unarmed lover lying helpless in the street, she acted without hesitation or fear. She ran to an upstairs room to obtain Bitter Creek's Winchester, then realizing that the doors of the hotel were covered by the lawmen, tied sheets together and let herself, with the rifle, to the ground. True to her expectations, the deputies held their fire as she ran across the street to aid and protect her fallen lover. Bitter Creek was helped into the saddle and escaped. Rose had saved her paramour from sure death, and later nursed him back to health. The Rose of the Cimarron's identity remained anonymous, as the deputies would not reveal her name, out of admiration for her bravery.

The author of *Oklahoma Outlaws* stated, in 1915, that Rose was a respected Christian woman, beloved as a wife and mother. As the script was enlarged to include these scenes, the cast was being gathered. Several cowboys from the Miller Brothers 101 Ranch Wild West Show acted in the movie. Tilghman took the role of the leading deputy marshal, with Nix, Madsen, and Bud Ledbetter performing their true parts. Roy Daugherty (Arkansas Tom) had obtained a parole in 1910, with the help of relatives and friends (including Nix and Tilghman). He played his own role, the main scene being his marksmanship and surrender at the Ingalls Hotel. Since the Jennings and O'Malley brothers were not invited to participate, Arkansas Tom was the only one of the old outlaws in the movie.

The amateur filmmakers started shooting the movie in January 1915, going to several of the actual locations to duplicate the original action. The production progressed without any major problems, and in late March they returned to Tilghman's ranch near Chandler to record the final scenes. On March 27, 1915, as they neared the completion of the film, they received word that another Oklahoma outlaw, Henry Starr, had just been captured at Stroud (fifteen miles from Chandler). Henry Starr and his gang were making their getaway, after robbing two banks at Stroud, when Henry was shot and captured. The Eagle Film Company immediately decided to use this double bank robbery as the conclusion of their motion picture.

Henry Starr was addicted to the thrill of robbing banks. Before he was twenty-one years old he had led a gang in bank robberies in Kansas and Arkansas. Twice he had been sentenced by Judge Parker to be hanged, for the murder of Floyd Wilson. (Henry had shot and killed Wilson as he was trying to arrest Starr.) The U.S. Supreme Court ordered new trials for the convictions at Judge Parker's Fort Smith court. In 1897, Starr was given a fifteen-year sentence for killing Wilson, and in 1902 President Roosevelt commuted that sentence. In 1909, Starr was tried and convicted of bank robbery in Colorado and was sentenced to the Canon City prison. While in the Colorado penitentiary, he wrote his autobiography, *Thrilling Events, Life of Henry Starr.* He was paroled in 1913, and eighteen months later he was caught at Stroud, pursuing his old profession.

The first showing of the movie was at Chandler, attended by an overflowing crowd of home folks. The first true test was the presentation in the Tabor Grand Opera House at Denver in September 1915. It passed with flying colors. It was soon noted that Bill Tilghman's talents included a slight flair as a showman. When Tilghman traveled with the show and gave a brief talk, the movie and the books were well received. Neither Nix nor Madsen were successful in this role and soon returned to their previous occupations. Tilghman assembled a display of pictures, rifles, and pistols to accompany the movie. As an added feature, Arkansas Tom would frequently travel with the show. Tilghman would introduce him to the audience; the attention and applause would delight the old outlaw. This combination of movie, lawman, outlaw, displays, and booklet was both popular and profitable.

The Eagle Film Company soon paid off all debts. Shortly afterward, Tilghman bought out Nix and Madsen to become the sole owner of the movie. Perhaps the memories stirred by traveling with the show were too much enticement for Arkansas Tom, and he returned to his old ways. He became involved with another bank robbery and, in 1917, was sentenced to eight years in a Missouri penitentiary. One of Tilghman's attractions was lost, but he continued with the show, traveling throughout the country on a profitable tour.

In 1919, Henry Starr was paroled for the Stroud double bank robbery conviction. Perhaps it was the general success of

Tilghman's *Passing of the Oklahoma Outlaws* that prompted Starr to become interested in a Tulsa motion picture firm. Henry was to receive an interest in the film company, in exchange for playing himself in a movie, *Debtor to the Law,* based on the events of his life. He also played major parts in two following movies. When Henry's partners cheated him out of his share of the profits, he learned that not all robbers held up banks. Once again, Starr turned to the thrill of robbing banks. His renewed career was rather short-lived, as he was shot and killed on February 18, 1921, while holding up a bank at Harrison, Arkansas.

Bill Tilghman continued to travel with the movie as his other interests permitted, but his other business required him to devote less and less time to the show circuit. Eight months after Henry Starr was killed, the other habitual bank robber, Arkansas Tom, was released from prison. He tried to refrain from repeating his past, but freedom to Arkansas Tom, like Henry Starr, seemed only to mean one thing, a chance to rob another bank. While trying to avoid arrest for his latest bank dealings, Arkansas Tom was shot and killed by law officers, on August 16, 1924, at Joplin, Missouri.

At the time that Arkansas Tom was in his final shoot-out, Bill Tilghman was being solicited by the citizens of Cromwell, Oklahoma, to accept the position of city marshal. Cromwell was an oil boomtown, filled with drug and whiskey peddlers and all of the other undesirables that flock to such a town that has no effective law enforcement. When the governor asked Tilghman to take the position, the seventy-year-old man became the city marshal. He was making progress in bringing law and order to Cromwell, but became a victim of his own efforts. While arresting and disarming a drunken federal prohibition officer for disturbing the peace, Tilghman failed to notice that the offender, Wiley Lynn, had a second pistol. As Tilghman started to lead his prisoner to jail, Lynn pulled his hidden automatic and shot the marshal at point-blank range.

The veteran of fifty years as an officer of the law died a few minutes later, on November 1, 1924.

With the death of Bill Tilghman, the movie *Passing of the Oklahoma Outlaws* was put on the shelf and seldom shown after 1924, except as a historical reference. Even though there were witnesses to the killing of Tilghman by Wiley Lynn, there was sufficient controversial testimony that the jury acquitted Lynn of murder. Lynn was suspended as a prohibition officer and continued his drunken sprees. He was frequently arrested for intoxication in various towns. On one of these binges, he saw Crockett Long, an off-duty police officer with whom he was upset because of a previous arrest. Lynn approached Long from behind and shot at him. The first shot missed. Then Long turned and fired. Each man killed the other in that gunfight at Madill, Oklahoma, on August 1932, eight years after Lynn had killed Tilghman.

The Al Jennings movie *Beating Back* never gained the popularity as did Tilghman's production, but it was sufficient to get Al accepted into the motion picture industry. In a world of pretense, the pretender is at home; and Al did find a home in Southern California, as Hollywood developed. He assumed the role of technical director of Western films and was accepted as an authority on the Old West gunfighter. After World War II, another movie, *Al Jennings of Oklahoma,* was made of his life. Again, he was portrayed as a brave man of gallant deeds. Al enjoyed the life provided by Hollywood and lived in that locale until his death in 1961, at the age of ninety-eight. Twenty-five years after Tilghman's death, a biography, *Marshal of the Last Frontier,* was published. This book was written by Zoe Tilghman, Bill's widow, and has been accepted as the best source of information about the author's husband.

CHAPTER 8

The Troublesome
Stevenson Brothers

John and Jim Stevenson were brothers who lived in Pickens County of the Chickasaw Nation, Indian Territory. The first several years that John and Jim resided in Pauls Valley, known as "The Queen City of the Washita", they operated saloons; later they were barbers. Over a span of some fifteen years, each of the brothers shot and killed a local officer of the law, and in another armed encounter John was killed by a city official. This story relates their major conflicts with lawmen and the repercussions, including the role of their shyster lawyer Moman Pruiett, whose success in defending Jim Stevenson on a murder charge at Norman triggered a mob to lynch four men in Ada.

The first of these instances occurred about 9:00 P.M. on August 22, 1893. Earlier that day, John Stevenson had been on the street displaying a knife in a threatening manner. When Pauls Valley Constable Joe Gaines was apprised of Stevenson's conduct, he deputized Bill Robinson (a local barber) to assist him in arresting the saloonkeeper who was reported to be somewhat inebriated. After Gaines and his aide took the knife-wielding man into custody and removed his weapon, the officer released Stevenson and advised him to go home.

Visiting in the Stevenson home that evening were Mr. and Mrs. Fred Waite. Fifteen years earlier, Fred had been a cohort of Billy the Kid in New Mexico. After running with the notorious

Chickasaw Street, Pauls Valley, Indian Territory, circa 1901. (Courtesy of the Railroad Depot Museum, Pauls Valley, Oklahoma)

young outlaw during the Lincoln County War, Waite left New Mexico and returned to the Indian Nation where a few years later he was elected to the Chickasaw legislature. Fred Waite had moved to Pauls Valley, and he resided there until his death in 1895. Upon John's arrival at home following his encounter with Officer Gaines, he hurriedly ate and briefly visited with the Waites. Stevenson then picked up his Winchester. With disdain for the constable bedeviling his mind, John returned to the street with rifle in hand.

Constable Gaines saw the rifle-toting Stevenson enter Bandy's Cider Joint. John had invited some of the boys to "have a drink with him." Moments later with a holstered revolver on his hip, the officer stepped inside the saloon. Sounding almost simultaneous, one shot was fired from each of the two weapons. Gaines's pistol shot hit John in the leg. The bullet from Stevenson's rifle fatally wounded the constable, and he fell to the floor.

John surrendered to Deputy U.S. Marshal E. H. Scrivner, who lived in Pauls Valley and was a neighbor of Stevenson. The commission of this type of crime in the Chickasaw Nation at that time was under the jurisdiction of the Federal court at Paris, Texas. Deputy Scrivner delivered the slightly wounded Stevenson to that Texas town, where the prisoner was jailed.

In December 1893, John Stevenson was indicted at Paris for the murder of Constable Joe Gaines (some accounts refer to Gaines as also being a deputy U.S. marshal). The accused man engaged Stillwell Russell and Jake Hodges, who were well-known attorneys in that area, to defend him in court.

While John Stevenson was awaiting trial for the murder of Officer Gaines, another murder case emerged against him. In May 1894, the newspapers reported that some three years earlier John had hired a Jack Shehan to sink a well on the Stevenson family farm west of Pauls Valley. While thus employed, the well driller suddenly disappeared. There were some suspicions in the neighborhood that Jack Shehan had met with foul play, but John's story about the young man having abruptly left the country was reluctantly accepted.

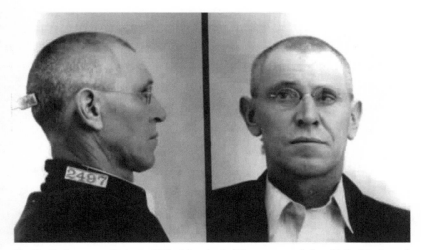

E. H. Scrivner, ex-Deputy U.S. Marshal. (Courtesy of the U.S. National Archives and Records Administration)

After the passing of many months, John's wife died, and later it became known that just before her death she acknowledged that her husband had killed Shehan and put his body in the well, then filled it in. When lawmen learned of this report, they went to the Stevenson farm and opened the well. As the officers excavated the site they found bones that they believed were the remains of Jack Shehan.

John's mother and brother Jim were arrested on suspicion of being accessories to the young man's murder. They were taken to Paris and put in jail along with John who was already celled in that facility.

Charges against the Stevensons for the murder of Jack Shehan were ultimately dropped because no skull was found, and the bones were never confirmed to be those of the missing man. Jim and his mother were released, and they returned to Pauls Valley, but John was retained behind bars to face the court as previously charged.

John Stevenson's trial for the murder of Constable Gaines

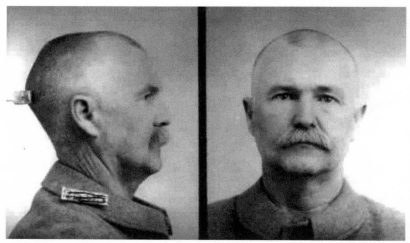

John Stevenson, the "Marshal Killer." (Courtesy of the U.S. National Archives and Records Administration)

came before the Paris tribunal in April 1895. He was found guilty of murder in the first degree and was sentenced to hang.

A few months after his conviction, the local newspaper reported that Stevenson had hired a "Judge" East, who was a prominent attorney in Washington, D.C., to assist in his appeal. In April 1896, the U.S. Supreme Court reviewed John's case. That echelon overturned the lower court's guilty verdict and remanded the case for a new trial.

John Stevenson's second trial was held at Paris, in December 1896. Again, he was defended by attorneys Russell and Hodges. This legal exercise resulted in a "hung jury," and a mistrial was declared.

In May 1897, Stevenson was tried a third time for the murder of Officer Joe Gaines. After hearing the case, the jury concluded that the accused was guilty of manslaughter and sentenced him to serve ten years in prison.

Following that conviction, Stevenson hired Moman Pruiett to represent him in the appeal process of his case. Pruiett had studied law while working for Jake Hodges at Paris, Texas. After being accepted to the bar, the young lawyer had moved to Pauls Valley, I.T. (Indian Territory), where he hung out his shingle and began his law practice. Pruiett was also the prosecuting attorney for the city of Pauls Valley. When Stevenson became aware that his defending lawyer also represented the city, which had some charges pending against him, he approached Moman on the matter.

Pruiett had just come out of a grocery store and was carrying two dozen eggs along with two loaves of bread when Stevenson inquired whether he intended to press the city's charges against him. Immediately upon Pruiett's response in the affirmative, Stevenson stepped back and kicked the sack of groceries out of his attorney's arms. Pruiett had been in numerous bare-knuckle fistfights and was known to be a brawler; however, at this time of the day, he was in no mood to tangle with John Stevenson. Shortly thereafter, John apologized to his lawyer for instigating the conflict and for his uncontrolled bad behavior.

Moman related later of the confrontation, "I stood there, yellow inside and out with egg yolk covering me." Knowledge of Stevenson's prowess with his fists was likely the reason that Officer Gaines had deputized Robinson to assist him in arresting the bartender.

In spite of having been roughly abused by his client, Moman Pruiett exerted every effort to gain relief of the conviction for John Stevenson. In March 1898, the U.S. Supreme Court ruled favorably on the young lawyer's appeal. After being granted a new trial again, John Stevenson was returned to Texas from the penitentiary at Detroit, Michigan.

John Stevenson's fourth trial for the murder of Joe Gaines came before the Paris court in April 1899. Almost six years had elapsed since the officer had been gunned down, when the jury yielded to the persuasive plea presented by Moman Pruiett and voted that the accused man was not guilty.

About six months after being acquitted of having murdered Joe Gaines, John Stevenson was involved in another shooting scrape in Pauls Valley. The particulars of his encounter with James Boyce that occurred in early November 1899 are not now known. It is not clear what the result of this armed fracas was; however, John Stevenson was charged with assault with intent to kill. The charge was later dropped.

During the criminal court proceedings at Pauls Valley in the spring of 1901, John and Jim Stevenson were convicted of introducing and selling liquor in the Chickasaw Nation. They were each sentenced to serve four years in the Federal penitentiary. John's neighbor, E. H. Scrivner (the former deputy U.S. marshal) was found guilty on the same charge and received a like sentence. These three and ten other men who were convicted in that term of court were delivered to the prison at Fort Leavenworth, Kansas, on May 29, 1901.

Some six years later, on Sunday, November 3, 1907, Jim

Stevenson (John's younger brother) shot and killed City Marshal Randolph Cathey at Pauls Valley. According to the newspaper reports of the fray, Stevenson was waiting in the dark, near the front door of a restaurant, and began firing his automatic pistol at Cathey when the officer came out after eating his evening meal.

Cathey fell to the sidewalk and, even though mortally wounded, he drew his pistol and fired five shots at his assailant as Stevenson continued to shoot until his weapon was empty. Stevenson was also wounded as two of Cathey's shots struck him.

The city marshal was a well-liked individual and much respected as an officer of the law. Those who knew Cathey became highly incensed when they learned that Jim Stevenson had shot him. Shortly after the populace became aware that Cathey had been killed and that Stevenson had been taken into custody, a group of citizens gathered near the jail. Their yen to avenge the murder of Cathey brought them to mingle and talk of hanging Stevenson.

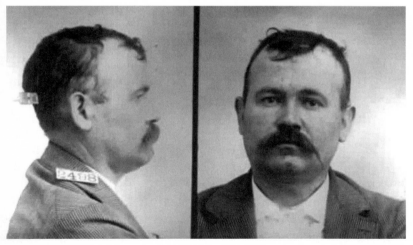

James Stevenson. (Courtesy of the U.S. National Archives and Records Administration)

To allay this mob, the doctor and lawmen spread the story that the assassin had been critically wounded by Cathey's bullets and would surely die. The discontented group accepted this tale and began to drift away. One newspaper reported, "The only thing that saved Stevenson from mob violence is the belief that he could live but a few hours." As soon as the crowd dispersed, Stevenson (whose wounds were not life threatening) was taken to the depot. The prisoner was delivered to the Ardmore jail to protect him from the mob that was thought might redevelop in Pauls Valley, when the citizens learned of Jim's true condition.

It was reported that Stevenson had held ill feeling against Cathey for some time, because of an accused liquor law violation at the saloon. Cathey had recently arrested Stevenson for drunkenness, and when Jim resisted, the officer had handled the inebriated man rather roughly in subduing him. This incident had further inflamed Stevenson's bad attitude toward the lawman.

At that time, saloons were commonly called "joints," and the operators were frequently referred to as "jointists." The next morning following Cathey's death, the mayor called a town meeting. After the leading citizens had gathered, a committee was appointed to notify all jointists in Pauls Valley that they had three hours to get their fixtures and merchandise to the train depot and ready to ship out, or their equipment and supplies would be destroyed.

The committee immediately took action, and soon the town was bustling with dray wagons as they hauled saloon fixtures and stock to the station in compliance with the directive. John Stump was the only Pauls Valley jointist who failed to obey the order. He was emphatically reminded and strongly urged to move out "lock, stock and barrel." Again, he defied the order and ignored the committee's edict. At that point his stuff was piled in the street, saturated with oil, and a match was struck. The local newspaper reported: "The whole was soon up in

R. W. Cathey, Deputy City Marshal, Pauls Valley, Indian Territory.
(From *The Daily Oklahoman,* November 6, 1907)

flames and Mr. Stump was poorer, yet wiser than a few minutes before."

A funeral was held at Pauls Valley for Randolph Cathey on Monday afternoon. Merchants shut their doors, and the schools were closed so that all could attend the ceremony. The officer's body was put aboard the train on Tuesday, to be returned for burial at Youngport, Texas.

A short time later, the local newspaper noted that during the two weeks between the day that the committee had run the jointists out of Pauls Valley and the time that statehood was proclaimed (when prohibition was invoked), not one arrest had been made in town. The article reported that prior to ridding themselves of the local joints, usually one man or more was arrested each day. The paper pointed out that prohibition was obviously the best policy.

Jim Stevenson hired attorney Moman Pruiett to defend him on the murder charge. Pruiett was able to get a change of venue from the newly formed Garvin County, and the case was transferred to Cleveland County. Jim Stevenson's trial for the murder of Officer Cathey was scheduled to begin at Norman in early December 1908, but his attorney got the case postponed to a later date.

On Monday, December 20, 1908, Pauls Valley marshal Joe Roberts observed John Stevenson receive some whiskey as Baldy Green delivered it to him at the Hill and Stevenson Barbershop. Roberts arrested Green. He then called for Stevenson to hand over the whiskey and to appear at the courthouse as a witness. At that point, John Stevenson began cursing Roberts and defiantly pulled his knife. With brisk motion the marshal drew his pistol and struck it sharply across John's head; the knife then fell to the floor. Stevenson was arrested and taken to jail.

John Stevenson was again on the street by Tuesday afternoon, and those who met and talked with him stated that he had vowed to kill Roberts at the earliest opportunity. Fifteen

Moman Pruiett, criminal lawyer, circa 1907. (Photo courtesy of the
Archives & Manuscripts Division of the Oklahoma Historical Society)

years earlier John had shot and killed Constable Joe Gaines, and only a year had passed since Jim Stevenson had killed Marshal Cathey in Pauls Valley. Knowing the disposition of the brothers, citizens throughout the area became concerned for Officer Roberts. One merchant reported an increase in the sales of handguns and ammunition.

About six o'clock on Christmas Eve, 1908, John Stevenson went into The Valley Grocery, where City Police Judge T. L. "Captain" Kendall was clerking at that time. Seeing that Stevenson was in a belligerent mood, Kendall ordered him to leave. This command infuriated the intoxicated visitor to a higher degree, and in stronger terms he continued his tirade upon the judge. Kendall was prepared for the inevitable, and when he saw Stevenson reach for his gun, the judge brought forth a pistol that he had already gripped and fired four shots into the abusive caller. After falling to the floor, the wounded man tried to fire his weapon, but Policeman Roberts had arrived on the scene, and he grabbed the gun in such a manner that the hammer snapped on the officer's finger. Stevenson was taken to the hospital where he died about two hours later. John was buried in the local cemetery.

The bond of five thousand dollars was immediately raised for the city police judge who had a clean record and an impeccable reputation. John Stevenson's previous troubles with the law were well known, and it was popularly thought that Captain Kendall would not have any difficulty in being freed of any charge that might result from his action. Kendall later served as mayor of Pauls Valley.

Jim Stevenson's trial for the murder of Officer Cathey came before the Cleveland County Court in April 1909. As the case unfurled, Moman Pruiett again preformed his wizardry for the defense. He reversed the roles from the original report. Pruiett advised the jury that Cathey had fired first, and his shot had knocked Stevenson down. The attorney emphasized his account of the shooting by acting out the claimed role of his

Capt. T. L. Kendall, Police Judge, who ended John Stevenson's reign of terror upon the good citizens of Pauls Valley, Oklahoma. (Author's collection)

client. He fell upon the floor, then pretended to fire a hand-gun only to defend himself from the attacking officer. Pruiett's dramatic presentation persuaded the jury to bring back a not guilty verdict, in the mid-afternoon of Saturday, April 17, 1909.

Years later the noted criminal lawyer recalled, "I crumpled up in front of that jury an' sprawled out. My damn head hit the floor so hard that I thought I had killed myself, an' I had to lay there. Ever'body thought it was a part of my act, my just layin' so still for so long, but it wasn't. I couldn't get up for a while." Pruiett acknowledged that it had been one of his most difficult cases. This trial had garnered a lot of notoriety because of the Stevenson brothers' previous troubles with the law. The not guilty verdict was typical of the cases in which Moman Pruiett was the defending attorney.

At the time that Jim Stevenson was on trial at Norman, some fifty miles southeast, seven men were in the Pontotoc County jail at Ada in connection with the recent murder of Gus Bobbitt. The victim had been a longtime, popular citizen of the area and had served as an officer of the law. One of the men in jail had admitted his guilt in the affair and had reported the roles that the others had played in Bobbitt's treacherous death.

Numerous citizens of Ada were aware that Moman Pruiett had been hired to defend the accused killer, Jim Miller. Some had also learned that the prominent attorney had recently accepted the cases of Jess West and Joe Allen, who were thought to have hired Miller to kill Bobbitt. Knowing Pruiett's reputation for getting juries to absolve his clients of any wrong-doing, those who were acutely interested in seeing that the men in jail pay for their crime anxiously awaited the verdict to be handed down to Jim Stevenson.

When the results of Stevenson's trial were received at Ada, it prompted the local citizens to assume that with Pruiett defending the ringleaders of the accused men, they would be acquitted of murdering Gus Bobbitt. With their minds plagued by this anticipated consequence, to insure that justice was done, a band of men broke into the Ada jail at about 2:00 A.M. on Monday, April 19, 1909, and removed Jim Miller, Jess West, Joe Allen, and Berry Burrell from their cells.

The mob took the four prisoners to a nearby barn and lynched them. One newspaper reported: "When the verdict of the jury at Norman clearing Jim Stevenson for the murder of Marshal Cathey, was made known in Ada, the general opinion seemed to be that it was not worth while to incur the expense of a trial with the probability of the murderers being freed."

Pruiett's victorious not guilty verdict at Norman had spared Jim Stevenson's life; however, it sparked a Pontotoc County mob into lynching four men some thirty-six hours later. This episode of Western-style justice enacted at Ada in April 1909 is well reported in the following books: *Four Men Hanging: The End of the Old West* by Welborn Hope, *Shotgun for Hire: the Story of "Deacon" Jim Miller, Killer of Pat Garrett* by Glenn Shirley, and *Jim Miller, The Untold Story of a Texas Badman* by Bill C. James.

When released by the court, Jim Stevenson returned to his barbering practice at Pauls Valley. He later settled in Cushing, Oklahoma, and operated a barbershop for years. Following his wife's death in 1942, he moved to Tulsa where he lived in a hotel.

During the morning of April 13, 1951, Jim Stevenson was found in his room after having been severely beaten. The eighty-four-year-old victim was rushed to the emergency hospital where the doctor reported that Stevenson had been savagely assaulted and had lost the sight of his right eye.

Stevenson could provide only meager information to the police about his attacker, whom he only slightly knew when he let the visitor into his quarters. After knocking the aged man about the room and kicking him numerous times, the assailant robbed Stevenson of fifteen dollars, then fled.

A couple of days later, Elmer McDonald, a crippled electrical repairman, was found dead in his shop at Tulsa. It was first thought that his death was accidental, the result of a fall. When an examination revealed that his skull had been crushed and his wallet was missing; the police began to suspect that he might be another victim of the culprit who had beaten up the elderly barber in his hotel room. (Later it was learned that McDonald's wallet had contained nine dollars).

Piecing together the fragments of information that Stevenson (who remained in critical condition) could provide, the police began a search for James Cristner, a local ex-convict and part-time cafe cook. The suspect was located at Muskogee, where he had relatives. Cristner was brought back to Tulsa, and when the police questioned him about the mayhem of Stevenson and the murder of McDonald, he acknowledged total guilt in both cases.

Jim Stevenson never recovered from the brutal beating. Less than a month later, while a patient in a rest home at Broken Arrow, he died on May 9, 1951. Jim was buried beside his wife Josephine in the Fairlawn Cemetery at Cushing.

James M. "Jim" Stevenson died as a result of one last violent encounter in 1951. The victim of a brutal beating at age eighty-four, he is buried at Cushing, Oklahoma. (Author's collection)

CHAPTER 9

Bits of History from Keokuk Falls

Keokuk Falls, Oklahoma Territory, was located in the pan-handle of northeastern Pottawatomie County and was named for the nearby waterfall on the North Canadian River. The waterfall though less than three feet high was unique, being on a major river in this region. The name of the falls had derived from Moses Keokuk, who was the chief of the Sac and Fox tribe, which had settled in that section of Indian Territory.

The first white man to visit the site was Capt. Thomas James in the 1820s. Each spring while operating out of Chouteau Trading Post (near Fort Gibson), Captain James would navigate a keelboat down the Arkansas River to its junction with the Canadian, then he would travel up the river to the "Keokuk Falls," where he would trade trinkets to the Indians for pelts. Washington Irving visited the falls, as he passed through the area on his "Tour of the Prairies" in 1832.

Shortly after the land run in September 1891, which opened that locale to white settlers, the little town began to emerge. In January 1892, the Keokuk Falls post office was established. The mail was delivered by stagecoach from Sapulpa (in the Creek Nation) to the Sac and Fox Agency (near present-day Stroud), then by horseback to the new settlement.

The location of Keokuk Falls (one quarter of a mile west of the Creek Nation, also across the river and a half-mile north of

The actual waterfall (on the North Canadian river) at Keokuk Falls, Oklahoma Territory, where adventurers discovered this natural campsite as early as 1820. (Photo courtesy of the Archives & Manuscripts Division of the Oklahoma Historical Society)

the Seminole Nation) made it an ideal site (Sec.26, T-11N, R-6E) to sell whiskey. Liquor was legal in Oklahoma Territory but was banned in Indian Territory. That feature gave birth to what became the town's most popular places of business, "the Seven Deadly Saloons." To provide suitable access to those facilities for the visitors from the Seminole Nation, a floating toll bridge was constructed across the river, below the falls. As the town (which was frequently referred to simply as Keokuk) grew, two distilleries were built in the settlement. Their products became staples at the local bars and were distributed to the more than fifty other saloons in Pottawatomie County.

D. N. Beaty, who had previously operated a like business in Choctaw City (present Oklahoma County), built the first tavern at Keokuk. Immediately upon opening the doors of his Black Dog Saloon for business, Beaty realized prosperity. Soon thereafter, Dr. Nicholas Stutsman approached him with an offer to

Keokuk Falls, Oklahoma Territory (in present-day Pottawatomie County, Oklahoma), famous for its "Seven Deadly Saloons" that provided whiskey to the citizens across the river in Indian Territory, where it was illegal. (Photo courtesy of the Archives & Manuscripts Division of the Oklahoma Historical Society)

buy the saloon. Beaty refused the proposal, which seemed to whet the rejected party's yen to own the establishment. Doc Stutsman made more offers to purchase the saloon or various interests in it, but they too were unacceptable to Beaty.

Stutsman then built a rival business, the Red Front Saloon. His new tavern drew a fair share of the trade in the ever-growing local market, and it is reported that he frequently delivered wagonloads of whiskey (illegally) into Indian Territory, unhampered by the law. Stutsman's success in those endeavors didn't seem to lessen his longing to own the Black Dog Saloon. If Dr. N. Stutsman (as his name was often cited and who became known simply as Doc) was a medical professional, his expertise in that field was wasted during this period of his life. He is reported only as being a gambler, saloon operator, gunslinger, and an illegal whiskey peddler. He frequently demonstrated his dexterity with a pistol by firing his weapon in Keokuk.

Stutsman and his hired hands created trouble for Beaty and his followers at every opportunity. Their armed clashes often entailed prolonged periods of shooting on the streets of Keokuk. At that time the closest available lawman was at Tecumseh (the Pottawatomie County seat), twenty-eight miles southwest of Keokuk. Once, Beaty sent a rider to report one of the ongoing wild melees to the county officials. Sheriff Jim Gill responded and went to the troubled little town on the North Canadian. One man had been killed in the current skirmish, and three dead horses littered the street. The sheriff and his deputies arrested nine men (three of whom were wounded) and loaded them in a wagon for the long haul to Tecumseh, where they were jailed and charges were filed.

Al Cook was the chief bartender at the Black Dog Saloon and a major supporter of Beaty, having also worked for him at his previous location. One morning Doc Stutsman observed Cook from a distance as the bartender was saddling his horse, preparing to ride out of town. Stutsman produced a pistol and fired at the bartender. Cook drew his weapon and shot at his attacker. Both participants were wounded in the exchange. Cook rode to Choctaw City and reported the incident to the officials. A few days later Stutsman was charged with the crime, but the case was disposed of in some manner before going to trial.

The constant conflict with Doc Stutsman was more than Beaty cared to cope with, and he sold out "lock, stock and barrel" to Aaron and John Haning, who had resided in Oklahoma City. The Haning brothers ran the tavern, and Aaron's wife Margaret opened a rooming house in Keokuk. After Beaty had "thrown in the towel," Doc renewed his effort to buy the Black Dog Saloon. Even though other bars were opening in town, and competition was keen, the Hanings were doing well, and they rejected Stutsman's offer. Doc did not appreciate their refusal and told the brothers that he felt toward them the same way he had felt toward the previous owner.

The interior of one of Keokuk Falls' "Seven Deadly Saloons" around 1898, where many a gunfight took place before law and order could take a stand. (Author's collection)

John Haning had been out of town for a few days, and when Aaron closed their saloon just before midnight, on July 1, 1896, he retired into a back room. The next morning Aaron was found lying on the floor of the drinking parlor, dead. An enlarged, mangled gunshot wound in the back of his head was evident.

As the citizens of Keokuk discussed the murder the following morning, Doc Stutsman spoke of suspicions. He insisted that a neighbor by the name of Bert Moneypenny was the killer and proposed that he be hanged. Doc had not been able to incite any interest to pursue his suggested course when Deputy Sheriff Jap Henry arrived on the scene about mid-afternoon. A few hours after Aaron had been killed, John Haning returned from his Arkansas business trip. John arranged for Sam Bartell (an acquaintance and former detective in Oklahoma City) to come to Keokuk and investigate Aaron's murder.

Two local doctors and another from Shawnee examined the fatal wound extensively. From their findings, along with other evidence, the officers concluded that the murderer feared that after being shot, Aaron was still alive. Further reasoning indicated that rather than risk firing another cartridge, which might bring out some curious neighbors, the killer had inserted a spike nail (that was used at the bar to stir drinks) into the wound. Gouging with that probe he lacerated the victim's brain, to insure his death. A gruesome murder indeed.

The evidence surrounding the murder of Aaron Haning that Bartell and the lawmen found didn't point at Moneypenny, but rather toward his accuser. Doc Stutsman was arrested, charged with murder, and jailed in Tecumseh.

In the November 1896 election, J .D. F. Jennings (father of the outlaw brothers Al and Frank) had been elected Pottawatomie County judge and Bill Trousdale had won the sheriff's office. Whether the result of that election was the reason or whether there was some other cause, shortly thereafter the Stutsman case was transferred to Oklahoma County. In April 1897, Doc was tried, convicted of murder, and sentenced to life imprisonment at hard labor.

Stutsman appealed the conviction and was granted a new trial. At each of Doc's trials confusion reigned, because the testimony of witnesses seemed to be spiked by suspicions, accusations, and acknowledgements concerning a romantic relationship between Deputy Sheriff Jap Henry and Stutsman's wife (and/or ex-wife) Bertha. At his second trial (December 1898, again in Oklahoma City), Doc was acquitted of the murder. After becoming a free man, he returned to Keokuk and sold his Red Front Saloon. Stutsman seemingly drifted into oblivion until recently when his gravesite was located in the Sparks cemetery some fifteen miles northwest of Keokuk Falls.

Lawmen were not normally seen in or around Keokuk, but occasionally one would venture into the vicinity. One such visit was by Deputy U.S. Marshal Bass Reeves, an African American, who was then operating out of Calvin (in present-day Hughes County). While on the trail of some bandits who had robbed a trading post, Reeves learned that they were holed up in a cabin near Keokuk Falls. To carry out his mission, the crafty deputy rented a yoke of aged oxen and an old wagon, because he wanted to appear to be a poverty-stricken tenant farmer when he approached the outlaws.

Upon nearing the suspects' abode while driving the dilapidated rig, Reeves deliberately got the wagon hung up on a tree stump. When the "wanted men" saw the downtrodden traveler's ox cart stalled close to their cabin, not wanting anyone to be lingering near their hideout they came out and physically lifted the wagon from the stump. As they positioned themselves to perform the generous gesture, Reeves stepped back out of the way. When they had completed their noble deed and looked around, they were confronted with two Colt 45 revolvers in the hands of the deputy marshal. Supposedly, there had been four men in the robbery of the store, the same number as had come out of the shanty to see that "the black hick got to going, on his way."

According to various reports of this incident, Bass Reeves handcuffed the men and chained them to the wagon. He searched the cabin and found some merchandise that had been stolen in the robbery. Taking the evidence aboard the wagon, then rechecking that the outlaws were securely chained to his conveyance, the wily lawman headed the oxen southwest, forcing his prisoners to walk. Upon reaching Tecumseh, he turned the robbers over to the county sheriff. Reeves then returned the rented rig to the accommodating owner, mounted his horse, and rode on, to dispense justice in his next assignment.

A man whose name was Martin worked at one of the local distilleries. One evening he was shot and killed at his home. Martin had lived alone at the north edge of Keokuk. One of his neighbors had seen two men riding toward his house about dark and had heard them call his name, then shots had sounded.

Deputy U.S. Marshal Bass Reeves, standing on the left with moustache. Photo taken at Muskogee, Oklahoma, on November 16, 1907. (Photo courtesy of the Archives & Manuscripts Division of the Oklahoma Historical Society)

Apparently, as Martin was in the doorway, silhouetted by the lamplight in the house, the night riders had fired away. The family who had become aware of the commotion found the victim a few minutes later, lying in the opened door, dead. Martin was an easygoing sort of fellow who was not known to have any enemies. It was assumed that the culprits (who were never apprehended) had carried out a grudge from some disagreement that had occurred prior to his moving to the little town on the North Canadian.

The murder of Martin would be more in line with what one might expect to have occurred in the average little town of that period, but it was not the typical case in Keokuk Falls. Most of the murders and other foul play in the subject town were reported to have occurred in the saloons; hence, the term "deadly" used in describing them. During Keokuk's heyday, it was on a stagecoach route. Numerous accounts report that when the stage arrived, the driver would announce, "Keokuk, we'll stop twenty minutes and likely see a man killed."

Keokuk Falls had more than its fair share of homicides, and it was routine for the guilty to beat the justice system. Seldom was anyone convicted of murder. That was not to be the case when sixty-year-old Zachariah W. Thatch was killed in May 1895, on Rock Creek, a couple of miles east of Keokuk.

As they traveled west, James C. Casharego apparently decided to slay his traveling companion; presumably for the wagon, team, and meager money that the elderly man carried. Casharego had grown up being a petty thief while living in Conway, Arkansas. Upon reaching the age of maturity he had been convicted of stealing and forging some bonds, for which he served time in the Tennessee State Penitentiary. After being released from that institution, his uncle had persuaded Thatch (a friend) to let James accompany him on his planned trip into Oklahoma Territory looking for a place to settle.

It is assumed that the twenty-five-year-old ex-convict had pulled a gun to shoot Z. W. Thatch, but the aged man grabbed the muzzle, and when the gun fired, two of his fingers were shot off. Casharego then hit "the old man" in the back of his head with an axe, splitting open his skull. Thatch fell upon the ground, dead. To dispose of the victim, Casharego tied stones to the body and dropped it in Rock Creek, about a half-mile upstream from where it emptied into the North Canadian River. To camouflage the discolored, blood-soaked spot where Thatch had fallen, the murderer built a fire to blacken the ground and cover it with ashes.

The bindings that held the rocks had loosened, permitting the cadaver to float to the surface and become entangled between some vegetation and a log. The odor that reeked from the body alerted a traveler that something was amiss, prompting him to stop and look for the cause. He found the victim's remains at the water's edge near the junction of the creek and the river.

Deputy U.S. Marshal Eddie Reed was assigned to the Rock Creek murder case. Eddie was the son of Jim and Belle Reed. Jim had "followed the outlaw trail" and had been shot and killed by a deputy sheriff in Texas. After her husband's demise, Belle became a notorious horse thief as she consorted with other out-laws. One of her cohorts on the foul side of the law was Sam Starr, whom she married in a Cherokee tribal ceremony.

Eddie's mother, Belle Starr, had been murdered in 1889, near Whitefield, I.T.; in fact, there had been some speculation that her only son was the triggerman. Nothing ever developed from that suspicion; however, Eddie was later convicted of two lesser crimes and was twice committed to prison. After serving his time and following his second release from the peniten-tiary, Eddie had not only obtained a pardon but had become a deputy, serving out of the U.S. marshal's office at Fort Smith, Arkansas. Judge Parker, who was known to be a staunch advo-cate of "law and order," had sanctioned that Reed be depu-tized, because he felt that the young man, having been raised by Belle Starr, had not received a fair chance in life. Eddie had served well as an officer of the law.

*Deputy U.S. Marshal Ed Reed, son of Belle
Starr. Reed served the Federal court in Fort
Smith, Arkansas, answering to Judge Isaac
Parker.* (Author's collection)

When Deputy Reed arrived at Keokuk, the corpse (with two
fingers missing) had been recovered and recognized as being
the older of two men who had been observed passing through
the country and who had camped on Rock Creek. The casualty's
younger companion had recently been seen in the area without
the elderly gentleman. Eddie was able to locate Casharego only
a few miles up the river from where Thatch's body had been
found. The young man had been using the name George
Wilson and upon being questioned, he claimed that his traveling companion was his uncle. Casharego further explained that
his relative had "gone on west" with a couple of men his uncle
knew who had stopped at their camp. He reported that the

three men were expected to be back shortly and that he was tending the horses and wagon, awaiting their return.

The suspect willingly accompanied Deputy Reed to the location where it was known that the pair had camped. As the lawman observed the campgrounds at Rock Creek, he noticed that in addition to a regular, well-used campfire site, there was a second spot nearby where a fire had burned. With the toe of his boot, Eddie had idly begun to kick the cinders from the smaller and less used fire site.

As his boot probed, a crack in the earth emerged (created by a drought season). The fault revealed a suspicious substance. While examining the clod, he recognized it to be dried blood. Eddie carefully dug, and from the crack in the ground, he removed clots of dried blood. The lifeblood of Z. W. Thatch, which flowed freely from his gaping head wound, had coagulated in the dry-weather crack in the ground. Following that discovery, Eddie found the murder weapon, the still bloody axe, in the old man's wagon.

Deputy Reed arrested James Casharego at the campsite where the crime had been committed. Eddie then took his prisoner to Fort Smith, where the suspect was put in Federal jail and charged with murder.

James Casharego was tried in December 1895 for the murder of Z. W. Thatch. The trial was held at Fort Smith with Judge Isaac Parker presiding. The native of Conway, Arkansas, was found guilty and was convicted. On February 18, 1896, Judge Parker sentenced James Casharego to be hanged. While addressing the condemned man, "the hanging judge" expounded: "Even nature revolted against your crime. The earth opened up, drinking the blood and held it in fast embrace until the time that it should appear against you. The water too, in the lowly creek, threw up its dead and bore upon its placid bosom bringing forth the foul evidence of your heinous crime."

James Casharego was hanged on July 30, 1896, and became

the last man to "meet his maker" on the gallows known as "the gates of hell" at Fort Smith. A few weeks later "Judge Parker's Court" was dissolved. Future cases were to be tried in Federal courts located in Texas, Kansas, and the "Twin Territories."

"Big Ed" Thomlinson and Mike Rooney jointly owned one of the local distilleries and one of the "Seven Deadly Saloons." In 1904, Big Ed (standing six feet four inches tall and weighing 250 pounds) shot and killed Jim Sweatte, the town's first marshal. The armed confrontation ensued when Sweatte became aware that Thomlinson was carrying on an adult affair with the marshal's young daughter, who appropriate for her age was attending the local grade school. At the resulting trial, Thomlinson convinced the jury that Sweatte had drawn his pistol first and that he had reacted only in self-defense. The panel acquitted the accused man.

In December 1905, while Big Ed was standing on the sidewalk of the little town, he was shot and mortally wounded by a Felix Grundy. In this latter case, Thomlinson had not fired a shot nor had he even shown a gun. Grundy was arrested and charged with the crime, but he won acquittal at his trial, due to the witnesses' conflicting stories, which created confusion among the jury.

The Hiram Thorpe family, who resided west of Keokuk, frequently visited the little town. Hiram's twin sons, Jim and Charlie (the latter died at age eight) had been born in 1888 at the Thorpe homestead, a few miles upstream from "the falls" and a mile north of the river. As a teenager Jim Thorpe attended the Haskell Indian Boys School in Kansas, and after completing it, he went to school at Carlisle, Pennsylvania, where he excelled in sports. Jim continued in that field and was recognized as "the most outstanding contestant of the 1912 Olympics" at Stockholm, Sweden. He later developed into a noted professional baseball and football player. Many consider that the young man "who hailed from the Keokuk community," was the world's greatest athlete of the twentieth century.

One of the more popular amusements in Keokuk was watching the swine that ran loose in the little town, when they gathered behind the Rooney & Thomlinson distillery, after the mash was dumped. The hogs would stagger, squeal, and maneuver about. Their gyrations would delight the observers; many of who were feeling the effects of the bottled spirits from the distillery's previous mash.

An unusual sight that the citizens of Keokuk Falls sometimes saw on their Main Street was "Rufe" Howard riding his seven-foot-tall ostrich, complete with small saddle. Howard was an auctioneer who lived at Vista, in Pottawatomie County, and he frequently rode the big bird to the sales that "he cried." Rufe and his ostrich were popular throughout the area and often visited Keokuk. Howard would routinely challenge a cowboy (typically in a saloon) to a race, then goad him into a wager. It is reported that when the contest was limited to one hundred yards, Rufe (mounted on his ostrich) always beat the horseback rider.

One of the many rank events that occurred in the little town began in the early morning hours of January 1, 1894. A band of Seminole Indians dressed only in breechcloths (in mid-winter) appearing to be young, wild, and on "the warpath," attacked the distillery that was owned by Jack Owens. They beat up the night watchman and after amply sampling the booze, they tore up the place. Their continuing havoc confirmed that the product was potent. The strangely garbed young hellions toted off a great deal of the powerful potion, as they unsteadily strode away, shortly before dawn.

Keokuk Falls had grown throughout the 1890s. Even though the Seven Deadly Saloons and two distilleries were considered to be the "centerpieces" and were the most publicized, other businesses had opened after the land run of 1891. Numerous stores, hotels, eating places, barbershops, livery stables, blacksmith shops, harness/saddle shops, one cotton gin, two grist mills, a telephone exchange, and even a coffin factory had

Rufe Howard's "Ostrich Races" on the streets of Keokuk Falls were a welcome distraction from the hardships of frontier life. (Author's collection)

been built and operated in the little town beside the North Canadian River. Keokuk never had a hospital, but when it was going full stride, three doctors and two drugstores prospered—much of their business was patching up customers of the saloons after fights with fist and/or gun. The little town never had a church, but religious services were regularly held in the schoolhouse. A local Masonic Lodge was well attended, and for a time the citizens enjoyed their weekly newspaper, the *Keokuk Kall.*

As the twentieth century unfurled, the railroads bypassed the little town, and its progress slowed. Keokuk was doomed in November 1907, when Oklahoma became the forty-sixth state, and prohibition was implemented. Many of Keokuk's other businesses shut their doors soon after the saloons and distilleries were forced to close. The post office continued to operate until 1918, when it too "bit the dust." The river has changed from its course of a century ago, and nothing recognizable from that period remains at Keokuk Falls, neither at the town site beside the river, nor in the flowing North Canadian. The isolated little cemetery (in the middle of a cow pasture, to which only a seldomused, grassed-over road leads) and a few bits of history are all that remain of the once exciting and prosperous Keokuk Falls.

CHAPTER 10

Dr. Beemblossom Becomes
a Sleuth

Following Oklahoma's Land Run of 1889, which opened the
area known as the Unassigned Lands, other sections of the state
were opened by the same method; however, these wild events
led to a multitude of personal conflicts, resulting in the death
of many of the disputing contenders. By 1900, the "powers that
be" decided that a lottery would be a more appropriate method
to distribute the land to the multitude of aspiring settlers.

The Kiowa, Comanche, and Apache lands, along with that
of the Caddo and Wichita, were authorized to be opened for
settlement in 1901, by implementing the lottery system. Those
people eligible to claim a homestead could sign up beginning
June 9, 1901, and the drawing was to commence some two
months later, on August 6.

As the date for the drawing approached, many of those who
had registered began to flock into Lawton, the site that had
been selected for the drawing. One of the interested parties,
who wanted to be on hand for the big event, was Dr. Zeno
Beemblossom of Oklahoma City. Two days before the disburse-
ment of the land was to begin, the physician and his eleven-year
old son, Joseph Phillip "Jay" Beemblossom, rode the train to
Rush Springs, near the western edge of the Chickasaw Nation.
At Rush Springs, they met Professor Esly of the Tulsa Indian
School, a Mr. Milder, and Harry Darbyshire, the doctor's

nephew, who was armed and provided the conveyance. The four adults and boy got into the carriage, and Darbyshire headed the team westward on the road to Lawton. After traveling an hour or so, they decided to camp early and enjoy the evening. There was no hurry as they had all the next day to cover the remaining thirty-five miles into Lawton.

The influx of hopeful homesteaders, who were gathering for the drawing, provided a golden opportunity for Bert Casey and his outlaw gang. Casey and his cohorts, Mort Perkins and George Moran, were busy hijacking the travelers who were en route to Lawton. Just after the Beemblossom party had pulled off the road into a grove of trees and was setting up camp, the outlaws rode in. They shouted to the surprised campers, "Hold up your hands." There was some delay in complying with the road agents' order. One of the robbers yelled, "Damn 'em, if they don't get their hands up, kill 'em." An instant later, a shot rang out. The

Sketch of the Casey gang holding up the Beemblossom party along the road to Lawton, Oklahoma Territory, circa 1901. (From *The Daily Oklahoman*, September 11, 1932)

bullet, which may have been intended for another of the party, took effect in the body of young Jay Beemblossom.

The slug entered the boy's back, close to his spine, and came out near his naval, then pierced his wrist. The highwaymen robbed Esly, Milder, and Darbyshire of their money and personal items, and then went on their way. While the doctor tended to his son, the others loaded their camping gear, hitched the team, and the party hurried back to Rush Springs. Jay Beemblossom died about midnight. The next day, Dr. Beemblossom returned to Oklahoma City with the body of his son. Jay was buried in the Fairlawn Cemetery in northwest Oklahoma City.

The murder of his son consumed Dr. Beemblossom with a vengeance. He vowed that he would do whatever was necessary to see that the guilty parties paid for their crime. He renounced his profession as a physician, and immediately commenced scheming to insure that the murderers were caught.

Zeno Beemblossom was of German descent. He was born in Iowa in 1855. After completing normal schooling, he took some advanced courses, and then taught school a few terms before starting medical studies. In 1878, Zeno Beemblossom married Florence Sheppard. He graduated from the Keokuk (Iowa) Medical College in 1881 as a Doctor of Medicine. Beemblossom practiced his newly earned profession in Iowa and later in Nebraska before moving to Oklahoma Territory. Dr. Beemblossom had arrived on the day of the run for the Unassigned Lands, April 22, 1889, but failed to obtain a claim. About a month later, he purchased the pending rights to a quarter section of land from two contesting claimants. Beemblossom homesteaded on his newly acquired land, northeast of Oklahoma Station, later known as Oklahoma City. He received the patent to his 160-acre homestead in 1894.

Beemblossom proved to be a successful farmer and stockman, as well as a doctor. As other settlers moved on, he pur-

Dr. Zeno Beemblossom gave up his medical practice to chase down Bert Casey and his outlaw gang who had murdered his eleven-year-old son. (Photo courtesy of Myra Woodside)

chased the farms that became available in the immediate area of his first farm—all had been in the vicinity of the present-day Lincoln Park Zoo and Remington Park racetrack. He made improvements to the land, erected buildings, and became very prosperous. The doctor sold some of these properties in 1900, and was eager for new adventures when the new lands were to be opened for settlement in 1901.

The tragedy that occurred on the road between Rush Springs and Lawton caused Beemblossom to drop all plans of expanding into the new territory. He was determined to see that the parties who were guilty of his son's death were brought to justice.

Deputy U.S. Marshal Chris Madsen was assigned to the boy's

Dr. Zeno Beemblossom's medical office in Oklahoma City, circa 1900. Dr. Beemblossom is seated at the desk, and his (unidentified) assistant stands. (Photo courtesy of Myra Woodside)

murder case. He traveled to Durant in pursuit of the three hijackers. Casey and Perkins were not with George Moran when Chris found and arrested him. Moran was not inclined to provide his captor any information about his companions, so Madsen returned with his lone prisoner and no clue as to where the other two outlaws were. Bert Casey and Mort Perkins were "long gone," and their whereabouts were unknown to the officers.

A few days after Jay Beemblossom was killed, Casey and Perkins robbed a cattleman's camp. Among the things that the outlaws stole was a lady's small gold watch that had belonged to the cattleman's daughter. Perkins then visited the farm home of his sweetheart in the Chickasaw Nation and demanded that she leave the country with him. She consented; however, her mother objected. Mort saddled the girl's horse, and she mounted. They were ready to leave when he told her to "kiss your mother good-bye 'cause you'll never see her again." This caused the girl to balk and dismount, instantly. She defied Perkins and dared him to lay hands on her. Perkins pleaded, threatened, raged, swore, and displayed a six-shooter, but the girl was mentally stronger than Perkins. She compelled the outlaw to ride away without her.

Beemblossom took to the trail of Bert Casey and Mort Perkins. He learned of their robbing the cattleman's camp. Zeno traced the pair through the Chickasaw Nation, then trailed them north past Table Mountain, Rainey Mountain School, Fort Reno, and into Kansas.

Casey had a girlfriend in one of the southern Kansas towns, where he and Perkins spent a couple of days. While there, the three of them went to a photography studio and had their pictures taken. Within a few days, Beemblossom acquired one of the photos and confirmed that Casey and Perkins were two of the men who had killed his son.

Zeno Beemblossom trailed the outlaw pair southward into what is now Kay County, Oklahoma, where Perkins had another girlfriend. He proposed marriage to her, and she accepted. He gave her the lady's gold watch that he had taken from the cattleman's camp. Before Perkins and the girl were married, he and Casey became alarmed and hurriedly left the area with Beemblossom only a few hours' ride behind them.

Beemblossom found Mort Perkins's second girlfriend. He searched her house and found the little gold watch that Perkins had given her. From the ranch house in Ponca City, Casey and Perkins rode the line of "hold out" sites into Seminole country, where they felt secure. After several more confrontations with law enforcement, Perkins was finally apprehended, charged, tried, and sentenced to a long prison sentence. Bert Casey was shot and killed by a fellow gang member, who had been released from jail and deputized to bring Casey to the authorities, or kill him, which he did.

To what extent Beemblossom's dogged determination and persistent efforts to hunt down the gang aided the officers to

The only known photograph of the notorious Oklahoma outlaw, Bert Casey.
(Photo courtesy of Myra Woodside)

Bert Casey's partner in crime, Mort Perkins. (Photo courtesy of Myra Woodside)

run the Casey gang "to ground" is not known. However, within two years, Dr. Zeno Beemblossom was credited with having done more to bring the gang to justice than any other man.

True to his vows, Beemblossom never practiced as a physician again. He established himself in the real estate business, tried politics for a while, and continued to work in law enforcement, when needed. Beemblossom continued to buy, improve, and sell farms very profitably in the Oklahoma City area. He served as Oklahoma Territory secretary of agriculture under Gov. Thompson Ferguson. Even then, he continued working in law enforcement, as a special deputy, especially on murder cases that had but scant clues. When Oklahoma became a state, Beemblossom ran for sheriff of Oklahoma County as a Republican; however, he was defeated.

One of his assignments as an investigative officer may have been the cause of his death. A man named Sam Connor had been killed at a country dance at the Balzar farm home, four miles northeast of Oklahoma City, near the corner identified today as Northeast 23rd Street and Martin Luther King Boulevard. Archie and Ivan Hawkins had been tried for the murder of Connor, but were acquitted. After they were freed, Dr. Beemblossom was assigned the case as a special deputy by Oklahoma County sheriff George W. Garrison to take over the investigation into the murder of Sam Connor.

J. C. Woodson had been a tenant for five years on one of the farms owned by Beemblossom; however, in December 1907, the forty-five-year-old Woodson moved his family to another farm. At that time, there was no known problem between the owner and the former renter.

During the morning of February 18, 1908, Beemblossom went to his vacated farm, where he found J. C. Woodson and Woodson's twenty-two-year-old son, Robert, loading some items that they had left behind when they moved away. Trouble developed within the trio when the fifty-three-year-old Beemblossom objected to Robert loading a grindstone. The farm owner and the former tenant each claimed that they had purchased the item. As the older men argued, Robert proceeded to load the grindstone on their wagon. To stop Robert, Beemblossom hit him over the head with the handle of the grindstone, and they started fighting. While his son fought with Beemblossom, J. C. pulled a .38-caliber revolver from his coat and fired one shot into the doctor's chest, the bullet entering near his heart. Beemblossom died moments later.

The only witnesses to this killing were the Woodsons. J. C. drove to the county jail and announced to Sheriff Garrison, "I guess that you have heard of the killing. Well, I am the man that did it." Officers went to the farm where the sheriff found the body of his deputy in the yard, as Woodson had reported. They noted that both coats the victim was wearing were buttoned, and his pistol was in his pocket.

Zeno's body was delivered to the Marshall undertaking establishment. He was buried beside his son, Jay, in the Fairlawn Cemetery.

Tombstone of Jay Beemblossom, located at Fairlawn Cemetery in Oklahoma City, Oklahoma. (Author's collection)

Beemblossom monument, located in Fairlawn Cemetery in Oklahoma City, Oklahoma. (Author's collection)

The newspaper article that reported Beemblossom's death provided a brief account of his life and noted that he had chased down the murderers of his son. It further stated that the doctor had recently been engaged as a special deputy in an effort to determine the person responsible for the killing of Sam Connor. The newspaper article's headline, "KILLS OFFI-CER WHO SOUGHT TO FIX A CRIME ON HIS SON," revealed that Robert Woodson was Beemblossom's main suspect in the death of Sam Connor.

The first trial of J. C. Woodson for the murder of Zeno Beemblossom ended in a hung jury and was declared a mistri-al. It was rescheduled for a later date.

At about nine-thirty on Saturday evening, September 18, 1910, Herbert "Bert" Beemblossom, Zeno's other son, shot D. T. "Tip" Woodson, the son of J. C. and younger brother to Robert Woodson. The shooting occurred at the Austin Dance Hall, on the second floor of a building at Second and Robinson Avenue in downtown Oklahoma City. Using the pistol that his father was carrying when he was killed, Bert fired two shots at the younger Woodson. His first bullet hit no one; however, the explosion of the cartridge set fire to the sleeve of the lady's dress with whom Tip was dancing. Bert's second shot hit Tip in his chest, passed near his heart, and exited his body at the left shoulder. Tip was rushed to the Rolator's Hospital. The first reports of the wounded man indicated that his condition was critical and his wounds would likely be fatal.

Meanwhile at the dance, a couple of men, who were on the dance floor, disarmed Bert. The police arrived and arrested young Beemblossom, leading him away to jail. And, as the band played on, the large crowd, who had gathered for the very popular Saturday night entertainment, disappeared into the night.

Witnesses reported that Bert had been there about an hour, and had sat quietly until he saw Woodson and Miss Ollie Wagoner dance nearby. He then stood and confronted the couple with his pistol. Ollie Wagoner reported that Bert's action was caused by his jealousy of her. Beemblossom stated to the police, "While discussing the matter of a partner with a man on the dance floor, I was struck by someone on the forehead with what I think was 'knucks,' and believe it to be Woodson. You can see the bruise over my eye. It stunned me and when I recovered, Tip was standing in front of me. Remembering that his father had killed my father and knowing that he had it in for me because of the prosecution, I drew my gun and fired."

The wound that Bert Beemblossom had inflicted on the son of his father's murderer, which was first believed to be fatal, proved not to be. Tip recovered from the gunshot, and Bert was held on the charge of attempted murder.

J. C. Woodson went on trial the second time for the murder of Dr. Z. E. Beemblossom on November 22, 1910, in Oklahoma City. J. C. took the stand and claimed that he considered it necessary to shoot Beemblossom to save the life of his son, Robert. Woodson stated that he knew Beemblossom had a revolver because he was a deputy sheriff and always carried a pistol. Furthermore, he had fired only after Beemblossom unloosened his overcoat and started to draw a revolver from his hip pocket. His testimony was contradictory to the evidence that Sheriff Garrison and his deputies had found at the site, that the victim's coats were still buttoned when they arrived. The jury was influenced by Judge George Clark's instructions, which included, "A man has the right to shoot and kill in defending the life of his wife, his sons, or servants." With but little deliberation, the jury reached its decision. On November 26, 1901, J. C. Woodson was found not guilty of murdering Dr. Zeno Beemblossom. The charge against Robert Woodson for the murder of Beemblossom was dismissed on November 28, 1910.

After the charges against Robert were dropped, it was rumored that Tip Woodson was willing for the case against

Bert to be dropped as well. The court was called to order the next morning for the trial of Bert Beemblossom for the attempted murder of Tip Woodson. Judge Clark remained as the presiding judge; however, this time the jury "deadlocked." and a mistrial was declared. The charges were ultimately dismissed, and no further action was taken.

CHAPTER 11

Ambush and Murder in Creek Country

Cicero Davis was born in Georgia and as a young man he and his family moved to Indian Territory. A fraction of Indian blood flowed within his veins, and he was listed on the Cherokee rolls. When Cicero married, he and his wife, Sidney, established their home a few miles outside the western boundary of the domain that had been allotted to those of his tribal heritage. The newlyweds resided on his Circle Bar Ranch in the Creek Nation, between Porum and Checotah.

Cicero was a prosperous stockman and was thought to be worth over a hundred thousand dollars. On Tuesday morning, September 11, 1906, the forty-eight-year-old, well-to-do rancher took his wife and their three daughters to Warner, so they could catch the train en route to Arkansas. The Davis children were to enroll in school at Fort Smith.

After the eastbound train departed with his family aboard, Cicero tended to some routine business in town. It was late afternoon when he climbed on his farm wagon and reined the team homeward. Three hours later, a rider galloped his horse into Warner bringing word that Cicero Davis had been found shot to death on the road about six miles southwest of town.

On Tuesday night, Deputy Bud Ledbetter and other lawmen from the U.S. marshal's office in Muskogee, along with some bloodhounds, were sent on a chartered train to Checotah. Jack

Cicero Davis, prosperous stockman of the Creek Nation, was murdered from ambush by unknown assailants. (Author's collection)

Deputy U.S. Marshal Bud Ledbetter, one of the best lawmen in the territory, was the principal investigator of Mack Alfred and his crimes. (Author's collection)

Davis, who lived in Muskogee and who was a younger brother of the murdered man, accompanied the officers. Two local men with horses met Ledbetter and his posse at the depot and guided them to the site of the crime, which was about fifteen miles east-southeast of Checotah and less than two miles from Davis's home. The officers reported that it appeared the victim had been shot twice with a Winchester and once with a shotgun.

While searching the murder scene for clues on Wednesday morning, the officers found the site where they believed the assassins had hid for some time. The grass had been trampled down. Ledbetter surmised that the snipers had chosen that location to wait so as not to be seen by Davis as he approached on his way home. The bloodhounds were unable to pick up a scent leading away from the area; however, the officers found two sets of tracks leaving the site.

The posse followed the tracks that had been made after a light shower had fallen the previous afternoon. The trail led the officers to Mack Alfred's house, which was about one and one-half miles from the place where Cicero had been murdered. The footprints were measured, and one set tallied with Alfred's shoes. A cartridge that had been found at the murder site matched the ones in his rifle.

Ledbetter arrested Mack Alfred (aka Mac Alford) along with D. King and Bud Roberts, who were visiting with Alfred when the lawmen arrived. The posse delivered the prisoners to Checotah, where the trio were put aboard a train and taken to Muskogee, that night.

As soon as Mrs. Davis learned of Cicero's death, she and their children caught the first train out of Fort Smith and returned to the homestead. Sidney arranged for her husband's remains to be transported to Fort Smith where his funeral was held, and he was buried in the City Cemetery (now Oak Cemetery).

When Ledbetter's posse got back to Muskogee, the three

prisoners were placed in Federal jail to be charged with the murder of Cicero Davis. For years, stories had circulated in the neighborhood about Mack Alfred having murdered a local resident referred to as "Old Man Spivey." Deputy U.S. Marshal Frank Jones, who lived at Checotah, had investigated that case; however, no one had ever been charged with the crime. Some local citizens also related a story that Alfred had previously killed another man and disposed of him by tying a large stone around his neck and dropping him in the Arkansas River.

Even though Mack Alfred's name had frequently been mentioned as the major suspect of previous homicides in the area, Davis was the first person that Alfred had been charged with murdering. The crime had been committed near the eastern boundary of the newly formed McIntosh County. As Oklahoma statehood was developing, criminals were transferred from Muskogee to the county jail at Eufaula.

Mack Alfred's trial came before the McIntosh County Court at Eufaula during the last week of February 1907. Charges had been dropped against D. King and Bud Roberts. King, who had been a tenant on one of Alfred's farms, had turned state's evidence and became a major witness for the prosecution.

When called before the court, King testified that Mack Alfred had told him about having killed Cicero Davis. He also stated that the suspect had explained to him about having wrapped his shoes with rags that had been heavily powdered with cayenne pepper, so that the bloodhounds would not follow his scent. The dogs' unwillingness to sniff out the tracks, and a bundle of rags that the officers found near the suspect's home, supported that contention. King's testimony also included a statement that the third shot was not from a shotgun, as the officers had speculated, but was an explosive bullet that Alfred had fired from his rifle.

Deputy Ledbetter testified that the tracks, which led away from the site where he believed the suspects had lingered while waiting for their victim, were traced to Mack Alfred's house and that one set of tracks matched his footprints. Ledbetter also described the loaded cartridge that he had discovered at the scene of the murder as "a sister shell" to those that were found in the suspect's rifle. Numerous witnesses testified that it had been common knowledge in the community for many years that bitter animosity existed between the accused man and the Davis family. Several local citizens, who were called to the stand, swore that they had heard Mack Alfred threaten to kill Cicero Davis.

Sam Shaddix, a neighbor of Alfred's, testified that the accused man had told him that he was going to kill Cicero Davis because Davis had talked to a banker at Warner and had prevented Alfred from obtaining a loan. Shaddix further stated that Alfred claimed that Deputy U. S. Marshal Frank Jones had urged him to kill Davis "just 'cause he needed killin'" and that Jones would help protect Mack Alfred. Cross-examination could not divert Shaddix from his story.

General Dunlap was a former deputy U. S. marshal, who, in recent months, had been charged with activities on the foul side of the law. He testified that while a prisoner in jail with the accused man Alfred had stated, "I killed the son of a b—— and I am going to beat the case, too." Bill Clark, who had been an inmate of the jail at the time, testified that he had overheard the conversation between the two men and confirmed that Alfred had openly acknowledged to Dunlap that he had killed Davis. Fifteen months after Dunlap testified at this trial, he was killed in the armed conflict that developed between Eufaula and Checotah over the selection of Eufaula as the permanent site for the McIntosh County seat.

After the testimony of Bill Clark, which corroborated the former deputy's account, the government rested its case against Alfred. The prosecuting attorneys reflected satisfaction with their presentation and confidence that the jury would issue a conviction.

Two of Mack Alfred's daughters, Susie and Fanny, testified

that their father was with them eating watermelon in their garden when the crime was committed. Susie further stated to the court that Tom Conger, a government witness, tried to intimidate her from taking the stand. She reported that Conger had threatened her that if she gave a false alibi for her father she would be charged with perjury. Other supporters of the defense claimed that King, the government's "key" witness, had told them that the Davis family had promised to pay him a five-hundred-dollar bonus and a dollar for each day that he was held in jail, if he would "stick" Alfred.

One local newspaper reported, "If Mack Alfred is guilty of having murdered Cicero Davis, he is the gamest man that has ever faced a jury from the prisoner's chair. If Mack Alfred is not innocent, he possesses that quality of brazen bravado that has redeemed the life of many a guilty man."

The case was processed to the McIntosh County jury on Wednesday, February 27. After fifteen hours of deliberation, the jury was stalled out. Seven of the jurors were staunchly supporting conviction, and five were insisting that the accused should be acquitted. Believing that the panel was hopelessly deadlocked, Judge Louis Sulzbacher declared a mistrial and released the jury.

Mack Alfred's case was then transferred to Muskogee County. In May 1907, he was tried the second time for the murder of Cicero Davis. His trial at Muskogee was much like the previous proceeding at Eufaula. After hearing the case, the jurors deliberated nearly forty-eight hours before they reached the verdict. On Saturday evening, May 11, the Muskogee jury declared that the accused man was not guilty.

Immediately after Mack Alfred was relieved of the Cicero Davis murder charge, he was arrested again and taken back to jail. Alfred was then charged with complicity in the murder of William Spivey, who had been killed four years earlier near Porum, Indian Territory. Mack Alfred was brought before the court in late June of 1907 on the Spivey murder charge. At a previous hearing on the case, Mack Alfred had turned state's evidence and had been given immunity for his testimony.

In his earlier deposition, Alfred had sworn that he held the horses while Bob Davis, Ben Graham, and Tuck Thornbury killed Spivey. He reported that after the three men had murdered the old man, they poured kerosene on the victim's clothing and house, setting the whole place ablaze with him inside. Alfred stated in his earlier testimony that Spivey's cache had been divided among the four; however, he insisted that he had taken no part in the crime—other than to stand guard and hold the saddled horses.

This second hearing, concerning Alfred's role in Spivey's death, was likely held because of confusion concerning the case, perhaps due to a lack of documentation and/or legal records that might have been misplaced while converting from Indian Territory to statehood. After reviewing the depositions and other records of the previous court hearing, the prosecutors dropped the indictment against Mack Alfred for the murder of "Old Man Spivey." The other three men—Bob Davis, Ben Graham, and Tuck Thornbury—were out on bond, and their cases were still pending.

Mack Alfred was released from jail on June 29, 1907. He had been confined as a prisoner for more than nine months. Shortly after he was freed, a local newspaper reported that Mack Alfred feared that he would be shot and killed if he remained in the country. So, he was planning to move to Mexico. Not only did Alfred fear retaliation from his numerous enemies, likewise some of the people who had testified against him in court had moved away to escape the anticipated revenge of Alfred's wrath.

Even though the court had acquitted Alfred on the charge of murdering Cicero Davis, there were rumors that the Davis family still considered him guilty as charged. Cicero had three brothers—Sam, Jack, and Bob—who resided in the area. It was reported that they had spent a fortune trying to get the accused man convicted. Some accounts related that the Davis family had hired special lawyers to assist the prosecution.

About a month after Mack had been released from jail, he went to Porum and, while dallying on the street after making his purchases, he talked with the town marshal. During that amiable discussion, Alfred told the officer that he intended to steer clear of the Davis brothers. He also advised the lawman that he planned to move into Checotah the following week. Alfred further commented that as soon as he could get his business in order and get through with the Spivey case he aimed to move his family to Mexico.

Not long after his conversation with the local marshal, Mack prepared to leave Porum in the company of two men and a boy. As the four traveled homeward, Alfred sat erect on the wagon seat with an automatic rifle across his knee, seemingly concerned and vigilant of the surroundings. When the evening sun was about one hour above the horizon, on Tuesday, July 23, 1907, the conveyance reached a point only one mile from Alfred's farmhouse and less than one-half mile from the place where Cicero Davis had been killed.

Suddenly, three shots rang out. One bullet hit Alfred in the head, and two struck his body. He toppled from the wagon—dead! None of the other three passengers had been hit.

Alfred's companions reported that immediately after the shots were fired, they heard horses' hooves clatter in quick retreat from a clump of bushes and trees beside the road. They had not seen anyone, but each claimed that more than one horse was required to make the noise they had heard. R. D. Lung, who was with the Alfred party, immediately rode to Checotah and reported the murder.

Less than a year after Cicero Davis had been murdered, Mack Alfred, who had been tried twice for the crime and acquitted, became a victim of the same fate. While traveling by wagon, three bullets had struck and killed each of the two

Never convicted of any of the murders he was charged with, Mack Alfred would later become a victim of an ambush murder not far from Porum, Oklahoma. As with the other murders, no one was ever convicted in his death. His grave can be found in the Twin Grove Cemetery. (Author's collection)

men, and both had been murdered about the same time of day and near the same site.

Mack Alfred was laid to rest in the Twin Grove Cemetery, not far from the place where he met his death. No one was ever arrested or charged with the killing of Mack Alfred. No one was ever convicted in the death of Cicero Davis. Had someone killed Mack Alfred because some still believed he had murdered Davis; or, was he killed because of his testimony in the Spivey murder case?

Could some outside party have murdered each of the men for his own personal reason and have gotten away, unsuspected of killing either or both men? Apparently, neither of the murder cases was ever solved, and, therefore, the incidences go down in history as an "Ambush and Murder in Creek Country."

Sometime after Mack Alfred was killed, charges against Bob Davis, Ben Graham, and Tuck Thornbury for the murder of William Spivey were dropped—due to the fact that the "key" witness against them had, himself, been silenced by "subjects unknown."

CHAPTER 12

Ira N. Terrill: Oklahoma's First Lawmaker/Lawbreaker

Ira Nathan Terrill was born on April 17, 1852, in Illinois. A few years later, his family moved to Sedgwick County, Kansas, where Ira was raised. He first appeared in Oklahoma Territory as one of David Payne's Boomers. Payne and W. L. Couch sought to open the territory for free settlement. Terrill (sometimes spelled Terrell) was a member of the force (more than two hundred men) that Couch led into the Unassigned Lands in December 1884. They set up camp on Stillwater Creek (now Payne County). This was the largest assembly that had attempted to establish a base in the area, which was off-limits for such habitation. When the army ordered Couch and his followers to disband and move out, they ignored the military command.

Col. Edward Hatch had the capability to dispose of the Boomer encampment, but rather than to attack their post and cause unnecessary bloodshed, he chose to blockade their site and cut off all supplies. His strategy was effective, and a few days later, they pulled up stakes and returned to Kansas.

Terrill's next known venture into Oklahoma Territory was on April 19, 1889, three days before the beginning of the official land run of that year. At that time, he led five men into the area where the Boomers had camped in 1884. This excursion was illegal, and the men claimed that they had encroached into the forbidden land by accident. They further stated that

Ira N. Terrill would enter the Twin Territories of what is now the state of Oklahoma in 1884 as one of David Payne's "Boomers," returning later to stake his claim in the land and in the history of the Sooner State. (Photo courtesy of the Archives & Manuscripts Division of the Oklahoma Historical Society)

when they learned of their actual location, they hurried back across the line; then on April 22 they raced along with the thousands who made "the run of '89."

Terrill staked a claim of seventy acres on the north bank of the Cimarron River, west of where the city of Perkins is now located. Their trek into the Unassigned Lands three days before the official opening date tainted the homestead claims of Terrill and his followers, who were then labeled "Sooners."

As soon as Ira could provide quarters for his family, he brought his wife (the former Eliza Jane Parsons) and their four children from Kansas to his homestead. While trying to "prove-up" on his claim, he decided to run for a seat in the territorial legislature. Terrill was a nonconformist and very vocal on political matters. He was impetuous and intensely temperamental. Ira supported the Populist Party and entered the race to become one of the Payne County representatives.

The election was held on August 5, 1890, and Ira Terrill won one of the twenty-six seats that made up the first Oklahoma Territorial House of Representatives. The legislature convened at Guthrie, on August 27, 1890.

Neither the Democrats nor the Republicans had seated a majority in the Lower House. Terrill was a leader of the five Populist members, which held the swing votes in the balance of power. Ira's support was sought by both major parties, which permitted him to exercise a prominent position on the issues that arose.

The first major subject to come before the legislature was the location of the territorial capital. After much heated discussion, it was decided (the vote was not along party lines) to leave the capital at Guthrie. Selecting the cities where the colleges were to be located also created an extensive debate. Terrill was instrumental in getting the Agriculture and Mechanical College (now Oklahoma State University) located at Stillwater (in Ira's home county).

Early in the session, the new legislature passed a bill that established a contract with the state of Kansas to house the territory's inmates. Representative Terrill was the leader enacting this law, which allowed Kansas to work territorial prisoners in its coal mines.

Mr. Terrill was extremely outspoken on the many issues that came before the House. On one occasion, he felt that the speaker was ignoring him, and so he walked out of the assembly. A short time later, Ira returned and laid a Colt 45 revolver on his desk, then announced: "Mr. Speaker, I am an American citizen and have the right to be heard as a member of this House. I am prepared to enforce my demand."

Concerned that a barrage of bullets might burst forth, House members ducked for cover as Sergeant-at-Arms James M. Jerome approached the irate representative. With the help of House messenger Rufus Razey, Jerome managed to gain control of the weapon. They persuaded Terrill to step into the hall, where the upset member calmed down within a few minutes. A short time later, Terrill returned to the chamber and apologized to his fellow officers.

A strong homicide law was enacted by the first legislature. This was one of Ira Terrill's pet bills, and he led it through the House, as the session was drawing to a close. The first Oklahoma Territorial Legislature adjourned on Christmas Eve 1890.

Some ten days later, on January 3, 1891, Terrill went with a Charles Cole to the land office at Guthrie. Cole was one of the five men who had been with Terrill when he ventured into the Unassigned Lands, three days before the official opening. Cole's claim was being contested, and Terrill attended the hearing as a witness in support of Cole's stake.

After attesting to Cole's rights, Terrill set forth to "prove-up" on his homestead. George M. Embrey was on hand to contest Ira's claim. The essence of Embrey's protest was Terrill's encroachment, three days before the run.

When Embrey (also spelled Embry and Embree) completed his testimony, he went into the yard. As he relaxed and leaned against a fence, Ira and his older brother David approached him. Moments later, harsh words were being exchanged between the Terrill brothers and Embrey.

Witnesses to the following action gave conflicting accounts of who (David B. Terrill or George Embrey) produced a gun. Most reported that the pistol was originally in David's hand. A struggle developed between the two elderly men over the weapon that had come into play. While David and George tussled for control of the revolver, Ira drew a pistol and fired four shots into Embrey. When the sixty-two-year-old victim slumped to the ground, Ira fired another bullet into his forehead.

Logan County sheriff L. T. Shockley arrested Terrill under the law that the Payne County representative had intensely advocated only a few days previously. Ira was looked upon with disdain by most of the citizens, as they considered that he was a "Sooner," a very derogatory term, at that time.

Terrill was especially unpopular in Guthrie because he had been most adamant in trying to move the territorial capital. Shortly after Embrey was killed, there was talk in Guthrie of lynching the murderer. Rather than confine Terrell in the local jail and risk an attempt by an angry mob to seize the known killer, Sheriff Shockley secretly took Ira to Oklahoma City, where he was held for a few days.

In July 1891, while confined awaiting trial, Terrill led an attempt to break out of the Logan County jail. The inmates had obtained a crowbar and were prying open the cell door when Sheriff John Hixon became aware of their effort. Hixon held a gun on the enterprising prisoners until deputies arrived. The officers were able to rearrange and secure the prisoners, before any of the inmates gained their freedom.

Terrill was tried in October 1891 for the murder of Embrey. The jury failed to reach a verdict. A mistrial was declared, and Ira was released on bond. Sometime later, one member of the jury who had served on the case was arrested and charged for having accepted a bribe to consistently vote "not guilty."

Ira's murder case was transferred to Payne County, and his second trial came before the court at Stillwater in September 1892. Terrill was convicted in his home county and was sentenced to life imprisonment at hard labor.

A local newspaper commented on Terrill's recent trial: "His hand helped to write, his voice advocated, his vote helped to enact many of the laws on our stature books. And he was especially active in the enactment of a proper murder law; looking over it with a critical eye, urging more stringent measures, yet he was the first one to break the law that he had strongly advocated and helped to enact."

Ira Terrill was delivered to the Kansas State Penitentiary, at Lansing, to serve his sentence and work in the coal mines. His attorney appealed the court's action. Two months after Terrill entered prison, his sentence was voided. Ira was granted a new trial and was returned to Payne County. While waiting to be tried again, he was permitted to "bond out" of the county jail at Stillwater, for an extended period of time.

Terrill's case was transferred to Noble County, and his next trial was held at Perry, O.T. In mid-December 1894, nearly four years after killing Embrey, Ira was again convicted of murder and was sentenced to serve twelve years at hard labor.

In keeping with the Christmas spirit, while still confined at Perry, during the evening of December 25, 1894, Ira was permitted to use the jailer's room to write some letters. While Terrill was enjoying this special privilege, J. M. Hart, the jailer, dozed off. When the deputy awoke, Terrill was missing. The convicted murderer had vanished into the night. Noble County sheriff John A. Hansen authorized a one-hundred-dollar reward for the arrest of the escaped prisoner.

A year later, J. M. Hart was indicted at Perry for having permitted Terrill to escape from the county jail. In mid-March 1896, the escapee was located at Fort Scott, Kansas. Ira had been using the name James Wells. J. A. Hollinger, who had known him for several years while both lived in Wichita, recognized him.

Hollinger was confident of Terrill's identity. He advised Officer Copes of the Fort Scott police that the person who claimed to be James Wells was actually the murderer Ira Terrill who had escaped from jail in Oklahoma Territory. Copes arrested the suspect and notified the authorities at Guthrie.

Sheriff Hansen departed from Perry, O.T., immediately. He found that the man in custody at Fort Scott was his missing prisoner. As soon as the legal papers could be processed, Hansen took charge of Terrill and, without delay, delivered him to the Kansas State Penitentiary at Lansing. In late March 1896, Ira was again put to work in the coal mines as convict #7718.

Terrill was a constant troublemaker for the prison personnel. He refused to work and called the coal mine labor "slavery." Ira's behavior was such that often he was forced to spend long periods of time in solitary confinement.

The former legislator was active as a jailhouse lawyer. He twice represented himself in appealing his case. While Ira did not win either appeal, he did get a great deal of publicity. A Wichita, Kansas, newspaper became interested in his cause and gave him some sympathetic coverage.

Shortly after the turn of the twentieth century, a rumor circulated throughout the territory reporting Ira's death. The news item was published in numerous newspapers in Oklahoma Territory and was headed: "IRA TERRILL HAS GONE MAD AND DIED IN PRISON." Later, it was learned that the report was untrue.

In September 1905, Terrill was declared "mentally ill". He was then sent back to Perry (the place of his conviction). Even though Ira had officially been deemed insane and supposedly was confined in the Noble County jail, he was permitted to act in his own behalf and appeal his case. Again, he failed to gain his freedom, but in May 1906, Oklahoma Territorial Governor Frank Frantz issued a parole (later a pardon) for Ira N. Terrill.

After being freed, the ex-convict concentrated his efforts on exposing to the public the hardships and injustices of forcing Oklahoma Territory inmates to work in the Kansas coal mines. Terrill wrote a play titled *From Paradise to Purgatory,* which delved into the foul treatment to which the prisoners were being subjected.

His efforts in this respect were credited with having a major impact on Kate Barnard, Oklahoma's first Commissioner of Charities and Corrections. After witnessing one of Terrill's tirades on the subject, she visited the Kansas penal facility and reported the conditions "to be intolerable."

In 1909, Ms. Barnard took action to bring Oklahoma prisoners back from Kansas, even though construction of the penitentiary at McAlester had hardly commenced. Not only had Terrill been a leader in enacting the law that sent the prisoners to work in the Kansas coal mines, and had been the first violator subject to serve under those conditions, he had also been instrumental in negating that arrangement.

Ira Terrill wrote several plays, some of which were based on figments that he had pondered extensively while in solitary confinement at Lansing. None of his plays became successful stage productions.

Even though they were sparse, Terrill had some supporters, and he did enjoy a certain following. In 1894, a post office was established at a small town in Pawnee County, Oklahoma Territory, which was named Terlton in his honor.

When the clouds of the First World War began to gather in Europe, and oil explorations became more popularly pursued throughout the area, he joined in the hunt for petroleum. Terrill was thought to be a geologist as he traveled about Texas and Oklahoma, dealing in mineral rights and promoting the industry. While carrying out this assumed role in the oil fields, he became a competent surveyor.

Ira and Eliza Terrill had eight children, and in 1919, following his wife's death, he established a residence in Wichita Falls, Texas. When Ira moved to that Texas city, he was devoting his

time and energy to inventing a rainmaking machine and form-
ing a company to manufacture and market his creation. Some
two years later, while still engaged in these projects, Ira N.
Terrill, Oklahoma's first lawmaker/lawbreaker, died, on
October 14, 1921. His death certificate shows that his expira-
tion was the result of heart trouble and records that he was a
surveyor by trade. He was buried at Columbus, Kansas.

CHAPTER 13

The McIntosh County
Seat War

While the Midwest was being settled, conflicts frequently arose between neighboring towns when they were competing for the county seat. Most of these county seat issues that arose in Oklahoma were resolved with no more strife than some ruffled feelings among the citizens and perhaps a heated election to mark the occasion. However, selecting the county seat in some of these locales created armed civil discord.

One of the most controversial and bitterly fought of these so-called county seat wars in Oklahoma emerged in McIntosh County. Both Checotah and Eufaula had many sincere and eager supporters. These boosters claimed that their town was more worthy than the other and should be named the McIntosh county seat. Each community thoroughly presented their cases before the public and the territorial legislature.

On Wednesday afternoon, January 9, 1907, a telegram was sent from Guthrie to Checotah stating that the legislative committee had selected Checotah to be the temporary McIntosh County seat. Realizing that being named the county seat on an interim basis would be an advantage in the selection of a permanent location, the Checotah citizens were elated when they learned of their good fortune. That evening they blew whistles, rang bells, passed out cigars, and danced in the streets.

This Checotah victory was short-lived. William C. Liedtke, an attorney from Eufaula, was a delegate to the constitutional conventional, which was in session at Guthrie. He disliked the decision that the committee had announced and brought the issue before the general assembly. Liedtke strongly favored his hometown for the county seat and gave a rousing speech in favor of Eufaula, on Thursday morning, January 17, 1907. He then called for a vote of the full House to decide the matter. The tally taken a few minutes later recorded that Eufaula had received forty-two votes and Checotah had got forty-one.

The news of this political maneuver was received at Eufaula about noon, and the townspeople reacted with merriment. In spite of the previous telegram and Checotah's celebration a few days earlier, Eufaula was officially designated as the temporary county seat of McIntosh County. Appropriate county offices were initially established on the second floor of a building located on Eufaula's main street. Years later, the structure was damaged by fire and was rebuilt as a single-story unit.

With this bitter loss the citizens of Checotah wailed, but soon they began to plan their course and set their sights on the election that would determine the permanent county seat. Not only did Eufaula and Checotah seek to be selected as the permanent site, also Stidham (located eight miles northwest of Eufaula) entered the race. The merits of the three competing locations were well publicized by their boosters, who actively campaigned in behalf of their hometowns.

The special election to select a permanent site for the county seat was held on Saturday, May 23, 1908. The preliminary count reported that Checotah received 1,647 votes, Eufaula 1,200, and Stidham 384. Checotah, having obtained 63 votes more than the total of both competitors, was assumed to be the winner.

The ballot boxes were delivered to the state capital in Guthrie, to confirm the tally. There had been a heavy rain during the day and night before the election, and Eufaula claimed that the flooded creeks and rivers prevented more than three hundred of its supporters from reaching the polling places. Alexander Posey, noted poet and Creek Indian leader, drowned in the Canadian River near Eufaula during that flood.

As the results of the McIntosh County election were being canvassed in Guthrie, a question arose about some sixty-five ballots that were referred to as "unaccounted for." This implied discrepancy cast a doubt on the election and created a controversy about the propriety of the earlier count, which had reported that Checotah was the winner.

In early June, the attorneys who represented Eufaula's campaign for the county seat obtained a hearing with Chief Justice Robert L. Williams of the state supreme court. They convinced him to issue a temporary injunction, restraining the removal of the county offices from Eufaula, until certain alleged discrepancies were resolved. One of the Guthrie newspapers described the pending situation in McIntosh County: "Checotah has a tail-hold and a down-hill pull but Eufaula has a bull-dog grip in the flank, and will hold on until the offices are moved."

W. F. "Frank" Jones, a former deputy U.S. marshal who lived at Checotah, had been one of the major boosters in seeking the county seat for his hometown. When the local citizens learned that the Eufaula promoters had blocked the county offices from being moved to Checotah; there was a swell of support to take up arms and obtain by force what they felt their town was being denied by unjust means.

On Sunday morning, June 7, 1908, a squad of well-armed men led by Frank Jones boarded a special train at Checotah for the fifteen-mile ride south. Upon arriving at Eufaula about noon, the armed force divided into two groups. A small band walked north from the depot and met McIntosh County clerk Edward C. Julian. The county clerk had lived near Checotah and favored that town to become the county seat. Ed Julian had keys to the county offices, which he relinquished to the

W. F. "Frank" Jones, a former deputy U.S. marshal. (Author's collection)

Checotah squad. They proceeded to the second-floor offices and began removing the county records, in preparation to take them to Checotah.

Jones led the larger group (estimated at some fifteen men) from the depot directly to the corner of Foley and Main. At that point, the Checotah force could cover the town's major intersection and the nearby courthouse. En route to that location they met Eufaula deputy marshals Kelser and Woods. Jones ordered the two Eufaula officers "to get off the street, else they would get the contents of his gun."

In view of the overwhelming force from Checotah, officers Kelser and Woods shied away and began alerting the citizens of Eufaula, about the armed squad that was raiding the courthouse. Word of this invasion spread throughout town, as many of the families were returning from church. Grabbing what firearms that were readily available, the men began to rally and join their neighbors to protect their county seat. One of the local hardware stores was opened, and the merchant passed out guns to those who needed weapons.

The first victim of the confrontation was Eufaula deputy F. M. Woods. He was shot by Special Deputy Sheriff Joe Parmenter, a noted gunman from Checotah. After Parmenter's first bullet struck Woods, he pumped two more slugs into the wounded officer. While the deputy from Checotah was shooting at Woods, several of the Eufaula defenders opened fire on him. Two bullets struck Parmenter as he reached shelter behind a watering trough.

One account relates that a messenger had been sent to the home of Grant Johnson, an African American deputy U. S. marshal who lived two miles from Eufaula, to bring him into the fray. The large force of Eufaula citizens that had gathered in the area welcomed the arrival of their local deputy U. S. marshal. Johnson found that they had already suffered one casualty (the seriously wounded Woods would die the following evening), and that his killer (the wounded Joe Parmenter who was hiding behind a horse trough) was being protected by the armed men from Checotah.

Frank Jones and Grant Johnson had worked together as officers of the law, and mutual respect had developed between the two. When Johnson saw Jones, he appealed to his former fellow officer that Jones cease his effort to abscond with the county files and surrender his men. By that time, the ex-lawman from Checotah could see that his force was outnumbered and that more Eufaula defenders were continuing to arrive. Frank Jones realized that his raid could not succeed. He then consented to a parley. Jones met with some of the Eufaula leaders, and arrangements were worked out for the Checotah squad to surrender.

Frank Jones was the key man in carrying out the terms of this submission. The Checotah men were required to relinquish their weapons. The disarmed squad would be held in the railroad depot until a train could come from Checotah and pick them up. All county papers would be left at Eufaula. Jones had to do a lot of coaxing to get his followers to surrender their guns and hand over the records that they had filched from the courthouse. By late afternoon these steps had been accomplished.

A train was on standby at Checotah, awaiting word from the invading force at Eufaula to come and pick up the raiding party, along with the documents from the county offices. The message that was received about the surrender was unexpected, and the train was slow in arriving at Eufaula.

The disheartened men were loaded aboard the coach, and the northbound train departed from Eufaula. The somber mood that hung over the depot when they arrived at Checotah was vastly different from the fanfare that had prevailed when they boarded the train at that location, some eight hours earlier.

A short time after the train had left Eufaula, General Dunlap, a former deputy U.S. marshal, who had been one of the guards at the depot, decided to seek out and arrest Edward

Julian. Dunlap believed that the county clerk had collaborated with the raiding party. He considered that Julian should be taken into custody and charged for his role in the affair. The former deputy marshal is reported to have been drinking when he set forth to apprehend the county clerk.

Dunlap located Julian's room on the third floor of the Foley Hotel at the intersection where the Checotah force had concentrated. The county clerk was aware of some commotion outside his door and overheard part of a conversation. He was prepared for trouble when the knock sounded. After Julian answered the door, only brief words were exchanged between him and Dunlap before the shooting commenced. Each man fired at the other, and Dunlap was mortally wounded, being struck by a bullet in his forehead.

Joe Parmenter survived his wounds, but two men had been

The Foley Building at Main and Foley as it stands today in Eufaula, Oklahoma. The major confrontation between the Checotah and Eufaula forces occurred at this intersection on June 7, 1908. General Dunlap was shot and killed on the third floor of this building. (Author's collection)

killed at Eufaula, on Sunday, June 7, 1908. Both F. M. Woods and General Dunlap were victims of the prolonged county seat controversy that had led to armed conflict.

Being cast in the leadership role, Frank Jones and his actions in this climactic chapter of the conflict were subject to widespread speculation. The failure of this drastic endeavor had left him open to a great deal of criticism.

Some two weeks after this debacle at Eufaula, Gov. Charles N. Haskell announced his findings of the McIntosh County special election. He reported that a review of the ballots revealed a total of 3,284 votes had been cast at the polls on May 23, 1908. Governor Haskell's tally showed that more of the voters preferred Checotah than Eufaula and Stidham combined. He declared that Checotah was the duly elected McIntosh county seat.

The governor's announcement had no effect on the matter, because an appeal was pending before the State Supreme Court. An injunction to forestall removing the county offices from Eufaula had been issued by the court. Ultimately, it was decided to hold another election to resolve the controversy.

Harry Beeler was a prominent Checotah real estate broker. He had arranged for his hometown's special train service of June 7, 1908, to Eufaula. Later, Beeler was elected to the state senate.

Shortly after the state legislature convened in January 1909, freshman senator Richard A. Billups from Cordell related in front of several witnesses a story about the election that the constitutional convention had held on January 17, 1907. Billups stated that he had come to the convention on that date to visit a friend who was a delegate but who was not present at the time that he arrived. The new senator said that he sat in his absent friend's seat and was impressed with the speech that William Liedtke had delivered. Billups stated that when the senate called for a vote, he (a mere citizen) had cast a ballot in his friend's name in favor of Eufaula.

Upon hearing Billups's story, Sen. Harry Beeler became quite disturbed. Beeler realized that Billups's illegal ballot had given Eufaula the one-vote margin that it had garnered in the forty-two to forty-one tally. This was the convention's vote that had prevented Checotah from becoming the county seat. It had set in motion the armed conflict and the bloodshed that ensued.

When Richard Billups became aware of Senator Beeler's reaction, he recanted his complete story. The senator from Cordell then claimed that he was only joshing about having voted in the January 1907 election. The effect of Billups's illicit vote that had been tallied some two years earlier was still being discussed when a second special election was held in McIntosh County.

In the February 10, 1909, election, only Checotah and Eufaula were in the race for the permanent county seat. Eufaula received 1,919 votes, and Checotah got 1,844. The result of this ballot seems to have initiated a waning in the heated conflict, which had been ongoing for years. Following this second special election, the controversy began to subside and slowly fade away. Today, almost a hundred years later, Eufaula still serves as the county seat.

Neither Joe Parmenter nor Edward Julian was convicted of the murder charges that stemmed from Checotah's armed attempt to grasp the county seat. Less than a year after that fiasco occurred in Eufaula, Julian was again serving as county clerk. Joe Parmenter was acquitted by a jury in June 1909.

Some thirty years subsequent to this county seat controversy, W. F. Jones assembled a book, which he titled: *The Experiences of a Deputy U.S. Marshal of the Indian Territory*. As the title suggests, Jones related many experiences of his long tenure as an officer of the law. He also told of some events that occurred after his retirement. Several of the activities that he wrote about happened in and around Checotah and Eufaula; however, the book makes no mention of the conflict known as "The McIntosh County Seat War."

CHAPTER 14

A Night of Vengeance
in Wewoka

This story relates the few-recorded highlights in the criminal career of John Cudjo, including limited information about his outlaw brother and two of their renegade friends. It also briefly tells of the three dedicated lawmen killed while in pursuit of these "wanted men" and provides the basic details of John's inglorious death.

John Cudjo, was an African American who was raised in the Creek Nation of Indian Territory. As John was growing up during the early years of the twentieth century, he became known as a thief with a mean disposition. It is likely that his reputation had previously been earned by stealing items of less value, but the first confirmed account of his banditry occurred in midsummer 1907.

John and his brother Morris (better known as Ned) broke into the Evans store and post office at Spaulding, Oklahoma (some six miles southwest of Holdenville). The Cudjo brothers robbed the combined establishments, on Wednesday night, July 17, and got away with seventy-five dollars in cash. The next day when John Morrison, town marshal at nearby Sasakwa, heard of the burglary, he deputized George Epley and M. J. Trout to accompany him as they began searching for the robbers.

Shortly after the Spaulding robbery, two more men of unsavory reputation, John Street and Jonas "Joe" Barkus (spelled

Barcus in some of the newspaper articles), joined the Cudjo brothers. Not long after these four foul characters got together, they became aware of the Sasakwa posse's pursuit. This news prompted the young hoodlums to position themselves in a grove of trees beside the road near Vamoosa (seven miles east of Konawa), so that they could watch for the approaching lawmen.

Late Thursday evening, Town Marshal Morrison (who was riding some distance ahead of his two deputies) advanced into the targeted area. At that point, gunfire erupted, and Morrison, who was also a deputy U.S. marshal, fell from the saddle; mortally wounded. The four black fugitives stowed their weapons and hurriedly departed, inadvertently losing a hat at the ambush site, which had the name John Street in it.

When word was received of the crimes of the Cudjo brothers in Spaulding, Oklahoma, City Marshal John Morrison of Sasakwa deputized George Epley and M. J. Trout to go after them; however, the hunt resulted in the marshal's death. (Photo courtesy of Al Ritter)

Morrison was a well-liked individual and much respected as a lawmen. His demise left a widow with two children. When word of his murder was received in the town of Seminole, Deputy U.S. Marshal John Cordell, City Marshal W. W. Thomason, Constable Tom Robertson, and Lighthorseman Dennis Cyrus formed a posse and started for the site of the shooting.

L. P. Dixon (often misspelled in the newspapers as Dickson) lived in Shawnee and worked throughout the area as a bank collector. He happened to be in Konawa the next day after Morrison was killed. When a local officer solicited recruits that Friday morning, Dixon and another man volunteered to join in the search for the murderers of the lawman. Shortly after this well-armed trio rode out of Konawa they met up with Deputy Cordell and his men from Seminole.

The two posses gathered in the road and discussed the case. After reorganizing their forces Dixon joined Cordell and Cyrus in search of the outlaws, while Marshal Thomason led the other officers in pursuit of the wanted men via another route.

Cordell and his two deputies had gone but a few miles when they came upon Elija Davis, a young black man who fit the description of the suspects. As the officers were questioning him, they became aware of a strange whistling sound coming from some distance away. Cordell asked Dixon to stay and guard the suspect while he and Cyrus went to investigate the suspicious noise and to talk with Elija's father.

Shortly after Cordell and Cyrus left Dixon with the young man, three black men (Ned Cudjo, Joe Barkus, and John Street) came walking along the road, approaching the deputy and Davis. Dixon called for the men to identify themselves. Instantly, Ned Cudjo raised his Winchester and shot at Dixon as the deputy was shouldering his rifle. The officer fired a cartridge at his attacker. Both shots sounded in rapid succession. Cudjo's bullet struck Dixon in the shoulder and raged downward, while Dixon's shot inflicted a wound in Cudjo's thigh.

Cordell and Cyrus had ridden some distance away when they heard the gunshots behind them. They raced back to where they had left Dixon guarding Davis, but they did not see their fellow deputy upon their return. Instead, the officers saw Elija, and at that same moment they realized the presence of three more young black men, one of whom had a weapon and was slouched against a tree, obviously wounded.

Upon arriving back at the site, the officers were asked to identify themselves. Cordell firmly replied, "We are deputy marshals," and continued riding directly toward the trio that had just come upon the scene. As Cordell neared the men, he dismounted and walked to Ned Cudjo, who offered no resistance when the officer took his gun.

While securing the three suspects, the lawmen heard moaning in the nearby brush. The sounds led them to some tall weeds where they found Deputy Dixon curled up on the ground with his rifle lying nearby. He was badly wounded, and Cordell sent for a doctor at Sasakwa. The medic came and tended the seriously injured victim, but Dixon died early the next morning. Two days later, his funeral was held at Shawnee, and he was interred in the local cemetery. Dixon left a wife and three children.

Late Friday evening, July 19, 1907, field deputies delivered Ned Cudjo, Joe Barkus, and John Street to Wewoka, where they were put in jail. The local officers became concerned that a mob might attempt to remove the prisoners from their cell to lynch them, but those who did gather and linger about did not undertake violence.

John Cudjo was noticeably absent from the group when the other three were captured. Shortly after Morrison was killed, John had separated himself from his brother and the pair who had joined them. About the time that Ned and his two allies were being jailed at Wewoka, other officers were tracing John into the vicinity of Earlsboro, about twenty miles north of Konawa, where his trail was lost.

The United States Federal courthouse, as originally built at Wewoka, Indian Territory. After Oklahoma statehood, it served as the Seminole County courthouse. (Courtesy of the Seminole Nation Museum, Wewoka, Oklahoma)

It was rumored that John Cudjo had fled to Earlsboro so that he could catch a train to travel farther west. For the next several days, all westbound trains were searched at Shawnee for the young black man who had escaped the posses in the field. Officers did not locate John Cudjo at Shawnee or anywhere else.

A few days after the three men were captured, Deputies Grant Cowan and L. B. Shahan took them to the Federal jail at Muskogee. Some time later, they were brought back to Wewoka where John Street and Joe Barkus were indicted for the murder of Marshal Morrison, and Ned Cudjo was charged with killing Deputy Dixon.

The Cudjo family had lived in the area of the Creek Nation

After John Cudjo and his accomplices killed Town Marshal John Morrison, they went on to kill posse volunteer L. P. Dixon, whose grave is located in the Fairview Cemetery at Shawnee, Oklahoma. (Author's collection)

that became McIntosh County, but in months prior to the Spaulding robbery; it was thought that the Cudjo brothers had hung out in the country between Holdenville and Wewoka. When John was not located trying to escape on a westbound train, it was assumed that he would return to Hughes County along the western edge of the old Creek Nation, where he had most recently lived. However, he was not found in that area.

Even after the other three suspects had officially been charged with murdering officers Morrison and Dixon, John Cudjo, the fourth member of this outlaw band, was still at large, and his whereabouts remained unknown.

In November 1908 (one year after statehood), Ned Cudjo was tried at Wewoka, on the charge of murdering Deputy Dixon. After hearing the case, the jury deliberated two days then rendered a verdict. They found that he was guilty of manslaughter and sentenced him to serve two years in the state penitentiary. No record of the disposition of the charges filed against Joe Barkus and James Street has been located to date.

It has not been determined where John Cudjo went after he left his brother and their two cohorts, following the murder of Deputy Morrison. For many years, the Cudjo family had been closely associated with the Creek Indians. It is likely that John Cudjo joined with many other blacks in following Chitto Harjo, better known as Crazy Snake, who was a rebel Creek leader.

Crazy Snake's allotted land was near the small settlement of Pierce; however, he and his followers often set up camp at the Hickory Grounds, a few miles northeast of Henryetta. Crazy Snake and his so-called Snake Indians (even though many of them were African American) were frequently sought out by county and Federal lawmen. In 1909 the National Guard was called out to quell the disturbances that the rebellious clan was instigating. Even though many of Crazy Snake's renegades (both black and Indian) were captured during this uprising that became known as the "Smoked Meat Rebellion," John

Cudjo was not recognized as being among those who were brought in.

The next confirmed report of John Cudjo was in March 1913, when his name again appeared in the Eufaula newspaper. The news item reported that "trouble had developed between a Negro by the name of Taylor and John Cudjo, also a Negro." The incident had occurred on Monday, March 24, near the small settlement of Hitchita in the northwestern corner of McIntosh County. The article continued: "The two became involved in a dispute and came to blows, when Cudjo drew a knife and stabbed Taylor, mortally wounding him. Cudjo who has the reputation of being a 'bad' negro [*sic*], is still at large."

Following the above account of John Cudjo killing Taylor, some seven months passed before anything more was reported about him. On November 1, word was received at the Seminole County sheriff's office in Wewoka that John Cudjo was staying with a relative who lived only five miles south of the county seat. Deputies Bud Brinsfield, Sanford Harvill, and John Dennis were immediately dispatched from the sheriff's office to the reported site to bring in the wanted man.

With darkness gathering that Saturday evening, the three officers arrived at the home of King Cudjo. As their automobile was slowing to a stop in front of the house, Deputy Sheriff John Dennis stepped from the car and began walking toward a fellow sitting on the front porch. When Dennis approached the man, he asked the party to identify himself. Without saying a word, the suspect (who was later confirmed to be John Cudjo) pulled a .45-caliber revolver and shot the lawman. Deputies Harvill and Brinsfield opened fire on the gunman, as he ran from the scene. Dodging and running in a hail of bullets, Cudjo raced away and made his escape.

The officers did not pursue Cudjo, as they could see that Dennis was severely injured and desperately needed medical attention. Being unable to stem the flow of blood, they tried to get Dennis to a doctor's office in Wewoka. The bullet had struck Deputy Dennis in the left hip and passed into his right pelvic area, severing the femoral artery in each leg. Less than an hour after being shot, the lawman bled to death.

John Dennis had been in law enforcement for several years, and since statehood had served as a deputy sheriff. He was well known, and the news of his being killed spread fast. The next day, officers from throughout the state began gathering, to search the area and bring in the murderer. Sheriff J. W. McCune and one deputy from McIntosh County along with some guards from the state prison at McAlester were among the arriving lawmen, along with several heavily armed citizens who joined the hunt for John Cudjo.

One of the posses came upon four young black men on Sunday evening, while they were searching among the trees and underbrush that grew along Little River. The lawmen began to query them. One of the suspects took exception to the questioning and started to pull his gun. Officer Rich Owen quickly drew and fired his pistol. The young man, who was later identified as Peter Carolian, fell dead. A couple of years later, the proficient gunman, Rich Owen, became the executioner at the Oklahoma State Penitentiary at McAlester, commonly referred to as "Big Mac." Carolian was but one of many whose life was ended by Rich Owen during Oklahoma's formative years.

All day Monday, posses combed the breaks along the Little River where it was thought that John Cudjo had taken refuge, but he was not found in the suspected locale. Bloodhounds from McAlester had been brought in for the hunt, but they were ineffective. Thinking that the fugitive might be trying to work his way back to McIntosh County, one posse began searching along the river southeast of Holdenville.

Early Tuesday morning, November 4, 1913, the Holdenville posse learned that during the night a horse had been stolen from a nearby farm. They began tracking the missing animal, believing that John Cudjo had ridden him away. About mid-afternoon, they located the horse and rider in a field. When Cudjo saw the pursuing lawmen, he started shooting at the posse, and they returned the gunfire. The fugitive wounded two of the approaching officers—one was hit in the leg, and the thumb of another was shot off. Cudjo attempted to escape, but after a short run the stolen horse was shot from under him. The officers closed in on the desperado, who had been hit by one of the lawmen's bullets.

The posse first took John Cudjo to Holdenville. Later in the evening, they loaded the wounded prisoner (whose injury was not life threatening) into a car and drove him to Wewoka. They arrived in the Seminole County seat about 8:00 P.M. Citizens came from every nook and cranny in town to peer at the villain who had killed their deputy sheriff.

The local newspaper article that reported the evening's events related that shortly after Cudjo was delivered to Wewoka, "He admitted his identity and realized that he was going to die." The news item continued by stating, "County Judge Norvell questioned him and [his] answers were being taken down for record. As this was in progress, a mob which had already gathered, slipped a rope over the negroe's [sic] head and he was strung [up] to a telephone pole in front of the courthouse." The article did not identify where the questioning had taken place, nor did it reveal what the judge and the recorder of the suspect's responses did as the lynching proceeded.

The newspaper's account of this homicide advised that some three hundred men, women, and children were on the street in Wewoka, watching as John Cudjo gasped his last breath. None of the men who had actively participated in the hanging wore masks, nor did any of the bystanders attempt to hide their identity.

Shortly after Cudjo's strangled body went limp, a shot was fired, and the corpse twisted and swayed from the impact of the slug. Soon, more guns were brought into play, and cartridges were triggered from half a dozen weapons, causing the carcass to swivel and swing with erratic movements. The suspended

Outlaw John Cudjo stayed at large from his 1907 killings until he murdered Seminole County Deputy Sheriff John Dennis in 1913. Deputy Dennis is buried in the Oakwood Cemetery in Wewoka, Oklahoma. (Author's collection)

cadaver gyrated for some time, while more than one hundred bullets were fired into the lifeless body of John Cudjo.

Mrs. Dennis, widow of the murdered deputy, had been brought downtown to observe the public spectacle. Across the street from the courthouse she and her seven (now fatherless) children sat in the front office of the *Wewoka Democrat* newspaper and watched as her husband's killer was lynched, then shot to pieces.

After the gunfire ceased and the corpse was limply swaying in the evening breeze, a placard was tied to the victim's dangling feet. On the card in large letters was written, TO THE MEMORY OF LEE CRUCE. This was a taunt at the state's second governor, who had a reputation of being extremely lenient in dealing with suspects and convicts.

It was planned that after the banner had been displayed a few minutes the lead-shredded carcass would be taken down, saturated with oil, and burned on the street. When Mrs. Dennis became aware of this intent, she pleaded that the body not be further desecrated. Her voice was heeded, and after the crowd milled around a while gawking at the bullet-riddled corpse, they began to drift away. Later they were all gone, and the town was quiet, only the hanging body of John Cudjo remained on the darkened street.

Seminole County Sheriff Moore and his posse, who had been out of town all night searching for John Cudjo, returned to Wewoka shortly after daybreak. They were indeed surprised when they rode into town and found the ravaged remains of the much-sought-after man, suspended by a noose in front of the courthouse. The sheriff's men cut the rope and lowered the mutilated mass to the ground.

Throughout Wednesday, there was talk that Governor Cruce would send a team to investigate the lynching. The local newspaper commented, "If these men come, they will receive scant courtesy. Even if the governor should come it will be made plain to him, what the people think about him commuting death sentences of negro [*sic*] murderers."

The "Whipping Tree" was a prominent site for punishment in the Seminole Nation. The tree has survived these many years and may currently be seen in front of the present-day Seminole County courthouse at Wewoka, Oklahoma. (Courtesy of the Seminole Nation Museum, Wewoka, Oklahoma)

There was no investigation into this lynching, nor did a band of blacks from Little River attack the town, as some people had forecast. Nothing of note followed this tragedy, and "A Night of Vengeance in Wewoka" merely faded into history.

Even though scores of people had witnessed his death, only the old newspapers record the demise of John Cudjo. There is no death certificate on file to document the passing of this murderer who became the victim of mob violence, nor has a copy of an obituary or the site of his burial been located.

CHAPTER 15

The First Prison Break at Big Mac

Upon becoming a state in 1907, Oklahoma made arrangements with Kansas to house its prisoners, until a suitable facility could be built. The state legislature authorized construction of the Oklahoma State Penitentiary, to be located at McAlester. A building site was selected, plans were approved, contracts were awarded, and construction was begun in 1909.

Kate Barnard, a very popular woman of the time, was Oklahoma's first Commissioner of Charities and Corrections. She did not approve of the treatment that the inmates were receiving at the Lansing, Kansas, facility. She tried to negotiate with the neighboring state to improve their care. Ms. Barnard was conscientious and dedicated to her duty. In 1909, when it became obvious that her efforts in behalf of the inmates' welfare were in vain, she ordered that they be returned from Kansas, even though construction of the new state penitentiary had hardly begun.

One group of the some seven hundred total returning prisoners was sent directly to McAlester, but the majority was celled in county jails throughout the state. As soon as temporary shelters could be erected at the new prison site, the remaining inmates of the state were transferred from the county jails to McAlester. Many of the convicts worked as indirect laborers in preparing the land and erecting the buildings. During this

Oklahoma State Prison, McAlester, Oklahoma. (Photo courtesy of the Archives & Manuscripts Division of the Oklahoma Historical Society)

period, barbed wire and armed guards provided the only security. While this makeshift arrangement was considered by many as likely to induce a massive breakout of the prisoners, no such disaster occurred. The guards maintained order and kept the inmates in the designated areas, without any uprising or major problems.

The first prison break from what became known as "Big Mac" was attempted early in 1914, well after construction of the penal institution had been completed. The three inmates who made the break were not considered to be among the most desperate of the lot.

The trio was led by Charley Koontz, inmate #2582, who was serving a forty-year sentence for robbing a bank at Crawford in Roger Mills County. Accompanying Koontz was China Reed, inmate #4622, who had previously been imprisoned and was currently confined for stealing a horse in Pittsburg County. The third member was Tom Lane, inmate #2610, who had been convicted of forgery in Garvin County and was serving six years.

Koontz had obtained a smuggled pistol and extra ammunition, then conspiring with Reed and Lane, he plotted the escape. About 4:00 P.M. on Monday, January 19, 1914, the three inmates approached prison guard J. W. Martin (the inner turnkey) and presented a forged pass, permitting them to visit the office of Parole Officer Frank H. Rice. Martin did not detect any fakery about the order and unlocked the gate. When the gate swung open, Koontz drew the hidden pistol and fired, hitting the guard in his cheek. As Martin fell, Reed grabbed the ring of keys from the lock, and the three convicts raced into the corridor that led to the main offices. The shot had resounded throughout the building and alerted everyone that something was awry.

After leaving the wounded turnkey on the floor at the opened gate, the first prison official seen by the escapees was H. H. Droves, a photographer and expert in the system of famed French criminologist Alphonse Bertillon. Droves had stepped into the hall to learn the purpose of the gunshot. Upon seeing the three armed inmates rushing upon him, he scampered to get back inside. Koontz fired the pistol and hit Droves, who then fell in the doorway to his office, mortally wounded.

Warden Robert W. Dick was not in his office when the shots sounded. At that time, Day Sergeant F. C. Godfrey was in the warden's office, along with former Federal Judge J. R. Thomas and his inmate client. The former judge was currently practicing law at Muskogee and was at the prison interviewing life-termer Frank Halkey to prepare an appeal. Upon hearing the shot fired near her workstation, stenographer Mary Foster began screaming and ran across the hall into the warden's office. Assuming that the screams identified her as a wounded victim of the shooting, Frank Rice, whose office was next to that of the warden's, rushed to aid her.

Immediately after Rice entered the warden's office, the armed inmates burst in. The trio of convicts seemed surprised at finding four men and one woman, but not Warden Dick. Wielding the weapon, Koontz ordered the five to line up against the wall. As four of them moved in compliance with the order, Sergeant Godfrey grappled with Koontz for control of the handgun. Another of the pistol's cartridges exploded, sending a fatal shot into Sergeant Godfrey.

The escapees then turned their attention to the three men and Ms. Foster. Judge Thomas pleaded that he was not an official of the institution, merely at the prison to talk with his client, Frank Halkey, who was still present. As Charley Koontz mumbled "that they could take no chances," he squeezed the trigger, and the aged jurist fell.

Guard C. B. Woods rushed into the office and was wounded in an exchange of shots with Koontz. Seeing that his action gravely endangered innocent people, Woods withdrew from the room. With Judge Thomas gasping his last breath, Deputy Warden D. C. Oates, armed with a shotgun and a pistol, entered the office and fired, wounding Koontz in the abdomen. As Koontz doubled over, he handed the weapon to his confederate, Reed. Lane and Reed then took cover behind Parole Officer Rice and Ms. Foster. Realizing the danger to the hostages, Oates quit shooting. The severely wounded Koontz ordered Reed to shoot Oates, even though the deputy warden had ceased firing. Following his leader's command, Reed fired the weapon, and Oates fell to the floor.

Lane went into an adjoining room and wrecked the telephone switchboard. Returning with some telephone cord, he bound Parole Officer Rice's hands. The escapees, then rearmed and still having Officer Martin's keys, prepared to depart from the warden's office. Using Rice and Ms. Foster (who had been hit in the thigh by a bullet) as shields, they began forcing their two hostages toward the front entrance, as Koontz stumbled along, holding his stomach and moaning in pain.

Upon nearing the front door, while shielded behind their hostages and holding a pistol at Rice's head, they shouted that they would kill him unless the guards laid down their guns. Seeing that any action on their part would be the same as "signing the parole officer's death warrant," the tower guards set their weapons aside. The two uninjured convicts were permitted to exit the building, with Rice (hands bound) and the screaming Ms. Foster (with blood running down her leg) as their hostages. Koontz followed them.

Near the front gate the desperadoes spotted a horse hitched to a small buggy, which they determined would become their conveyance. When they reached the one-seated hack, Reed forced the woman to sit on his lap and Rice was placed on Lane's lap. Koontz, in agony, hunkered into the space behind the seat, and Reed reined the horse west on the farm road.

As soon as the convicts had left the warden's office, guards and trustees rushed into the room where three men lay and gave aid to the victims. Morton, a trustee, applied his ingenuity to repairing the damaged switchboard, and he soon had it in operation. A phone call was placed to Sgt. R. J. Ritchie, who was in charge of the bloodhounds at the kennel, which was located northwest of the main building. Ritchie was informed that the escapees were in a buggy, going west on the farm road.

Ritchie mounted the only readily available horse, a small pony, and raced toward a prominent rock formation along the roadway about one mile west of the main building. As the sergeant rode, he observed the loaded buggy on the road in the flat. Seeing that the escapees' animal was being urged to its fullest and would press him to reach the rock in time to halt their escape, Ritchie prodded his puny horse faster. Nearing his destination ahead of the buggy, he left his winded mount in some trees and ran to the rocks. Just as the prison guard reached the site, he saw the weary animal pulling the hack. The escapees were at the crest of the hill.

Sergeant Ritchie was unaware that some of the occupants of

the buggy were hostages, and assumed Ms. Foster to be an escaping inmate from the women's prison. Her screams held his attention, and he then noticed a man's head peeking from under her arm. When the buggy was within a few feet of Ritchie he shouted, "Surrender." Reed responded by shooting toward the hidden officer.

With his well-aimed rifle, Ritchie fired at the peeking head. Reed tumbled from the buggy. Ritchie's rifle failed to accept another cartridge in the chamber and merely snapped when triggered again. The sergeant reached for his pistol but it had dropped from his pocket while running to the rock. Ritchie again manipulated the rifle, and a bullet slid into the chamber. By this time the buggy had passed and was some distance away. The sergeant drew a bead and fired twice. Two men fell from the buggy. The spent horse plodded on a few steps before stopping. Ms. Foster was still in the buggy.

Ritchie checked the first man who had fallen and confirmed that Reed was dead. Another guard arrived as Ritchie cautiously walked toward the other two men who lay on the ground. Parole Officer Rice lay motionless and silent, fearing that any movement or yelling on his part might prompt the rifleman to shoot him. When the guards stepped close, Rice spoke to them. Immediately they recognized and untied the parole officer.

The officers determined that Lane, the other man on the ground, was also dead. Moving to the buggy, they checked the man whose body was slumped behind the seat. Koontz had died from the gunshot wound he received from Deputy Warden Oates.

Neither Mary Foster nor Frank Rice had been hit by any of the bullets that had been fired by Sergeant Ritchie. He was later quoted as saying, "How I came to shoot the convicts and not Rice, I can never tell. It is one of those things that we do not understand."

Seven men had been killed on January 19, 1914, in the first prison break at Big Mac. The dead were: D. C. Oates, deputy warden; F. C. Godfrey, day sergeant; H. H. Droves, Bertillon expert; J. R. Thomas, former judge; Charley Koontz, convict; China Reed, convict; and Tom Lane, convict.

Three more persons had been wounded during the attempted escape: Mary Foster, J. W. Martin, and C. B. Woods. The outcropping of rocks where the escapees were shot and killed became known as "Ritchie's Rock." It may be seen a few hundred feet north of Highways 1 and 270, between McAlester and the Indian Nation Turnpike.

CHAPTER 16

Outlaw Tom Slaughter

Tom Slaughter applied his adopted trade of robbing banks, stealing cars, and escaping from jails, during a period that is not commonly thought of as an "outlaw era." Perhaps that is the reason that he has been overlooked and that very little has been written about his outlaw career, leaving him almost forgotten today. While our nation's attention was focused on World War I and its aftermath, Slaughter ran his crime spree through Texas, Oklahoma, Arkansas, Louisiana, Tennessee, and Kentucky.

Tom was the son of T. L. and Georgia Slaughter. He was born in Louisiana in 1892. Tom's father was a carpenter, and during the first decade of the twentieth century, T. L., his wife, and their six children moved to Dallas County, Texas.

One account reports that Tom's first crime was stealing a horse near Russellville, Arkansas, and he was sentenced to serve time in the State Boys' Industrial Home, from which he escaped. His first conviction in Texas was for stealing an automobile in Dallas, and he was sentenced to one year in the prison at Huntsville. That incarceration would be the only time that Tom would serve his full sentence.

Shortly after being released from Huntsville, he was convicted of another crime. On that occasion Tom was sent to the prison at Rusk, Texas, and typical of his following criminal

Tom "Curly" Slaughter, outlaw/bankrobber, 1892–1921. (Author's collection)

career, he broke out of that facility. He was later located and arrested in Carter County, Oklahoma, and was taken to Ardmore, where Texas officers picked him up and took him back to the Lone Star State. While being held in a Texas jail awaiting trial, Slaughter also found a way out of that lockup.

The first crime that Tom Slaughter is reported to have committed in the Sooner State was in June 1918. While a fugitive from Texas, he stole an automobile from a Mr. Montgomery who lived near Centralia, Oklahoma (Craig County). Slaughter was caught, arrested, taken to Nowata, and put in jail. Lee Jarrett and William Creech, local badmen of some notoriety, were inmates in the Nowata County jail at the time that Slaughter was brought in. They too were being held on automobile theft charges.

When jailer Lee Brady entered the cell of the three alleged car thieves on Wednesday evening, July 10, 1918, Tom Slaughter produced a pistol. He commanded the officer to put his "hands up." As Brady obeyed, Jarrett grabbed the jailer's keys. Slaughter, forcing Brady in front, entered the sheriff's office and confronted Deputy Jim Hendrix. Before Hendrix realized what was happening, the three escapees had him covered with Slaughter's weapon and Brady's revolver, which they had found on the jailer's desk. Both officers were locked in the recently vacated cell.

Taking two high-powered rifles from the sheriff's office, the now well-armed trio left by the front door. They ran north from the jail to the O. T. Garage, where they robbed an employee, stole a car, and made their getaway. Within a few minutes, two quickly formed posses were in pursuit of the outlaws. The first group sped north to the Kansas line, but found no trace of the trio. Another posse went east from Nowata and searched the area, but they too returned, with no information about the escapees.

Nowata County sheriff Bill Gillespey alerted officers throughout the area that three inmates had broken out of jail. He further advised that they were armed and dangerous. Tom Slaughter's wife, Myrtle (she and Tom had married at Dallas in

1914), was located and taken to Nowata. The officers questioned her thoroughly, but she was steadfast in denying that she knew anything about how her husband came by the pistol or where he might be.

Some six weeks after the Nowata jailbreak, Tom Slaughter was recaptured while in the company of Mable (a lady friend whom Tom sometimes introduced as his wife). Officers also nabbed John Connor and his wife Lena, who were camping with Tom and Mable. The couples were located with two cars and were arrested south of Wirt, Oklahoma (Carter County), in late August 1918 by Deputy Sheriff Will Ward and Constable Charlie Jones. Tom was acquainted with that vicinity, having worked on drillings rigs in the area during the Healdton oil boom. Once before, while on the lam from Texas, he had been found and arrested in the same locale.

When Slaughter was brought into Ardmore, Carter County officials notified the Dallas police that they had their man in jail—again. There were numerous charges pending against Slaughter in Texas and other states. He was, however, sent back to Nowata to answer for his more recent crimes.

William Creech had been arrested near Centralia about a week after the Nowata jailbreak. With the return of Slaughter, only Lee Jarrett was still at large. Because of Tom's numerous jailbreaks, Sheriff Gillespey had a second lock installed on his cell door, to help insure his continued confinement.

Soon after Slaughter's return to the Nowata hoosegow, some of the plumbing in his cell was found partially disassembled. His efforts to fabricate tools in preparation for another escape had been detected before he could spring his plan on the security personnel. The sheriff then doubled the guard at the jail.

Shortly after that additional security step was taken, the sheriff's office received word from the Dallas police that some of Slaughter's friends and relatives were planning a raid on the calaboose in northeastern Oklahoma to rescue the Texas desperado. Sheriff Gillespey then placed an armed guard on the courthouse balcony to watch for the arrival of suspicious-appearing visitors, until he could make arrangements for his escape-prone inmate to be confined elsewhere.

Tom Slaughter was secretly transported to the Washington County jail at Bartlesville on September 19, 1918. The Bartlesville jail was considered to be a more secure facility, as the cells were on the third floor of the courthouse, and the public was not aware of the prisoner's presence. Less than six weeks after being incarcerated in the Bartlesville lockup, the crafty prisoner freed himself again. During the night of October 30, 1918, Tom Slaughter and another prisoner, Henry Fourt, who was being held on a robbery charge, sawed the bars from their cell window. They tied their bedclothes together and lowered themselves to the ground, which enabled the pair to escape the area before daylight.

Will Creech had been released on bond from the Nowata

Washington County courthouse, Bartlesville, Oklahoma, which was built in 1913. Tom Slaughter escaped from the jail on the third floor. (Photo courtesy of the Archives & Manuscripts Division of the Oklahoma Historical Society)

jail, and while awaiting trial he became involved in a shooting fray near Lenapah in January 1919, during which his "right eye was shot out." Creech's trial for breaking out of the Nowata jail with Slaughter and Jarrett the previous July was held in late March 1919. He was convicted and sentenced to serve six months in the state penitentiary.

The whereabouts of Tom Slaughter for several months after his escape from Bartlesville can not be confirmed. He and Lee Jarrett were frequently named as suspects in bank robberies throughout the country.

About noon on Tuesday, August 26, 1919, while some of the employees were out eating lunch, three men drove up to the First National Bank in Lindsay, Oklahoma (Garvin County). They entered the building, drew their pistols, and called for the money to be handed over. Miss Winifred Gardenhire, a bank employee whose desk was located in the back of the building, happened to be near the rear exit when she saw the men come in and pull their guns. She immediately ran out of the back door and into a nearby store, alerting everyone that the bank was being robbed. The bandits were aware that she had got away and surmised that she was drawing attention to their endeavor. They grabbed the $727 that was in the till, but did not take time to raid the vault.

The robbers hurried to their car and sped out of town. Local officers and citizens were soon in pursuit of the outlaws, but lost their trail near Criner (McClain County).

A couple of weeks after the Lindsay bank heist, two of the robbers were captured in Hugo (Choctaw County). They gave their names as Jack Adams, an alias of Jim Baldwin, who was experienced in hitting banks, and Charles Lofton. The surname of the third outlaw was cited as "Stone," which was an alias that Tom Slaughter routinely used. Later it was learned that in recent months, Slaughter had hid out at the Baldwin Ranch (in McCurtain County) and had often teamed up with Jim Baldwin in looting banks. In September 1919, the two captured outlaws were tried and convicted for robbing the Lindsay bank. Baldwin was sentenced to thirty years in the state penitentiary, and Lofton was sent up for twenty years. Slaughter remained at large.

Officers in Hot Springs, Arkansas, were informed that five men and two young women were camped about seven miles east of town. The informer advised the lawmen that the camping party was thought to be from Oklahoma and that their actions were suspicious. Upon receiving another similar report, three officers were dispatched. On Sunday morning, October 10, 1920, Deputy Sheriff Roy Brown, Constable Will Wilson, and Deputy Constable R. D. Adams went to investigate the camping party.

The officers found three of the men and two teenage girls in camp and questioned them. They advised the lawmen that the other two men were in town, but were expected to return soon. Deputy Brown decided that they would leave the five in camp, drive back closer to the highway, and wait for the two men to return from town and talk with them.

The lawmen had waited but a few minutes when they saw the described roadster pull off the highway. Brown waved his arms and signaled for it to stop. The driver did stop the car, and as both of its occupants got out, each of the men brought forth a rifle. They ordered Brown and Wilson (who were ahead of Adams) to throw up their hands. Officer Adams later reported that Wilson drew his weapon, but it was instantly shot from his grasp. Deputy Brown had also pulled his pistol and fired once before being struck by bullets fired by the two bandits. Adams got off one shot and believed that he hit the larger of the two men in the shoulder. That suspect retreated and got back into the vehicle. The driver then jumped into the car, and the two men raced away. Both Brown and Wilson were critically wounded. The outlaws escaped.

Deputy Sheriff Roy Brown died a short time after being shot. Wilson recovered from his wounds. The driver of the car was identified as Tom "Curly" Slaughter, and the other one was thought to be Fulton "Kid" Green. The three men in camp were identified as Lee Jarrett, Albert O'Connor, and Paul Witters.

Fulton "Kid" Green, Tom Slaughter's bandit buddy. (Author's collection)

Less than a week later, Slaughter struck again. The bank at Alluwe, Oklahoma (Nowata County), was robbed during the afternoon of October 15, 1920. A man entered the bank and pulled a pistol. He covered the cashier, a bookkeeper, and a customer (only three people were in the bank at the time) and demanded money. After stuffing some two thousand dollars in currency and three thousand dollars of liberty bonds into a canvas bag, he ran from the bank and jumped into a car that had a waiting driver with engine running. The automobile quickly raced out of town.

A few minutes after the bank robbery, a speeding vehicle loaded with officers who were in pursuit of the robber's car, ran over and killed Frank Beau, a six-year-old boy, three miles north of Alluwe. Posses chased the bandits throughout the night, into Kansas, then back into Oklahoma. They pursued the robbers over endless miles of back roads before losing their trail in western Mayes County. Nowata County sheriff Gillespey announced that the holdup man had been identified as Tom Slaughter.

On October 29, 1920 (two weeks after the Alluwe bank robbery), Chautauqua County undersheriff A.Y. Buckles and two deputies captured Tom Slaughter at Sedan, Kansas. Slaughter considered pulling his pistol in an attempt to get away, but seeing that the lawmen's hands were on their weapons, he surrendered.

The same day that Slaughter was nabbed, Kid Green and a Frank McGivens were arrested in Cedarvale, some twenty miles west of Sedan. Evidence was found that revealed the three men were planing to rob banks in the two towns, which are just north of the Oklahoma state line. The officers thought that McGivens had recently joined the outlaw pair and had not yet participated in any of their crimes.

The information that led to the arrest of Tom Slaughter and Fulton Green had been obtained from one of the teenage girls, who had been taken into custody at the outlaws' camp near Hot Springs. She revealed to the officers that they were to meet the men in Sedan, Kansas.

Slaughter and Green were wanted in several states for bank robberies and larceny of automobiles. The Texas desperado acknowledged to having participated in bank robberies in Texas, Arkansas, Louisiana, Tennessee, Kentucky, and Oklahoma. As well as the heists at Lindsay and Alluwe, Slaughter had also robbed the bank at Frederick, in the Sooner State.

Arkansas's charges against the pair included the murder of Deputy Sheriff Roy Brown, and the state filed a request to have the outlaws returned to be tried. Both bandits realized that if convicted of murder they would likely incur more severe sentences than they would receive for the other pending crimes, so they hired lawyers to block being extradited to face those charges. Their effort proved inadequate, and Arkansas's claim prevailed. The two outlaws were taken to Hot Springs.

In November 1920, as the state prepared to try Slaughter and Green for the murder of Deputy Roy Brown, a National Guard machine-gun company from Pine Bluff was called to active duty and was posted at the Hot Springs courthouse and jail. During the trial, S. D. Caldwell identified Slaughter and Green as the bandits who held up his bank in Cave City, Kentucky, on April 6, 1920. Slaughter readily agreed to return a valuable gold watch to the banker, which he had taken during the robbery. While the trial was in progress, a knife and a makeshift saw were found in the defendant's jail cell. Again, Tom's preparation for escape had been discovered before he could take action.

Slaughter took the stand in his own defense and claimed that the officers had not identified themselves (they were not in uniform) and that he mistook them to be hijackers. While his self-defense claim did not convince the jury to acquit the pair, it may have been a factor in gaining for them a sentence of life in prison at hard labor, instead of the death penalty, which was popularly expected.

Slaughter and Green were sent to the Tucker Prison Farm, which was the state's major facility for those who were to serve "hard time." Raising cotton was the main enterprise at the farm, and to keep the cost of operation at a minimum, the prisoners were shackled in long rows while in the field, and trusties (armed with shotguns) manned the "first line guard." The convicts who had worked up to being "armed trustees" were spaced about fifty feet apart and approximately a hundred feet behind the chain gang of toiling inmates. The armed trustees were in turn followed by a line of horseback-riding state officers who carried rifles. If a "first line guard" showed any hesitancy in using his shotgun on a disruptive inmate, the trailing horsemen immediately went into action. The riflemen targeted both the rebellious worker and the inept armed inmates who permitted the display of unacceptable conduct.

The security at Tucker held Tom for about a year, but chains and guards were not to deny Slaughter his fight for freedom. One Saturday afternoon, in November 1921, as the prisoners were lined up for their weekly bath and change of clothes, he grabbed a hidden rifle from under a pile of garments and began firing at the convict guards. Tom shot two of the armed trustees (both died within a few minutes), before he was subdued by a trustee (a convicted murderer) who clubbed him down from behind, then placed the muzzle of his shotgun in the pit of Tom's stomach.

Slaughter was immediately thrown into solitary confinement. Within a few days of his foiled attempt, he had been tried, convicted, and sentenced to be electrocuted. Soon thereafter, he was transferred to "The Walls," as the state prison at Little Rock was then known. While awaiting his finale with the executioner, Tom was placed on death row. Two armed trustees were posted outside of his cell.

During the early morning hours of December 8, 1921, eight days before his scheduled execution, Slaughter appeared to become very sick and in great pain. He called for a medic to be sent to his cell. A nurse arrived, examined the inmate and gave him some medicine, then departed. A few minutes later, Tom began to shake violently, as if severely chilled, and he asked for a blanket. One of the guards tried to pass a blanket through the service slot in the cell door but found that it was too bulky for the restricted opening. At that point, the trustee unlocked the cell to lay the blanket inside. As the cell door opened, Slaughter jumped from the cot with an automatic pistol in hand. The startled guard obeyed the outlaw's order to "stick 'em up." Tom grabbed the guard's gun. Now in possession of two pistols, the prisoner stepped through the unlocked door, confronted the other guard, and took his weapon.

Slaughter then herded the two disarmed trustees ahead of him to the point where only they could be seen by the guard who was manning the door. Being unaware of the situation, at their request the officer opened the door for the trustees to exit. Slaughter lunged upon the guard and ordered him to drop his weapon, which he did. Tom took the stockade keys from him and placed his two trustee captives in a cell. He then unlocked the cellblock where the African American prisoners were quartered and invited them to come with him. Several of the black inmates jumped to their feet, anxious for any chance to leave the prison. Slaughter selected five of the prisoners to join him, and as they left the area, he gave his extra weapons to his new recruits.

Forcing the hostage guard ahead of him and flanked by the five black prisoners, Slaughter directed the party to the steel door that gave access to the prison offices. While he and his allies stood back, not to be seen, he ordered his captive to approach the door and request entrance. His hostage complied, and as the door opened, two of the men with Slaughter rushed forward and shoved their captive into the guard who was opening the door, sending both of them sprawling to the floor. Two of his black cohorts took the office guard to the stockade and locked him in, while Slaughter plotted a plan to cope with the guards in three prison towers.

Taking some of his followers with him, the experienced escape artist later returned with the tower guards in tow. The captured guards were marched to the stockade and locked up. Slaughter then led his men to Warden Dempsey's house, which was on the prison grounds. The warden, his wife, two of their children, and a granddaughter were taken from their sleep and forced into the prison compound. To highlight his success, Tom locked the warden in the same cell from which he had recently escaped.

Tom Slaughter had completely taken over the prison. He then went to the stockade where the white inmates were celled, and a Jack Howard, who was serving a three-year sentence for forgery, joined the fleeing party. Before departing they gathered cash from all available sources and groceries from the commissary. Five hours after Slaughter had pulled the pistol (later confirmed to have been empty) on the guard in his cell, he and his six cohorts flamboyantly departed from the Little Rock prison, through the front gate aboard a state owned Model T Ford.

The fleeing party encountered no problem as they maneuvered the heavily loaded vehicle, until they reached Benton, some thirty miles southwest of the prison. Police at Benton had been alerted and were watching for their arrival. As the escapees' car approached, the officers opened fire on the motley lot. One of their bullets hit Slaughter in the face, shooting away part of his jaw. Two of the black prisoners were wounded, but the desperate men drove the "Tin Lizzie" through the gunfire. After traveling about twelve miles southwest of Benton, they stopped the automobile in an obscure location in the "hill country" to hide from the posse that was in pursuit. They took stock of their situation and checked the wounds of their comrades.

There are conflicting stories about what happened at that remote site before the posse of Saline County sheriff J. J. Crow located and captured the band of escapees. The sheriff found

E. H. Dempsey, warden of the Arkansas State Prison at the time of Slaughter's infamous break, was locked in a death cell with members of his family. (Author's collection)

Jack Howard, fugitive convict who ended Tom Slaughter's crimson career, was paroled and presented with a reward for his services to the state. (Author's collection)

Slaughter dead, and one of the black prisoners was dying, as his deputies rounded up the other five convicts in the immediate area. Jack Howard claimed that he had accepted the invitation to leave the prison with Slaughter in order to see that he and the other prisoners were returned to the penitentiary. Howard told the officers that "he had shot and killed Slaughter to keep him from killing all of the Negroes."

As the lawmen learned that some of Howard's other stories were not credible, they began to doubt his version of the bandit leader's death. The officers then surmised that Slaughter had died from the bullet wounds that had been inflicted by the officers at Benton. They further speculated that Howard had later fired three bullets into Slaughter's lifeless body, hoping to be credited with killing the noted outlaw, collect a reward, and gain favor with the parole board.

After having heard the evidence presented, a Saline County grand jury indicted Howard for the murder of Tom Slaughter, and he was returned to the prison. He was never tried for Slaughter's murder, as Arkansas governor Thomas C. McRae soon granted him freedom and issued a parole for his earlier sentence. Jack Howard was twice sent back to prison in Arkansas, to serve time for crimes that he later committed, for which he was charged and convicted.

At the time of his death, one newspaper briefly listed Tom Slaughter's escapes from the following facilities. On one occasion he had got out of the Dallas jail. Twice he had broken out of the prison at Rusk, Texas. While being transported as a prisoner, he had got away from officers at Greenville, Texas. He had escaped from both the Nowata and Washington County jails in Oklahoma. After being confined in Arkansas, he had killed two guards while trying to break out of the Tucker Prison Farm, and later he had escaped from the prison at Little Rock.

Tom's wife Myrtle had remained loyal to her husband throughout his criminal career, in spite of his cavorting with other females. She was available, whenever steel bars and cell doors permitted, or whenever her husband could free himself from those restraints. Tom took Myrtle along on his capers when he desired her company, instead of Mable or one of his other lady friends. When Myrtle learned that her husband had been killed, she made funeral arrangements, and Tom was interred at Little Rock.

Nora Brooks, a teenage girl who was known to travel often with Tom Slaughter, lived in Ponca City, Oklahoma. He received numerous letters from her, also many from his wife, and several from Mable during his tenure at the Tucker Prison Farm. A lot of the shady characters in Kay County were acquainted with and catered to the wanted man. Ponca City policemen were reported to have known that Slaughter often walked their streets and spent much of his time in that vicinity. Following Tom's death, there was a great deal of activity in the Osage Hills (a few miles east of Ponca City) by men searching for a cache that they believed the noted outlaw had stashed near the Arkansas River. It is not known whether any of Slaughter's ill-gotten cash has ever been found. Perhaps, it remains intact to become the treasure trove of someone who, until now, had never heard of "Outlaw Tom Slaughter."

CHAPTER 17

Ed Lockhart, an Outlaw
from Sallisaw

Four well-armed men arrived at Harrison, Arkansas, on Friday morning, February 18, 1921. Before entering the Boone County seat, they drove completely around the town and cut all of the telephone lines. After isolating the Ozark Mountain village from outside communications, they stopped their late-model touring car in front of Harrison's leading financial facility, The People's National Bank.

With drawn pistols the four desperadoes entered the building and announced that they were robbing the bank. The bandit leader started gathering money from the tills and putting it into a sack. Sixty-year-old W. J. Meyers, who had served as president of the bank, happened to be visiting with one of the employees and was standing near the safe when the robbers appeared. Upon realizing their mission, he stepped into the vault and grabbed a rifle that had been kept there in readiness for this type of occasion. The thieves had not seen the former bank official, and from the doorway of the walk-in vault, he fired one cartridge. The bullet struck the outlaw leader in his right side and severed his spine. With money sack in hand the robber fell to the floor, mortally wounded.

Those who are acquainted with Oklahoma banditry of eighty years ago will recognize the above-described episode as the finale of Henry Starr. The notorious outlaw died a couple of days after being shot during that attempt to rob the Harrison bank. This story is not about Henry Starr, of whom a great deal has already been written, including one book that he authored. Instead, the subject of this story is Ed Lockhart, who was one of the men who accompanied Henry on that ill-fated day.

When Henry Starr fell after being shot by W. J. Meyers, Lockhart and the other two would-be robbers fled from the bank. The escaping trio ran to their car and sped away. Some local citizens gave chase in another vehicle. A few miles out of town, those in the pursuing car came upon the bandit's auto-mobile, which was in flames, but the robbers were nowhere to be seen. Later, it was learned that the three men had set their car on fire and then run into the woods. The bandits mounted some horses that they had hidden in the trees and made their getaway across the hilly terrain, via a remote route. The out-laws escaped the area without encountering any lawmen.

It has been written that the attempt to loot the bank at Harrison, Arkansas, was the first such job in which Ed Lockhart had participated. No record of a previous crime has been locat-ed; however, the only information that has been found about the subject's vocation prior to that escapade are mere reports that he had served in the army during World War I and that he enjoyed "betting on the horses." If the attempted robbery of The People's National Bank was Lockhart's first such venture, one might wonder why that fiasco (with the bandit leader being gunned down, and the others getting away without any money) did not deter him from further pursuit into that field, but such was not the case.

Following the death of Henry Starr, Ed Lockhart became the leader of the remaining members of the bank-robbing gang. Their chosen profession also included stealing horses and cars to provide transportation for their enterprise. The name of the new leader was Dave Edward Lockhart, as etched on his tombstone; however, his prison record identifies him as

"Ed (alias Dave)" Lockhart, and the newspapers usually referred to him simply as "Ed Lockhart." He was born in 1890, in the Cherokee Nation; the location later fell within the bounds of present-day Sequoyah County. After Ed became a "wanted man," numerous accounts report that he hid out in an isolated area north of Marble City, Oklahoma, near the junction of Sequoyah, Cherokee, and Adair counties.

From this backwoods retreat in the Spavinaw Hills, Lockhart and his cohorts would hit the banks throughout the area. Typical of his operation is the following account. About one o'clock on Tuesday afternoon, December 20, 1921, two men dismounted and tied their horses in the alley behind the Farmers Bank of Illinois at Gore, Oklahoma. The pair (without masks) promptly entered the bank and ordered the cashier and two customers (all who were present) to hold up their hands and face the wall. As the three complied with the command, the robbers began to sack up the money, then ordered the trio into the vault and shut the door.

An early-day picture of Marble City, Oklahoma, a frequent hideout for the outlaw Ed Lockhart. (Courtesy of the Sequoyah County Historical Society)

Farmers Bank of Illinois, Gore, Oklahoma. (Courtesy of Paul W. Eichling of Gore, Oklahoma)

With some two thousand dollars in their moneybag, the robbers ran from the bank, mounted their horses, and raced out of town. The vault entry had not locked when the bandits closed the door, and the three hostages were able to free themselves. Several minutes elapsed before any pursuit was undertaken, and the robbers got away. Lockhart was the prime suspect in this heist, which was the fourth time in recent months that the bank had been looted, and as yet no one had been convicted for the thievery.

Another instance of Lockhart's operation repeats the same pattern and is reported to have occurred at about noon on Friday, January 20, 1922. While some of the employees were out eating lunch, three armed men walked into the First National Bank at Hulbert, Oklahoma, and stated that they were robbing the place. After sacking the money from the tills, they quickly left the bank. The robbers mounted their horses, then hurriedly rode out of town. Cherokee County sheriff

George R. Gourd and posse scoured the country for miles around the little town, but the bandits had escaped into the hills.

About a month after the Hulbert bank robbery, Ed Lockhart and Jack Brodie (also spelled Bodie and Brody in the newspapers) rode into Huntsville, Arkansas. The mounts that they were astride were recognized by local officers as having been reported stolen from near Marble City. The Arkansas lawmen arrested the suspected horse thieves, and their capture was reported to Oklahoma officials. The pair was then recognized as being wanted on bank robbery charges. Jack Brodie was released to Oklahoma officers and was taken to Sallisaw to be charged with robbing the bank at Gore. The Arkansas officials would not release Lockhart, as they wanted him in connection with the attempted bank robbery at Harrison and for looting a bank at Eureka Springs.

Lockhart was being held at Harrison, Arkansas, awaiting trial on charges of robbing the local bank, when on Monday evening, March 13, 1922, he broke out of the Boone County jail. While he was being held in that lockup, a pistol had been smuggled to him. Choosing an opportune time, he drew the hidden weapon and threatened the jailer, forcing him to unlock the door. The outlaw then locked the officer in the cell and fled. Those who went in pursuit of the escapee were not able to find any trace of him.

Ed Lockhart was of slight build and weighed about 135 pounds. He had black wavy hair and dark eyes that peered from deep sockets. His cheeks were sunken, and he appeared to be a victim of tuberculosis. On one occasion Sheriff Jim White had arrested Lockhart at Barnsdall, Oklahoma, but the elusive fugitive had managed to escape while the officer was taking him to the Osage County jail, at Pawhuska.

About 3:00 A.M., on Tuesday morning, February 20, 1923, Perry Chuculate, the "night watchman" at Sallisaw, discovered two men trying to steal a car at the home of Bert Cotton.

Chuculate drew his weapon and ordered the pair to hold up their hands; he then called out for help. Bert Cotton, who happened to be the Sequoyah County under-sheriff, got out of bed and came to the assistance of the city night watchman.

A .45-caliber automatic pistol was removed from each captive. As the officers were taking the two men to the county jail, Cotton recognized Ed Lockhart as the noted bank robber. Ed's accomplice was identified as Matt Charlie. Lockhart explained later that he had conceded to the night watchman and held up his hands as ordered, "thinking that he would have a better chance to escape from the lone lawman later, not realizing that another officer would be on site immediately."

Perry Chuculate (left) and Bert Cotton (right) were dedicated lawmen in Sallisaw, Sequoyah County, Oklahoma. (Courtesy of the Sequoyah County Historical Society)

About an hour after nabbing Lockhart, Chuculate and Cotton located and arrested Ed's brother Sam in Sallisaw. The Ford roadster that Sam was driving was stocked with money sacks, high-powered pistols and rifles, along with scads of ammunition. Three years later, Chuculate was killed by the outlaw brothers Matt and George Kimes at a roadblock near Sallisaw.

A few days before Ed was arrested in the Sequoyah County seat, the Sallisaw Bank and Trust Company had gone broke and was forced to close. It had been reported that the First National Bank of Sallisaw was being infused with more than one hundred thousand dollars to handle the anticipated increased demand on its business.

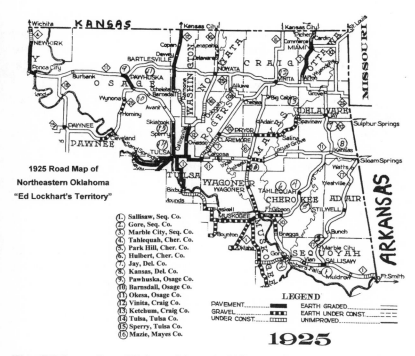

1925 Road Map of
Northeastern Oklahoma
"Ed Lockhart's Territory"

1. Sallisaw, Seq. Co.
2. Gore, Seq. Co.
3. Marble City, Seq. Co.
4. Tahlequah, Cher. Co.
5. Park Hill, Cher. Co.
6. Hulbert, Cher. Co.
7. Jay, Del. Co.
8. Kansas, Del. Co.
9. Pawhuska, Osage Co.
10. Barnsdall, Osage Co.
11. Okesa, Osage Co.
12. Vinita, Craig Co.
13. Ketchum, Craig Co.
14. Tulsa, Tulsa Co.
15. Sperry, Tulsa Co.
16. Mazie, Mayes Co.

LEGEND

PAVEMENT
GRAVEL
UNDER CONST.
EARTH GRADED
EARTH UNDER CONST.
UNIMPROVED

1925

This Oklahoma State Highway Map of 1925 indicates many of the sites visited in Ed Lockhart's bandit career. (Author's collection)

Sequoyah County sheriff John E. Johnston surmised that Lockhart had heard of this bonanza and had come to Sallisaw to rob the First National Bank. The sheriff further speculated that the trio had damaged their car while maneuvering it over the mountain trails when leaving their hideout in the Spavinaw Hills and had decided to steal an automobile in Sallisaw, rather than risk a getaway in their impaired vehicle.

Regardless of the events that had led to the arrest of Ed Lockhart at Sallisaw, Sheriff Johnston reflected satisfaction that the bank robber was in the county jail. The officer knew of the inmate's reputation for escaping from behind bars, but he appeared confident that the outlaw would not be able to get out of his facility.

Not only was Lockhart facing charges of attempting to steal an automobile, he was also wanted in Sequoyah County in connection with robbing the bank at Gore on two occasions and was thought to have stolen horses numerous times in the area. The county prisoner was wanted on bank robbery charges at other locations in Oklahoma, as well as in Arkansas, Kansas, and Missouri.

A few days after Ed had been confined in the Sequoyah County jail, the local newspaper reported that he had sent for his chauffeur (Mack Moore of Sperry) to bring his automobile to Sallisaw. The article described the vehicle as a new 1923 Sport Model Buick Runabout and hinted that Ed might "have hopes of using the high-powered car in getting away, if he can break-out of the local jail."

About a month after the noted bank robber was arrested in Sallisaw, it was discovered that he was sawing the bars of his cell. The officers became fully aware of his continuing preparation to escape from the county jail. When it came time for Lockhart and his companions to make their dash to freedom, nothing happened. It was later learned that the prisoners had been tipped off that the county lawmen were onto their plan, and they feared that any attempt to escape would have been "sure death." (One source advises that according to folklore, one of the local lawmen had provided the saw blades to the inmate so that he could undertake that endeavor).

Officials of the state of Arkansas had been urging the governor of Oklahoma to release Ed Lockhart to them, for trial on charges of robbing the banks at Eureka Springs and Harrison, and for breaking out of jail at the latter place. A few days after the foiled jailbreak at Sallisaw, Ed learned that Oklahoma governor Jack Walton was yielding to Arkansas and would sign the papers, which would send him to face the pending charges in that state. Lockhart was well aware that Arkansas frequently sentenced its prisoners to "hard labor," which meant that they would be assigned to the Tucker Prison Farm, near Little Rock. It was common knowledge that inmates at the prison farm were forced to work long, hard hours in chain gangs as they toiled in the cotton fields. The notorious outlaw felt that Arkansas would deal with him more severely than would Oklahoma.

Jack Brodie, who had been arrested with Lockhart at Huntsville, Arkansas, had been brought back, tried, and convicted of the Gore bank robbery. He had been sentenced to serve ten years in the Oklahoma State Penitentiary. To preclude being subjected to the strenuous punishment that Lockhart feared Arkansas would levy upon him, he stepped forward and pled guilty to the December 1921 bank robbery at Gore (the same robbery for which Brodie had been convicted). In response to Ed's guilty plea, Sequoyah County Judge J. H. Jarman sentenced him to twenty years in the Oklahoma State Penitentiary. Sheriff Johnston and Deputy Cotton delivered Ed Lockhart to the prison at McAlester on April 10, 1923.

Not only did Ed have a knack for breaking out of jail, but apparently he also had a talent for gaining freedom from the penitentiary. Some four months after Lockhart had been sentenced to serve twenty years in prison, Governor Walton signed a release on August 22, granting him a leave of absence (the newspapers reported that he was released for ninety days, but his prison record shows that it was for six months). The governor claimed that he had granted the leave to Ed because his family, who Walton said lived in St. Louis, Missouri, was in destitute circumstance, and he was desperately needed at home.

When the populace learned of the convict's release, they blasted the governor's office with complaints. Criticism of the governor's action increased when the bank at Mazie, Oklahoma (Mayes County), was robbed, and Ed Lockhart was the major suspect. Only two days after Governor Walton had magnanimously issued the order, he cancelled the leave of absence; however, that withdrawal did not lure the absentee to honor the governor's change of mind. Lockhart did not report back to McAlester.

Some newspaper articles stated that Ed Lockhart was running wild, and implied that he and Al Spencer were collaborating in some of their evildoing. It is believed that the two outlaws were well acquainted, but there is nothing to indicate that they conspired together. Al Spencer and his gang pulled off the big train robbery at Okesa on Tuesday, August 21, 1923, possibly the last train robbery in the Sooner State. This event happened the night before Lockhart was released from prison.

More than a month had passed since Lockhart's leave had been cancelled, and his name continued to head the prison's "missing list." On Sunday night, September 30, 1923, a car was stolen in Cherokee County, and the thief was identified to be the noted bank robber, who was still on the lam. A couple of days later, the Delaware County sheriff's office in Jay received a tip that some strange men were being harbored on the Pete Baker farm, some six miles east of Kansas, Oklahoma (Delaware County).

On Thursday, October 4, 1923, Sheriff Ben Smith and Deputies G. C. Monroe and Jack Carey, along with Deputy U.S. Marshal Bill Meeks of Vinita, drove from Jay to Baker's farm, where they captured Lockhart, whom they found asleep in the barn. A shotgun and a new automatic pistol were found, stashed near where the outlaw was taking a noonday nap. In talking with the officers later, Lockhart commented that they had caught him unaware and that "he had no intention of being taken alive." Three automobiles were found at the farm; the engine number of each vehicle had been "scratched."

Lockhart was placed in the Delaware County jail, and the officials at "Big Mac" were notified of his capture. Before prison guards arrived at Jay to pick up the missing prisoner and return him to the penitentiary, the conniving convict escaped—again.

This jailbreak occurred late Sunday evening, October 7, 1923, when five masked men arrived at the Delaware County sheriff's office. A friend (Perry Arthur) was visiting with Jack Carney, the jailer, when the armed squad abruptly entered. The leader of the attackers, who appeared to be the youngest of the lot, ordered the surprised officer to lay his gun and keys on the table. While the other four men posted themselves about the jail, the leader of the quintet picked up Carney's gun and keys. The young man unlocked Lockhart's cell and handed the officer's pistol to the freed prisoner. The jailer and his friend were then locked in the confines that the bank robber had just vacated. Moments later, six men ran from the jail to a parked car and sped out of town.

Officers were unable to locate the elusive escapee, and some three months later Lockhart struck again. When W. C. Cantrell and F. X. Hess opened the First National Bank at Shidler, Oklahoma (Osage County), for business on Wednesday morning, January 2, 1924, to commence the New Year, a pair of bandits immediately appeared on the scene. The cashiers were ordered to lie down on the floor, and they promptly obeyed.

After gathering up some eight thousand dollars, the robbers forced Cantrell and Hess, along with another bank employee, W. C. Hinton, who had entered the building while the robbery was in progress, into the vault and closed the door. The three hostages were able to gain their freedom from the walk-in vault in short order; however, the robbers had jumped into a waiting vehicle and had already vanished. Osage County sheriff C. A. Cook was summoned. and he organized a posse, but the outlaws had got away.

In addition to these heists, Lockhart was thought to have robbed banks at Fairfax, Ketchum, Park Hill, and Bethany in Oklahoma, and others out of state. One newspaper reported that he had escaped from three jails. It is not believed that Lockhart was ever tried and convicted for any crime, as no record has been found of Ed's having been brought to trial, other than the time when (in preference to being extradited to Arkansas) he pled guilty at Sallisaw.

Ed Lockhart's criminal career came at a time when the people were converting from reliance on horses for transportation and had started using automobiles for many excursions. Ed was one of the last horseback outlaws in Oklahoma; he was also one of the first to use cars (then known as "devil wagons") in his bank-robbing business. On occasions he combined the two means of transportation, as he and the gang had done at Harrison, Arkansas, when Henry Starr was killed.

Mont Grady, a lawman with some fifteen years' experience, became a McAlester prison special officer early in 1924. He was assigned the Lockhart case, and immediately started trying to locate the missing inmate. Grady, who was of Choctaw Indian heritage, got a tip and began spying at the Fred Walker farm, which was a few miles west of Sperry. Late one evening, the officer observed (from a distance) Ed Lockhart drive up, get out of a car, and enter Walker's farmhouse. The special agent reported his findings to Tulsa County sheriff Bob Sanford and solicited his help in raiding the place to capture the "wanted man." After counseling, Sheriff Sanford, Officer Grady, and five deputies planned to hit the farmhome about daylight, Wednesday morning, March 26, 1924. Due to having four flat tires on their cars while en route to the farmhouse, it was much later than anticipated when the lawmen reached their destination, and all were aboard one vehicle. The bad luck that had delayed them on the road continued to plague their effort. The officers' car got stuck in front of the farmhouse, and they were unable to drive into the backyard, where they had intended to launch their attack.

When Grady realized that the car with its seven passengers was unable to proceed, he called for the others to "take cover." As the sheriff and his deputies were abandoning the stalled vehicle and seeking refuge, the prison officer walked to the house and knocked on the front door. A woman opened the entry and spoke to the caller; suddenly Ed Lockhart poked his rifle into the officer's ribs. While nudging Grady with his weapon, Lockhart called for him to hand over his pistol and enter.

Seeing that others were in the house and circumstances being as they were, the officer obeyed. He yielded his weapon to the outlaw and slowly stepped inside. Grady closely watched as Lockhart placed the officer's pistol in the left pocket of the fugitive's coat. Along with the bandit and the new captive, there were two women and two children in the house. Suddenly, Tulsa County deputy sheriff Jack Quest burst through the back door with weapon in hand, hoping to surprise Lockhart and gain control of the situation. The "wanted man" was prepared for the officer's intrusion and while using Grady for a shield he threatened to shoot his hostage, thus forcing the deputy to retreat.

Grady and the two women tried to talk Lockhart into surrendering, telling him that he couldn't possibly escape from the lawmen on site. The outlaw was not receptive to that idea and expressed confidence that he could get away. Grady considered grabbing for his pistol, but fearing that a gunfight would ensue, in which one or more of the women and/or children might be injured, he decided not to risk such an attempt.

A few minutes later, Lockhart began to work his way out of

the house using Grady for protection. As the outlaw walked backward he forced Grady to do the same, by gripping the hostage's left wrist with his left hand and holding a rifle in his right hand. The pair's progress was slow and awkward as they retreated toward a grove of trees that the outlaw hoped would provide cover, so that he could escape from the posse.

Suddenly, Lockhart and Grady saw movement by one of the officers (Sheriff Sanford), which prompted the outlaw to quickly raise and fire his rifle. That "wild shot" provided Grady the opportunity that he had been waiting for. While the outlaw was momentarily distracted, the officer quickly twisted to his left and with his right hand he grabbed the butt of his pistol that extended above Lockhart's pocket. Without removing the revolver from the coat, Grady turned the muzzle of the weapon into the desperado's side and pulled the trigger.

Immediately, the bullet took effect, and Lockhart was overcome by a violent tremor. The victim started shaking intensely and fell to the ground. With his last breath the outlaw haltingly muttered, "You've killed me." Grady fired another round (into the air) to call the posse's attention that "the fugitive had been done in."

The officers found a serviceable vehicle at the farm and freed their automobile. The posse loaded the fallen felon; then using the two cars; they drove back to Tulsa and delivered the dead outlaw to the Mobray Funeral Parlor. The fatal bullet, a soft-nosed, .38-caliber cartridge, was removed from below the kidney of the cadaver. When the undertakers got the body ready and "laid out for display," hundreds of Tulsans came to view Ed Lockhart, the notorious bank robber, as he lay in death.

A total of sixty-six hundred dollars in rewards were posted for the outlaw at the time he was killed. The newspaper reported that all of the bounty would go to Grady but expressed the opinion that he planned to share a portion of the dividends with the sheriff and his five deputies who had accompanied him on his mission.

Maude "Alma" (nee Sitton) Lockhart, Ed's twenty-five-year-old wife, who lived in St. Joe, Arkansas (twenty-five miles southeast of Harrison), arrived in Tulsa to claim the body of her husband and arrange for his funeral. Mrs. Lockhart had been raised in St. Joe. She and Ed had got married there, shortly before he had gone into service. While Ed was overseas, his bride remained in her hometown, and after he returned, she continued to "keep house" in that village. The couple had two children, Donald and Carthal (ages five and three), who lived with their mother. While "robbing banks and fleeing from the law," Ed had often visited his wife and children at St. Joe.

Mrs. Lockhart arranged for the deceased to be taken to Sallisaw, where her husband's funeral was held. While in the army, Ed had courageously served his country in six major engagements in Europe, and his funeral included full military honors, which were presented by the local American Legion and the VFW posts. Realizing the widow's economic condition,

Ed Lockhart's tombstone in the McCoy Cemetery, Sequoyah County, Oklahoma. (Author's collection)

the veterans' organizations also helped pay the funeral expenses. Ed was buried beside his father "Cal" in the McCoy Cemetery (some five miles northwest of Sallisaw). The noted bank robber was laid to rest in the neighborhood where he had been born and raised.

A little more than ten years after the demise of Ed Lockhart, another outlaw from Sallisaw, who had garnered a great deal of national notoriety, was also killed by lawmen. He too was brought back home and interred in Sequoyah County. Charles Arthur "Pretty Boy" Floyd, known locally as "Choc", was buried on Sunday October 28, 1934, in the Akins Cemetery, which is situated in the midst of the vicinity where he had been raised and is located eight miles east of Ed Lockhart's grave site.

CHAPTER 18

Joe Davis: Often Charged, Seldom Convicted

Few fans of Oklahoma outlaw and lawman history will recall ever hearing of Joe Davis, yet there was a time when his name routinely appeared in the newspapers, as he was often suspected of felonious acts. He was frequently arrested and often charged with crimes. The numerous cases that were filed against Joe Davis included stealing livestock, train robbery, bank robbery, and murder. The 1910 census record of the Creek Nation lists Joe as nineteen years old and living with his father Jack Davis near Eufaula.

There are indications that Joe Davis had previously been in trouble with the law, but the first documented account occurred on Monday, May 29, 1911. On that date a posse of more than thirty Anti-Horse Thief Association (AHTA) members (some were reported to have been wearing masks, while others wore dresses to disguise themselves as women), rode to the house of Pony Starr (cousin of the infamous Henry Starr) at Porum. The AHTA wanted Starr and Davis in connection with the theft of some cattle. As the posse expected, Joe Davis was at Starr's home when they rode in. What they did not expect was the accurate barrage that the two "wanted men" fired at the arriving posse.

While Starr and Davis were battling with the posse, Pony's wife ran to the barn and saddled their horses. As she was leading the mounts to the house, one of the posse members who was near-by, fired his revolver at her four times, but each shot missed. Then in disgust, he threw the weapon at her. Mrs. Starr was no "shrinking violet." She retrieved the tossed pistol, then shot the two remaining cartridges at the disgruntled man, as he spurred his horse to get away.

During this attack, George Maxwell, a well-known stockman in the area, was killed, and five other members of the posse were wounded. Some accounts of this encounter report that six men were killed. When the posse retreated, Starr and Davis mounted their horses, and while flourishing their weapons they boldly rode though the streets of Porum, then headed south.

Joe Davis was later arrested, and the case against him for stealing livestock in McIntosh County was transferred to McAlester. Jack Davis's brother Bob had been convicted at Eufaula for stealing the cattle, and Joe readily admitted having helped drive the herd. Joe's attorney claimed that his client was merely helping a relative and was not aware of how his uncle had obtained the cattle. After deliberating, on October 24, 1911, the jury voted that the defendant was not guilty. Whether Joe and Pony were tried for their hostile reception of the AHTA posse's visit to Starr's home is not known.

As the southbound Katy Number 9 Limited approached Wirth (five miles south of Eufaula), before dawn on Tuesday, October 29, 1912, the engineer saw a fire on the track ahead and braked the train to a stop. Robbers immediately appeared on the scene and uncoupled the engine, baggage car, and express car from the others. They climbed aboard and ordered the engineer to cross the burning trestle, leaving the passenger coaches on the brink of the Canadian River. The blazing span collapsed shortly after the engine and two cars cleared. Once across, the bandits ordered the engineer to stop, and they commenced their planned task. The robbers used four charges to blow the safe, which badly damaged the express car.

Joe Davis, outlaw. (Courtesy of Jerry D. Thompson, Dean of the College of Arts and Humanities, Texas A&M International University, Laredo, Texas)

After placing the loot from the safe into a sack, the robbers shot out the engine's headlight, then fled into the wooded hills.

One of the thieves had ridden a horse that was missing a shoe. This clue led Sheriff John W. Cune and posse to Blocker (twenty miles southeast of Eufaula), where a horse, missing one shoe and belonging to Joe Davis, had been located.

Two days after the robbery, Joe Davis and Buck Burdoff (one source incorrectly reports that Buck was Joe's brother) were arrested. Each claimed that they were not near the site at the time of the robbery, but were asleep in Blocker. An arrest warrant was also issued for Bob Worthman, who was an employee of the Jack Davis ranch. A John McClure was later brought in as an accomplice.

A change of venue was granted the robbery suspects, and the preliminary hearing was held at McAlester on December 2, 1912. At the hearing, the United States commissioner asked that the case against the four young men (Davis, Burdoff, Worthman, and McClure) be dismissed. The prosecution did not reveal what evidence had led the law officers to arrest the men, nor what had prompted them to drop the charges. This action left the government with no suspects in custody, and the Katy train robbery remained a mystery.

Four months later, Joe Davis was again apprehended in connection with the Wirth train robbery. Davis was arrested in March 1913 when it became known that he had been buying cattle in the area and paying for the stock with one- and two-dollar bills. The bulk of the money that had been taken in the train robbery was in those denominations.

Buck Burdoff, Bob Worthman, and a Tom Spencer were also charged with robbing the Katy Number 9. Bonds were established, and the suspects were released until their trial. Davis tried to get the case transferred from McIntosh County to Pittsburg County, but the request was denied.

The four accused men were brought to trial at Eufaula in

early October 1913. The state presented a great deal of damaging evidence and several solid witnesses. The defendants produced witnesses who claimed that those being tried for the crime were in other locations at the time of the train robbery. Some of the witnesses for the defense became confused when cross-examined by the prosecution. Those who had heard the full testimonies during the weeklong trial were greatly surprised when the not guilty verdict was announced.

The defendants were released, but before Joe Davis, Buck Burdoff, and Bob Worthman could leave the courthouse, they were arrested on horse theft warrants from Osage County. The trio was taken to Pawhuska and charged with stealing three horses from Charles Whitehorn, who lived near Hominy. Each of the three men posted a five-hundred-dollar bond and was released, awaiting trial.

The three stolen horses had been found in a thicket beside the railroad, along with two bottles of nitroglycerine. A fire was burning on the track, near where the saddled horses and the explosives were located. Lawmen surmised that the horse thieves had planned to rob the Katy passenger train, three miles south of Hominy, on September 4, 1913, but for some reason had become frightened and had not carried out their intent.

A broad-brimmed hat had been left, hanging on one of the saddles. The hat was marked as having been merchandised by The Model, a store in McAlester. The proprietor of The Model recalled having sold a hat like it to Joe Davis.

In November 1913, Joe Davis and Bob Worthman were tried at Pawhuska for stealing horses and attempting to rob a train. Much of the state's case stemmed from the hat that had been sold in McAlester and found with the stolen horses. Joe Davis appeared in court wearing an identical piece of headgear. Davis and Worthman were acquitted of the charges.

On October 9, 1914, a body was found, partially hidden, in a remote area near Blocker. The body was identified as that of Fred Spess (aka Tom Spencer). Fred's brothers, Walt and Gus

Spess, confirmed the identification and claimed the body. Joe Davis was arrested a month later at McAlester and charged with the murder of his former confederate. When arrested, Davis had five hundred dollars hidden in his sock. Officers thought that Davis had led the gang that had robbed the Central State Bank at Kiefer (Creek County), on October 1, 1914, and that Tom Spencer had absconded with the proceeds of that heist. They further surmised that Davis had overtaken Spencer, then killed him to recover the loot.

The Spess brothers did not appear at the hearing held in late November 1914 at McAlester. Without the state's main witnesses, the prosecution dropped its case against Joe Davis for the murder of Tom Spencer.

Jack Davis (Joe's father) had moved from Eufaula to Hugo but was always on hand to defend his son. The senior Davis told bystanders around the Pittsburg County courthouse that the three Spess brothers had robbed the Kiefer bank. Jack claimed that Walt and Gus were trying to use the recently found body of Tom Spencer to account to the law for their brother Fred, who had simply left the country, to escape the numerous charges pending against him.

The Spess brothers' less than shining reputations is explained in a newspaper article of a few years earlier and quoted in part: "The Spess brothers and their gang comprise the last sad relic of Indian Territory barbarity. The Spess boys are a cheap imitation of old time outlaws, merely ignorant, cultureless and irresponsible country louts, who have an inbred spirit of viciousness which must of necessity arise to the surface at stated intervals."

Following his release at McAlester for the murder of Tom Spencer, Joe Davis was turned over to Creek County sheriff Henry King. He was then taken to Sapulpa, where he was to be charged with robbing the Kiefer bank. When the officials of the bank failed to identify Joe as one of the robbers, those charges were voided, in late November 1914.

Joe Davis was then transferred to Pawnee County, as a suspect in the robbery of the First State Bank at Keystone, which had occurred on September 5, 1914. At the time that Joe was taken to Pawnee and jailed, he was also wanted by Kansas officers as a suspect in a bank robbery at Baxter Springs.

In mid-January 1915, the charges against Joe Davis in Pawnee County for robbing the Keystone bank were dropped due to lack of evidence. A few days later, Oklahoma governor Lee Cruce announced his refusal to honor the requisition from Kansas for Joe Davis.

In view of the many failures of the prosecution to proceed with charges against Joe Davis, one newspaper reported: "The officers scratch their heads and say that Davis is undoubtedly the man they want, but they seem unable to get the evidence to pursue the case and obtain a conviction."

In February 1915, Buck Burdoff, Bob Worthman, and Joe and Jack Davis were tried at Muskogee for obstruction of the United States mail. These Federal charges were in connection with the Katy train robbery near Wirth, back on October 29, 1912. Three of the men being tried for interfering with the mail service had been acquitted of the train-robbing charge in McIntosh County, at their trial in October 1913. The forth man, Jack Davis, had not previously been charged with that crime.

The government did not claim that the robbers had taken any of the mail from the train, but that the holdup had delayed delivery of the mail. Even though the charges were technically different from those for which three of the men had previously been tried and acquitted, the case was much the same. The court proceedings at Muskogee were practically a repeat of the trial that had been held fifteen months earlier at Eufaula. Many of the same witnesses were called, and their testimonies sounded like echoes from the past tribunal.

There was one major difference, however; after twenty-four hours of deliberation, the jury voted that the defendants were guilty. Joe Davis, Buck Burdoff, and Bob Worthman were each convicted on two counts: (1) taking part in the holdup, and (2) conspiring to obstruct the United States mail. The jury determined that Jack Davis was not an actual participant in the robbery, but it did find him guilty on the second charge, conspiracy. The men were held in the Federal jail at Muskogee.

A week later, attorney S. M. Rutherford, who had represented Joe Davis in many of his previous cases, filed a motion for a new trial on behalf of the four convicted men. While this appeal was pending, Jack and Joe Davis were "bonded out" of jail.

Joe Davis was a suspect in the attempted robbery of two banks at Stroud, Oklahoma, on March 27, 1915. Henry Starr, the leader of the gang, was shot, wounded, and captured in that endeavor. Lewis Estes, another member of the gang who was captured and turned state's evidence, named Joe Davis and Lige Higgons as the two of the outlaw gang who got away.

Some twenty months later, at about 6:00 P.M. on Monday, November 27, 1916, as the patrons of the Pollock boarding house in Purcell were gathering for their evening meal, four officers entered the dining room. The lawmen arrested Joe Davis, W. F. Wells, John Brogan, John Courtney, and a woman named Lula Cobb, who was thought to be Joe Davis's wife.

Officers had been searching for Joe Davis, thinking that he and the others, who were arrested with him, had been involved with two recent train robberies. The Rock Island's Golden State Limited had been robbed near Apache, Arizona, on September 6, 1916. Also, a Santa Fe train had been held up near Bliss, Oklahoma, and Percy Norman, a mail clerk, had been killed, on October 18, 1916.

The five suspects who were arrested at Purcell (some were later identified by other names) were transferred that evening by special train to Oklahoma City and were booked into jail. At Oklahoma City, a long-bladed knife that had been overlooked in the earlier search was found hidden in the clothing of Joe Davis. The appeal of the previous conviction (interfering with the United States mail) was still pending, and Joe Davis remained under the ten-thousand-dollar bond. He was transferred to Muskogee. It appears that the government considered that its case against the younger Davis for the Apache robbery was stronger than the case in the train robbery and murder near Bliss, and so it sought to extradite him to Arizona. Attorney S. M. Rutherford argued that his client, Joe Davis, was still under the jurisdiction of the Eastern District of Oklahoma because of his conviction and pending appeal for interfering with the mail in the Wirth train robbery case; therefore, he had to remain under the direction of that court.

In early December 1916, Federal Judge Ralph Campbell of Muskogee ruled that Joe Davis had to answer the charges in Arizona. Again, Jack Davis was on hand to protest the court's decision and support his son's claim of innocence. Joe's father also emphatically denied that Lula Cobb, who had been arrested with Joe at Purcell, was his son's wife. He said that she was a twenty-year-old country girl from the Checotah area. Jack Davis is quoted as saying: "Lula Cobb is just a plain, ignorant little country gal, who doesn't know enough to come in out of the rain, let alone to plan robberies as has been intimated by the newspapers. And they are playing her up and running her picture as a bandit queen."

Joe Davis was delivered to Prescott, Arizona, where he was jailed on December 12, 1916, and charged with the train robbery, near Apache. The trial for Joe Davis and his comrade Jeff Spurlock was scheduled to be held at Tucson in mid-February 1917.

To face the train robbery charges in Arizona, Joe Davis selected attorney Moman Pruiett of Oklahoma City to represent him, and Spurlock hired Charles Owen of El Paso as his attorney. Owen was no pantywaist in the legal profession, having defended Mexican bandit Pancho Villa in his conflict with the United States. Pruiett was well known as a criminal lawyer who could get his clients off, regardless of the circumstances or evidence against them. The two lawyers made a formidable pair, and the prosecutors expected to be confronted with a strong defense.

According to Moman Pruiett's account of the case that he related years later, he was late getting to Tucson, due to illness in the family. Pruiett was informed by an ex-con that he had previously known and met again while en route to Arizona that Tucson was teeming with Federal agents and that they were in position to learn of any shenanigans that the defense planned. Upon his arrival, two days before the trial, Pruiett was advised by Jack Davis that "he [Davis] had arranged for a bunch of witnesses and they had cost a lot of money."

Pruiett had a reputation of being very creative with evidence and witnesses, but he was hesitant to practice any deception in this case. He respected his informant's insight into the local conditions. Pruiett suspected that their rooms were bugged and that everyone that he met was spying on him. Feeling that the prosecution knew of the arrangements that Jack Davis had made for some witnesses, Moman refused to go to court with that defense.

Jack Davis then tried to get Charles Owen to represent his son. Owen refused to participate in the case unless Pruiett led the defense. Reluctantly, Jack and Joe Davis agreed for Moman Pruiett to proceed, without the staged witnesses.

As the trial unfurled, Pruiett attempted to discredit the prosecutor's presentation, but had very little defense to offer. On February 24, 1917, the jury found Joe Davis and Jeff Spurlock guilty of the September 6, 1916, Arizona train robbery.

Years later, Pruiett reported that after the trial, as he was on his way to the Tucson train station, he was approached by Mr. Flynn, the Federal prosecutor in the case. Flynn apprised him that the prosecution was aware of the defense's plot to present a perjured testimony, and of the conspiracy, and that if Pruiett had proceeded with that plan, the government was in position to indict all that were involved. The prosecutor complimented Pruiett for wisely discarding the plotted defense.

A few days after his conviction, Joe Davis was sentenced to serve twenty-five years for robbing the United States mail. He was incarcerated on March 1, 1917, in the Federal prison at Leavenworth, Kansas.

On June 22, 1921, Joe Davis and fellow inmate Roy Sherill stole the prison doctor's car and escaped from the penitentiary. Within a few days, Joe was recaptured in Topeka and was returned to the Leavenworth pen. Sherill was arrested later and taken back to the Federal prison.

Joe Davis was released from the penitentiary on February 3, 1931, and discharged from supervision on March 16, 1933. No further information has been discovered about Joe Davis after he completed his Federal sentence.

CHAPTER 19

Bank Robbery Fiasco at Salt Springs

The adventures of the horseback outlaws have always stirred a fascination with the "Old West." The following episode occurred in the later years of the horseback outlaws ands contains scenes that are reminiscent of a silent movie featuring the Keystone Cops.

Cashier A. E. Clothier was the only person in the Citizens State Bank at Salt Springs, Oklahoma, when a man entered about three-thirty on Wednesday afternoon, March 30, 1921. Assuming that the arriving caller was a customer who wanted to transact routine business, the cashier issued his usual greeting and offered his assistance.

The visitor did not produce a check to be cashed as Clothier had anticipated; instead the cashier found himself facing a stranger with two pistols and being ordered to "hand over the money." The ready weapons prompted the bank employee to obey the command, with but slight delay.

While the cashier was relinquishing the bank's money and laying it on the ledge, the thief started to put the bills in a bag. Seeing that the robber was distracted as he "sacked the loot," Clothier decided that was the time to tackle the commandeering intruder. During the ensuing roughhouse melee, guns were knocked askew and the money was scattered as each man pelted the other with his fists. The cashier's performance as a brawler excelled that of the robber and resulted in the latter being badly battered.

Believing that he had beaten the bandit into an unconscious condition, Clothier picked up one of the revolvers and opened the front door of the building. He then fired two shots into the air to attract attention to the trouble at the bank.

While the cashier was thus engaged in the doorway, the stunned robber regained his dazed senses and, after retrieving his other gun, commenced shooting at his nemesis. Clothier then turned his weapon upon the thief. When the cylinder of the cashier's pistol revolved to the emptied chamber, he scampered from the bank to escape the bandit's bullets.

While wiping away the blood that blurred his vision, the befuddled robber grabbed some of the meager remains of the scattered loot and then limped to his horse. According to reports at the time, "He made his get-away by the same route that he had entered, via a fleet steed. It is said that he snapped his empty gun at all of the residents who were close-by."

First estimates were that the robber had got away with about $250, but it was later determined that only $60.25 was missing. After crossing Buffalo Creek, the weakened rider was last seen heading in a southeastern direction. He was described as a dark-complexioned man with black hair, about five feet ten inches tall and weighing approximately 165 pounds. The bank robber had been seen loitering in town on previous occasions.

Two days after the heist, a man named Joseph Heirholzer, who had recently received a gunshot wound in his side, was being visited by three men in a remote shack in Woodward County. Peace officers had been tipped off about the shanty and its inhabitants. The Woodward County posse located the shack and arrested the injured man (Joseph Heirholzer) along with the others who were present. They were identified as Charles Brankel, Bennett Highfill, and Thomas Dickson.

The four men were suspected of being involved in the Salt Springs robbery, and Harper County authorities were immediately notified. Twenty-eight-year-old Heirholzer was then placed in the Harper County jail at Buffalo and was charged with the larceny. The other three men were charged as accomplices in the Salt Springs bank robbery, and the bond for each was fixed at thirteen thousand dollars. None of the three were able to raise the bond, and they were kept in jail, along with Heirholzer.

While the crime had all of the amateurish earmarks of a first-time solo effort, it seems even more poorly conceived, considering that four men had been involved in planning the job. The quartet was so inept that none of them had prepared a suitable means of transportation to carry out their felonious plan.

The officers learned that the horse, which the robber had ridden in the ill-fated holdup, had been borrowed by one of the allies from a Charles M. Madden. When the lawmen determined that Madden knew the purpose for which the horse was to be used, he became the fifth man implicated in the recent bank robbery. The owner of the horse, who lived near Curtis, Oklahoma, was then arrested, and his bond was set at eighteen thousand dollars.

Why Heirholzer used a horse in the robbery is uncertain, since he was well acquainted with and had a fondness for the "Tin Lizzies" of the time. He had previously been arrested in New Mexico for stealing cars and was being held in the Clayton, New Mexico, jail when he and three other inmates escaped, some two months before the robbery at Salt Springs. The other three escapees had been captured and returned to New Mexico, but Heirholzer had eluded the posse after finding sanctuary in an obscure Woodward County canyon. (Perhaps that hideout was the same one in which the posse had recently found him).

Prior to Heirholzer's run-in with the law in New Mexico, he had served time in a Colorado reformatory for larceny and perhaps had been incarcerated elsewhere for other crimes. The gunshot wound that Heirholzer had sustained in the bank

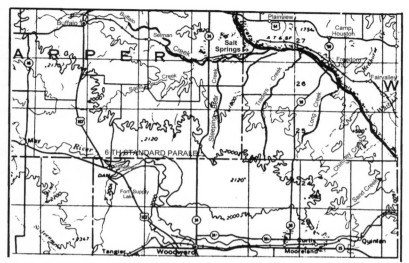

Map of southern Harper County and northern Woodward County. Salt Springs is located on Buffalo Creek near the junction of Buffalo Creek and the Cimarron River. Salt Springs is also on the railroad line between the towns of Buffalo and Freedom. The land between Salt Springs and Curtis, to the south, is marked by several creeks and canyons. (Author's collection)

robbery proved not to be serious. His three sidekicks in the recent heist lived in the local area and were well known. The older two of these men had been suspects in previous crimes in the vicinity.

A preliminary hearing of the evidence against Brankel, Highfill, and Dickson was held in April 1921. Madden's hearing was held the following month. Judge Walker ruled that all four of the suspected allies were to be bound over for trial at the next term of district court, as was Heirholzer.

Bennett Highfill was the first of the suspects brought to trial in the court at Buffalo. In June 1921, he was tried, convicted, and sentenced to ten years in the state prison. Highfill was released on bond, pending his appeal.

Thomas Dickson's trial was some three months after

Highfill's, and it developed the same as the earlier case. Dickson also appealed his conviction and posted bond.

When the cases against Joseph Heirholzer and Charles Brankel came before the court, they pled guilty to their roles in the robbery. Judge Arthur G. Sutton sentenced each of the men to ten years imprisonment. They were received at Big Mac on September 29, 1921, and were assigned numbers 11646 and 11647. Brankel was paroled on November 18, 1922, and Heirholzer was released on December 24, 1926.

Both Highfill and Dickson lost on their appeals, and each was then sent to McAlester. Highfill arrived at the prison on July 10, 1924, and was paroled on July 6, 1929. Dickson was received in Big Mac on September 8, 1924, and was paroled on September 3, 1929. Charles Madden, owner of the fleet steed that was used in the robbery, had also been tried and convicted in September 1921 and was sentenced to five years in prison. He too had appealed his case, and it appears that his determination to resist prevailed, as there is no record that he was sent to prison.

The man of the hour, bank cashier A. E. Clothier, likewise dropped from view. His daring-do had disrupted the ill-fated plan and, coupled with the efficiency of the county lawmen, had terminated Joseph Heirholzer's career as a bank robber. He would never attain the notoriety associated with other Old West desperadoes. Whether Clothier faded into the sunset or continued to exercise his expertise with fist and gun is unknown.

This episode that featured a foiled bank robbery, a free-for-all brawl, a gunfight, an empty pistol, a borrowed horse, and a spunky but addled bank robber, brought down the curtain on this segment of the Old West as this colorful period neared its finale in Oklahoma. Salt Springs was located in eastern Harper County, in northwestern Oklahoma. The small town had a post office from 1920 to 1928. It has since withered away.

CHAPTER 20

The Oglesby Brothers and the OCPD

The subjects of this chapter hailed from Callahan County, Texas, and were the sons of Charles F. and Dollie (Newton) Oglesby. The Oglesby boys were first cousins of the Newton brothers of Uvalde, Texas, who became quite active bank and train robbers. In recent years a book has been written and a movie produced about the Newton boys (Willis, Doc, Jess, and Joe), which has added to their notoriety.

The Oglesby brothers followed their Uvalde, Texas, cousins, who later lived in Tulsa, into the criminal world. Charles and Dollie's sons participated in the most lucrative (two million dollars) train robbery in history. The Newtons planned and carried out the big train robbery at Rondout, Illinois (near Chicago) in June 1924. While each of the Oglesby brothers developed extensive criminal records, this account of their felonious activities will focus on their encounters with officers of the Oklahoma City Police Department (OCPD).

As the third decade of the twentieth century unfolded, a rash of car thefts and service station robberies was plaguing Oklahoma City. On Monday morning, May 3, 1930, Oklahoma City Detectives A. J. Roberts and J. M. Mabe were in hot pursuit of a suspect who was thought to be an active participant in the popular crimes of the time. While Officer Mabe sped their police car to overtake the escaping vehicle, Detective Roberts

In the early 1930s, officers of the Oklahoma City Police Department (OCPD) and the various county sheriffs' offices had to go it alone in their ongoing efforts to fight crime and criminals, as evident in their dealings with the Oglesby Brothers. (Courtesy of Al Ritter)

fired his weapon out the window at the suspect's car. As the two automobiles raced into an oil field section in the south part of the capital city, one of the lawman's shots hit the driver. Immediately upon being struck by the officer's bullet, the suspect wrecked his car.

After being pulled from the wreckage and arrested, the wounded but not seriously injured man told the officers that his name was John Clark. While the suspect was being held under guard at the Oklahoma City General Hospital where he was being treated, the police were trying to determine his true identity. They soon learned that his fingerprints and Bertillon makeup matched those of a John Oglesby, who was wanted for highway robbery and criminal assault in Tulsa County and who had served prison time in Texas and Illinois.

While the captive was still in the Oklahoma City hospital, it was determined that, indeed, he was John Oglesby. His criminal record revealed that he had been convicted in Illinois for having been involved in the Rondout train robbery. Oglesby had been paroled after serving only one year of that sentence, because he had provided information that resulted in other arrests. It was also recorded that he had been convicted in 1927 for several burglaries in Texas and had been sentenced to serve four years, but he had been paroled in 1928.

Since larceny and assault charges had already been filed against Oglesby in Tulsa County, and it appeared that the county had a strong case against him, it was decided that he should be returned to that locale to be tried. In June 1930, John Oglesby was brought to trial at Tulsa (then known as the Oil Capital of the World) for having robbed three young couples and for the attempted rape of two of the girls on Turkey Mountain, near Tulsa, in October 1929. Shortly after that crime had been committed, Tulsa County deputies had arrested John Oglesby and his younger brother Weldon (who was still being held, awaiting trial), but John had escaped from the officers.

The prosecution sought the death penalty in the case. When it appeared to Oglesby that the jury was being impressed with the county attorney's presentation, he pled guilty to forestall the maximum sentence of death in the electric chair being imposed. In response to the plea, Judge Saul Yager sentenced him to life imprisonment in the Oklahoma State Penitentiary. Two months after having a run-in with Oklahoma City police officers, twenty-three-year-old John Oglesby was behind bars at Big Mac facing a life sentence.

A little more than two years after John had become a long-term inmate in the state penitentiary, his older brother Elbert Oglesby drove into Oklahoma City. On Monday afternoon,

October 17, 1932, Officers Gerald "Jerry" Campbell and George Baker were working the area just south of downtown. The two policemen were assigned to the stolen car division and as always, they were alert to locate "hot cars" and the thieves who had stolen the missing vehicles.

As the pair of officers cruised in the 700 block of South Robinson, they noticed that two men had been sitting in a car for some time. The vehicle had caught their eye earlier, because it displayed a Kansas license plate. The officers circled the block again and pulled up behind the out-of-state car.

The policemen got out of their vehicle, and one walked to each side of the parked automobile, where they began questioning the two occupants. The men's responses caused the officers to become more suspicious, especially of the one who was sitting in the driver's seat, so they began checking the vehicle. Finding that the engine number had been altered, the officers arrested both men.

Officer Baker took one of the men with him to the patrol car, and Jerry Campbell told the other occupant to stay behind the steering wheel. When Campbell got in on the passenger side of the front seat, he told the man to drive to the police station. The Kansas car then pulled from the curb and started up the street, with Baker and his captive in the police car following close behind. Immediately after heading north on Robinson, Campbell noticed a hump under the rear floor mat. He reached back to examine the cause and found that under the mat was a sawed-off shotgun, which he left as it lay.

Realizing that Campbell had seen his stashed weapon, the suspect dropped his left hand from the steering wheel, and the officer ordered him to keep both hands on the wheel. Campbell later reported that an instant later the driver pushed a pistol to his chest and that he shoved the gun aside, just before it fired. The officer then whipped out his revolver and triggered four cartridges, inflicting fatal wounds in the suspect's jaw, neck, shoulder, and chest. The car ran onto a curb and hit a parked automobile before stopping. Officer Campbell got out of the vehicle holding his revolver in one hand and the outlaw's pistol in his other.

The dead man was identified as Elbert Cole Oglesby. His criminal record revealed that he was twenty-seven years old and had taken part in the big train robbery in Illinois. He was wanted in Texas on a murder charge at Abilene and for robbing banks at Canton and Paradise. He was also sought in Mississippi in connection with a bank robbery, during which a policeman had been kidnapped.

The party who had been arrested with Elbert Oglesby was not aware that the person who was trying to sell the automobile to him was a "wanted man." He was released after confirmation that he was an employed local citizen, with a wife and two children, and had no criminal record. Officers learned that the car that Oglesby was driving had been stolen in Shawnee two days earlier.

Just over a year after Elbert Oglesby had been shot and killed by a city police officer, his brother Ernest arrived in Oklahoma City. About six o'clock on Sunday morning, December 2, 1933, while scout car officers Douglas Gates and Webb Campbell were chatting with a friend on North Lincoln, they observed a new Chevrolet coupe speed away from the tourist court. Campbell jotted down the tag number and started checking it against the list of stolen cars that the officers carried with them. He located the number on the list and advised his partner that the license plate was from a sedan that had been stolen at Weatherford the previous month and had later been found, abandoned and burned, near El Reno.

Gates put the patrol car in gear, and the officers began racing south after the suspicious vehicle. They observed the blue coupe turn right as it neared the state capitol, and when the suspect stopped at the N.W. 23rd and Robinson traffic light, the officers pulled up behind it. Campbell got out of the police car and walked to the right side of the new Chevrolet, where

OCPD Officer Webb Campbell (above) and his partner, Douglas Gates, tangled with Texas badman Ernest Oglesby, resulting in a wild pursuit and shoot-out in December 1933. (Courtesy of Richard E. Jones)

he asked the driver if that was his car. In a rather harsh tone, he replied that it was.

When Campbell walked behind the car to approach the man on the left side of the vehicle to question him further, the driver revved the engine and released the clutch. As the automobile lurched forward, Campbell grabbed the spare tire that was mounted on the rear of the blue coupe. With the tires spinning through the intersection, the athletic adept officer swung his body upon the trunk of the car and braced his leg against the tire rack. While in this partial-prone position Campbell pulled his service revolver and, pointing it at the driver's head, he shouted, "Stop or I'll shoot."

Before the officer carried out his threat, the driver quickly produced a pistol and, directing it over his right shoulder, he fired. The rear window shattered, imbedding slivers of the broken glass into Campbell's face and forehead. As the flowing blood began to blur his vision, Campbell fired his weapon twice. One of the officer's bullets struck the driver's arm, and the vehicle swerved into the path of an oncoming car, causing them to collide. Upon the impact of the two vehicles, Campbell was thrown from the back of the coupe and fell upon the street, where he lay, momentarily dazed. Gates was following close behind in the police cruiser. When the outlaw's car struck the other vehicle, Oglesby jumped out and started firing at the arriving officer. Gates tried shooting at the desperado through the window of the police car. One of the bandit's bullets was deflected, having hit Gates's badge, but another cartridge broke the policeman's collarbone and passed into his neck. The outlaw then jumped onto the running board of a nearby Willis automobile that had arrived on the scene and ordered the driver to proceed.

A few seconds after Campbell was thrown to the pavement, he aroused and, while wiping blood from his face, tried to get a shot at the fleeing outlaw. Hearing someone shout that there were children in the car that the bandit had commandeered, the officer held his fire, letting the desperado escape.

Officer Campbell, whose head was severely bleeding, got into another passing car and directed the driver to follow the course that the bandit had taken. When Campbell did not see the car with the gun-wielding escapee aboard within a few blocks; he had the driver deliver him to a fire station at Northwest 16th and Pennsylvania, where he called police headquarters and reported the tragic encounter.

Campbell was then taken to the General Hospital, arriving there shortly after the mortally wounded Douglas Gates had been brought in. It was first thought that Campbell's cuts had permanently damaged his vision. A few minutes after the police officer had called and reported the disastrous incident, the driver of the Willis automobile phoned the police station and advised them that the bandit had departed from his car in the vicinity of Northwest 14th and May.

As the police converged into that area, they met a milkman who had just completed his morning delivery route in a horse-drawn wagon. When asked, he reported having seen a man with a wounded arm in the 2900 block of Northwest 12th Street. Police began a house-to-house search in that vicinity. Ernest Oglesby was located in a home that he had rented a couple of days earlier at 2921 Northwest 12th Street.

Oglesby was arrested about two hours after his shoot-out with the officers. Four spent cartridges and a set of keys to the blue coupe were found in his coat pockets. He had a flesh wound on his arm, and his pistol was found, stashed in a bathroom heater.

Officer Gates died that afternoon. Webb Campbell later recovered, with no permanent damage, other than some scars from his facial cuts. Oglesby denied being involved in the gunfight, but the evidence—eyewitnesses, his own injury, a ballistic test, fingerprints, and other confirmation—left no doubt that he was the guilty party.

A contingent of nearly one hundred Oklahoma City policemen and sheriff's deputies escorted the body of Douglas Gates back home to Fort Cobb in Caddo County, where he was laid to rest in the family plot, beside his brother Jack. Jack Gates was Douglas's younger brother and had been shot and killed in the line of duty as an Oklahoma City police officer, some three years earlier and about ten blocks south of the place where Douglas had been fatally shot.

Not only was the little town of Fort Cobb brought into the limelight of this tragedy because it had been the hometown of the victim, but another factor was soon revealed. A strange coincidence in the case was unveiled when it was reported that the new blue coupe, which Oglesby was driving when overtaken by the officers, had been stolen from the showroom of the Chevrolet agency in that small western Oklahoma town.

Ernest Oglesby had a lengthy criminal record, especially in Texas. He had twenty-two felony convictions in the Lone Star State and was serving time in the Huntsville prison when, in April 1933, Gov. Miriam A. "Ma" Ferguson granted him a full pardon. She developed a notorious reputation for issuing such unwarranted releases.

Oglesby was brought to trial in Oklahoma City for the murder of Police Officer Douglas Gates. The jury accepted the testimony and evidence that was presented against the outlaw from Texas as sufficient to warrant judgment. After only thirty-five minutes of deliberation, on Friday, January 12, 1934, Ernest Oglesby was convicted and sentenced to death in the electric chair.

At the age of twenty-six, Oglesby was taken to the Oklahoma State Penitentiary at McAlester, to await his fate. Shortly after midnight on the morning of Friday, January 4, 1935, the executioner threw the switch, and "Ol Sparky" shot forth the electrical jolt that ended the life of Ernest Oglesby. The widow of Douglas Gates, Gates's partner, Webb Campbell, and a large contingency of law-enforcement officers traveled from Oklahoma City to witness the execution.

The prison records of the outlaw sons of Charles and Dollie

Rich Owen, longtime executioner at the Oklahoma State Penitentiary at McAlester, is seen at the controls of the prison's electric chair. This photo was taken three months after Owen executed Ernest Oglesby in 1935. (Photo courtesy of the Archives & Manuscripts Division of the Oklahoma Historical Society)

Oglesby reveal that their boys had created a multitude of troubles in the Southwest, extending over a long period of time. There is no known connection in the inducements that had brought their sons to Oklahoma City on the three separate occasions mentioned. Of the three Oglesby brothers, who were reported to have visited Oklahoma's capital city, all had deadly encounters with local police officers. Their run-ins with the OCPD resulted in the deaths of one officer and two of the Oglesby brothers, leaving the third member of the outlaw family in prison with a life sentence.

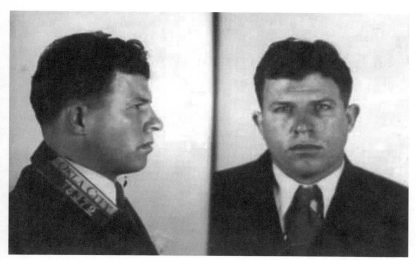

Ernest Oglesby was executed on January 4, 1935, for the death of Officer Douglas Gates in December of 1933. (Courtesy of Richard E. Jones)

Five years later and only five blocks from the spot where Douglas Gates had been fatally wounded, his partner on that ill-fated day, Webb Campbell, fell victim to a like fate. About 10:00 P.M., on October 29, 1938, Detectives Campbell and McCurdy responded to a report of a prowler on Northwest 24th Street. Unaware that two detectives had already arrived on the scene, Campbell alit from his slowing patrol car and ran to the back of the apartment house, while his partner, who was driving, looked for a place to pull over. Officer Lawrence Bush, already on the scene, saw a man run around the corner of the building. In the dark, he mistook the plain-clothed detective, Campbell, as the prowler and fired. Neither Bush nor his partner was aware that the other two officers had arrived on the scene. Detective Sergeant Webb Campbell died that night, having been struck in his left side by the bullet. Although Bush was cleared of the killing of his fellow officer, he resigned from the force a few months later.

CHAPTER 21

The Cunningham Brothers

The subjects of this story were the sons of Burl (also spelled Burrell) and Addie Cunningham. The boys' given names were: Forrest, called "Doc"; John; Manuel (Emanuel), called "Skinny"; and Jess, called "Jake." The Cunningham family (four sons and two daughters) had lived in Jefferson County, Oklahoma, for several years before moving to Levelland, Texas in about 1925. A couple of years later they moved back to Oklahoma and settled in Stephens County, some seven miles east of Comanche.

If there was a particular cause for the downfall of the Cunningham brothers it is not now known, nor is the date known when they entered into crime. Their first confirmed felonious activity occurred on July 30, 1928. Shortly after nine o'clock that Monday morning, two young men entered the bank in Hastings (Jefferson County), Oklahoma. Only John R. Reynolds (the cashier) and J. H. Ross (a customer) were in the bank when the armed pair walked in, displayed their weapons, and demanded money. After gathering up some fifteen hundred dollars from the tills, the bandits left the Oklahoma National Bank and made their getaway in a Buick sedan.

Citizens and lawmen gave chase, but the robbers got away. It was believed that four men were involved in the robbery, because the two bandits had been seen in town a half-hour before the heist in the getaway car, with two other men of similar appearances. A deposit slip from a bank at Plainview, Texas, was found where the bandits' Buick had been parked. An officer called the Texas bank and learned that the man whose name appeared on the slip had been robbed a few days earlier.

At about 2:15 P.M., on Friday, December 21, 1928, while Christmas shoppers milled the streets, three men entered the Bank of Manitou (Tillman County), Oklahoma. The robbers ordered those present (two employees and four customers) into the teller's cage. R. D. Campbell, a customer who was hard of hearing and not fully aware of what was happening, started to leave. One of the gunmen grabbed the unconcerned customer to keep him from walking away. While the robber was distracted with Campbell, the cashier, W. D. Jones, was able to hide a package containing several hundred dollars under the counter. The robbers did, however, get away with more than fifteen hundred dollars in currency. One of the bandits remained in the doorway until the others had reached the car. He told those in the bank not to follow because they had machine guns in their automobile.

Manitou mayor R. F. Hill commandeered a car and raced after the bandits' Buick. He had to give up the chase a few miles east of town, because of a puncture in one of the tires on the confiscated vehicle. The robbers made good their escape. This bank robbery at Manitou was reported to have been the first such heist in Tillman County.

Harold Johnson escorted Mayre Chancellor to the Methodist Church in Lawton, on Sunday evening, February 24, 1929. When the nineteen-year-old Johnson and his companion returned to his car after the service, two armed men stepped forward. One of the thugs forced the girl into the back seat with him, and Johnson was told to drive. The other hoodlum scooted in beside Johnson and poked a gun into his ribs, then ordered him to "follow that car," which had two men in it who then began to drive away.

Numerous people were in the church parking lot, and some were nearby when the kidnapping occurred, but no one noticed the criminal activity in progress. Johnson followed the gunman's orders. After driving some three miles out of town, the lead car stopped, and the four desperadoes began transferring guns from it into the trailing automobile. When their weapons and personal gear were loaded into Johnson's new Buick, the four young hoodlums stepped to the side and held a discussion.

The kidnapers had not physically harmed either of the victims. Following the bandits' brief parley, one of them informed Johnson that after they had left, he could drive the abandoned car and take the girl back to Lawton. They told him that the car they were leaving had been stolen in Vernon, Texas. A short time later, Harold Johnson and Mayre Chancellor arrived at the county sheriff's office in Lawton, driving the stolen car from Texas. The young couple excitedly related their ordeal to the officers.

Shortly after 10:00 A.M., on Friday, July 26, 1929, four young men walked into the First National Bank in Hooker, Oklahoma (Texas County). The heavily armed bandits ordered the employees and customers who were in the bank to lie on the floor. The pistol-wielding robbers carried away nearly ten thousand dollars, as they ran out of the bank and got in two cars, a Buick and a Ford. C. E. Wilson, a bank cashier, fired two shots that demolished the taillight of the robber's Ford. Citizens, who had become aware of the bank heist, had gathered nearby and fired several shots at the two getaway cars. These shots were answered with a volley from a machine gun in the Buick sedan, but none of the local citizens were hit.

During the skirmish in Hooker, a bullet had struck one of the bandits. After traveling a few miles east on Highway 64, the bank robbers stopped at a farmhouse. They asked the lady who answered the door for some rags and turpentine. When they explained that their brother had been injured by a broken car window, she gladly provided the requested items, and they drove away.

A few miles farther, the Ford roadster became inoperative and, after everything was put in the Buick, the Ford was abandoned. The robbers were followed to a point south of Boyd (Beaver County) where Hooker city marshal Tattu's car ran out of gas. No further trace of the bandits' Buick could be picked up. Officers learned that the abandoned Ford had been stolen a few days earlier in Electra, Texas.

During the period of these bank robberies, there had been numerous robberies of filling stations and country stores throughout southwestern Oklahoma. The bandits who pulled those petty thefts and hit these three banks were not wearing masks, yet no names were associated with the crimes. The newspaper articles that reported the thefts gave basic descriptions of the robbers, but there was no mention of their suspected identities.

At about 9:00 P.M., on Monday evening, May 12, 1930, the Checkerboard filling station at the south side of Lawton (Comanche County) was robbed by four young men. The robbers got away with a carton of Camel cigarettes, one box of cigars, one small sack of meal, a plug of Tinsley chewing tobacco, eleven gallons of gasoline, four quarts of oil, a box of cartridges, and a few coins.

Shortly after the filling station robbery, Lawton officers telephoned the Stephens County sheriff's office that the bandits were last seen heading east. Upon receiving this information at Duncan, Stephens County sheriff Waldo A. "Wal" Williams, Duncan police chief I. B. Gossett, Undersheriff Ed Sumrill, and policeman W. F. McKinzey jumped into the undersheriff's car and sped away to intercept the fleeing robbers. With Sumrill driving, they met the suspects' car some five miles north of Duncan and with special effort hailed them down.

When both cars came to a stop, the four officers got out of their vehicle and approached the suspects' car with its four occupants. As his cohorts began to get out of their vehicle, the driver of the flagged-down automobile asked, "Who are you fellows"? Chief Gossett replied, "We're the law, and we want to search your car." While the driver of the suspects' sedan was getting out of the car, he drew his pistol. At that same moment, one of his confederates grabbed the shotgun that was being held by Chief Gossett, and the shooting commenced. It was dark, and no one claimed that they could relate the full particulars of the gunfight that ensued, but it is believed that all eight men participated in the deadly encounter.

When the shots ceased, Sheriff Williams and Chief Gossett were each severely wounded. Neither Sumrill nor McKinzey had been hit. Twenty-seven-year old Forrest Cunningham was dead. His brothers John and Manuel were badly wounded, each having been hit by two bullets, and Jess, though uninjured, had run from the scene.

Sheriff Wal Williams had three bullet wounds. He died the following afternoon and was buried in the Marlow Cemetery. Minnie Williams, the sheriff's wife, was appointed to fill his position. Chief Gossett did recover and return to work after having been shot in the abdomen.

Typical of the Cunningham brothers' operation, the car that they were driving was a Buick that had been stolen in Texas. Jess Cunningham escaped the area by stealing a car from a George Miller, whose home was not far from the site of the bloody gunfight. Two weeks later, Jess was captured near Gunnison, Colorado, and was returned to Stephens County.

Forrest Cunningham had taken an aircraft course in Oklahoma City and had recently begun to build an airplane. His death certificate lists his trade as an airplane mechanic.

Each of outlaw brothers was led to believe that he was the only survivor of the four-member family gang. John (and later Manuel) admitted his involvement in the previously described crimes. After being identified by witnesses from Kansas, the brothers also acknowledged that the Cunninghams were the quartet that had robbed the bank at Kiowa, Kansas, of thirty-five hundred dollars, on March 24, 1929.

In late June 1930, the surviving Cunningham brothers made a plea bargain and accepted life sentences rather than go to trial for the murder of Sheriff Williams. The three were also facing charges of bank robbery, stealing automobiles, kidnapping, and numerous petty crimes. The Cunningham boys were received at the McAlester Penitentiary on June 28, 1930. They were recorded as Jess, age eighteen, who was assigned number 22154; John, age twenty-five, became number 22155; Manuel, age twenty-three, entered as number 22156.

Sheriff Waldo "Wal" Williams was a well-respected officer and was very popular among his constituents. To honor their fallen sheriff, the citizens of Stephens County raised funds and placed a granite monument near the site where Williams had been gunned down. The monument is located at the intersection of U.S. Highway 81 and State Highway 7, six miles north of Duncan, and is inscribed:

ERECTED IN HONOR OF
THE SERVICES OF ALL PEACE OFFICERS
AND DEDICATED TO THE MEMORY OF
SHERIFF W. A. (WAL) WILLIAMS
1869–1930
WHO GAVE HIS LIFE IN THE
COURAGEOUS PERFORMANCE OF HIS DUTY
MAY 13, 1930

In the gunfight with the police, John had been shot in the stomach, and the injury could not be completely corrected. Two years after being incarcerated, on July 29, 1932, John Cunningham died in the prison hospital of obstruction of the bowels and adhesions. At that time, Manuel Cunningham was described as paralyzed from the waist down and confined to a wheelchair.

Author Ken Butler standing beside the monument, located six miles north of Duncan, Oklahoma, which is dedicated to the memory of Sheriff W. A. "Wal" Williams. (Author's collection)

On May 13, 1936, twenty-four inmates who were working in the brick plant rioted and killed the brickyard superintendent, Charles D. Powell. Two guards, Tuck Cope and W. W. Gossett, were injured during this McAlester prison break. Ten of the convicts were wounded and taken into custody at the site. Six others were recaptured shortly after the break. One of the many bullets that were fired at the escaping prisoners had hit Jess Cunningham, but he managed to get away along with seven others. Two days later, Jess was located by four officers in a vacant house one mile south of Antlers (Pushmataha County). Even though he was alone and feverish from his hip wound having become infected, he tried to reach his rifle when the officers burst in. Jess was captured and returned to the penitentiary.

Manuel served his time at McAlester without any behavioral problems and was paroled on April 12, 1945. Three years after he had been released, his mother and father with their partially paralyzed son were involved in a car wreck in Texas. Burl, Addie, and Manuel were killed in a car accident in August of 1948. Their bodies were returned to Oklahoma, and they were buried beside their sons, Forrest and John, in the Duncan Cemetery, Duncan, Oklahoma.

Jess's role in the 1936 prison break delayed his parole four years, after his brother Manuel had been released. Jess was paroled on May 3, 1949. A few months after getting out of prison, he was caught in Altus trying to steal an automobile. Jess Cunningham was held in the Jackson County jail for some time awaiting determination of his parole, which was revoked on March 6, 1950. Four days later he was returned to the McAlester Penitentiary.

In July 1952, Jess and two other convicts undertook a prison escape that nearly cost them their lives. The three were sealed in separate reinforced cardboard soap barrels just before they were loaded on a truck to be taken to Fort Supply. One of the escapees, W. L. Hall, managed to cut an opening in his container so that he could get some air. While the truck was still on the McAlester prison grounds, picking up canned goods, a guard noticed the hole in the barrel from which a man's hair was visible. After unsealing the container and finding Hall, the other two barrels were opened. Jess Cunningham and a L. E. Goddard were each dragged from their concealment, unconscious and nearly suffocated. Prolonged artificial respiratory efforts were required to revive the pair.

In May 1958, Jess was charged with conspiracy, attempting to have contraband brought into the penal institution. He received his second parole on March 10, 1965. Three years later, Jess was released from supervision.

Thirty-eight years after the Cunningham brothers robbed the Lawton filling station of a few dollars' worth of merchandise and were caught in the deadly gunfight that took the lives of Sheriff Williams and Forrest Cunningham, Jess, the lone surviving Cunningham brother, became a free man.

CHAPTER 22

Bessie's Heroic Banker

The town of Bessie (Washita County), Oklahoma, is located in the far western part of the state, about halfway between Clinton and Cordell on today's State Highway 183A. The little hamlet was founded in 1895 and was first known as Boggy; a name taken from a creek that ran nearby. Some three years later, it was renamed Stout. In 1903, the Blackwell, Enid and Southwestern Railroad, which was fondly called "The Bess," built a roundhouse at the site. In appreciation of the new industry the name was changed to Bessie.

Most of the early settlers in the community were farm families of German origin. Typical of the small towns that are found in the predominately rural area of western Oklahoma, it has a population of around 190. However, it differs from other rural communities in the state due to the striking sight of an eighteen-foot granite monument on the small town's main street. Unlike other monuments or statues dedicated to the memory of war heroes, historical or political figures, or fallen police officers, Bessie's imposing monument is dedicated to a local banker. Bessie's main street monument was dedicated in 1929 to the memory of Ben Kiehn.

A few years after his birth in 1889 at Lehi, Kansas, Ben's family moved to Oklahoma Territory and settled on a farm near Boggy Creek, where he was raised. His early years were typical of a rural childhood that included the beginning of the twentieth century. After completing the eighth grade during a time period when achieving a sixth-grade education was considered an accomplishment, young Kiehn joined the army. He served on the Mexican border during the period when Pancho Villa was creating troubles for the United States.

In 1917, when the country became involved in World War I that had broken out in Europe, Ben Kiehn was among the first American troops sent into combat. His talent and devotion to the army earned him a promotion to officer status. Even though Ben was of German heritage, he was proud to serve Uncle Sam in defeating the Kaiser's troops. Lieutenant Kiehn bravely led his men into numerous engagements in France.

After the armistice, the young veteran was discharged from service, and he returned to his old hometown of Bessie, Oklahoma. Ben became the vice president of the local bank and a leader in the community. He was the driving force in getting a community auditorium erected in Bessie. Ben was on the school board and an active member of the local Masonic Order. He also served as vice commander of the American Legion post at Clinton.

The tranquility of conducting routine business in the rural western Oklahoma town was interrupted on Tuesday morning, January 24, 1928, when two armed men entered the Bessie State Bank. They ordered bookkeeper Georgia Stehr and bank vice-president Ben Kiehn, who were the only people in the building at the time, to lie down on the floor. As the two bank employees obeyed, the robbers began cleaning out the tills. After gathering up all the money that was easily available, the bandits told Kiehn and Stehr to get up and go into the vault. At that time a customer, Henry Dyck, arrived at the front door to enter the bank. He was also put into the walk-in safe.

The vault door had a hidden catch that prevented it from completely closing, and a slight opening remained after the robber tried to shut the door. Kiehn had stashed a pistol in the vault just in case this kind of situation occurred. He grabbed the revolver and began shooting through the crack in the door. As Ben fired four shots at the robbers, one of the bandits began shooting at the banker. A slug from the robber's gun hit the edge of the door then glanced through the slight opening and struck Ben Kiehn just under his left eye.

While trying to lock the hostages in the vault and during the flurry of gunshots that followed due to the brave action of Ben Kiehn from inside the bank vault, one of the robbers was hit by one of Ben's bullets. Immediately after the desperado was struck, the robbers left the bank. The first one who reached their waiting Jewett automobile got behind the wheel. The driver then paused as his wounded companion at a slower pace made his way to the car and climbed into the back seat. The automobile then sped out of town.

Miss Stehr rushed to the telephone and called the doctor while Henry Dyke ran out on the street and shouted for help. Numerous local citizens hurried to the bank where they found

A view of the main street in Bessie, Oklahoma, taken around the time of the bank robbery in which Ben Kiehn was killed. (Photo courtesy of the Archives & Manuscripts Division of the Oklahoma Historical Society)

Ben on the floor of the vault, still holding his weapon. The banker had received a fatal wound, and he died a few minutes later.

After leaving Bessie, the outlaws drove a half-mile north then two miles west, where they turned north again and their trail was lost. They had gotten away with eight hundred and sixty dollars.

Washita County sheriff John Miller was notified of the robbery and murder. A few minutes later the news was broadcast over radio stations in the area. A posse including an airplane was soon searching for the pair of robbers. But the bandits were not located. Shortly after dark that evening a stranger walked to the home of Buster Peck, who lived a few miles west of Bessie. This caller advised the farmer that there was a "sick man down in the ravine who wanted to get to town." As Peck was walking with the man toward the gulch, the stranger suddenly broke and ran away. The farmer continued to the designated site where he found "the sick man" covered with an overcoat lying near the creek. When Peck saw that the man was armed and had a gunshot wound, he rushed to town and called the sheriff.

Sheriff Miller and a deputy responded. They took the injured, half-conscious man to the Cordell hospital. While en route to that facility, he told the officers that his name was Fletcher Rickard and readily acknowledged that he had participated in robbing the Bessie bank. He reported that his cohort was a man named Jack Brown.

The wounded man claimed that Kiehn had been shot by Brown, and that they had escaped in a Maxwell automobile. In fact, the vehicle was a Jewett brand, and in retrospect it is assumed that the name Jack Brown might have been given in an effort to hide the true identity of the wounded bank robber's accomplice. The officers were unable to question him further, as Rickard lapsed into a state of unconsciousness and died about two o'clock Wednesday morning.

Some twelve miles northeast of Elk City, an abandoned

Jewett automobile was discovered on Wednesday afternoon. Not only did it fit the description of the bandit's' vehicle, but also the rear seat was stained with blood, which assured the officers that it was the bank robbers' getaway car. The lawmen believed that the driver had deliberately ditched it and ridden off with someone, whom he had arranged to meet at that location, because the vehicle was still in operating order. The car had been stolen in Oklahoma City the previous Sunday night, and it was taken to Cordell for further checking.

Hundreds of people attended the funeral of Ben Kiehn. The services were held in the recently completed auditorium that he had so diligently sponsored. His funeral was held on the same day that he had been scheduled to deliver the main address, dedicating the building to the community. Ben was buried in the Bessie Cemetery.

Base of the downtown monument to Ben Kiehn's bravery during a January 1928 bank robbery in Bessie, Oklahoma. (Author's collection)

The imposing eighteen-foot granite monument on the main street of Bessie, Oklahoma, is dedicated to the memory of Ben Kiehn, who died defending the citizens of the community. (Photo courtesy of the Archives & Manuscripts Division of the Oklahoma Historical Society)

One local newspaper reported: "Ben Kiehn is Washita County's hero. He was shot down by bandits while attempting to perform what he considered his duty in protecting the property that had been placed in his trust. In the same unselfish manner in which he risked his life before the enemy's guns in World War I he faced the bank robbers in a gunfight that led to his death. He did what few other bankers would have done."

Ben Kiehn had been a popular member of the State Bankers Association, who voted to establish a marker in his honor. During their meeting at Tulsa in December 1928, the association awarded a three-thousand-dollar contract to the Pellow brothers of Granite, Oklahoma, to erect a stone at Bessie in reverence to Ben Kiehn.

The mahogany granite monument was dedicated on Memorial Day 1929 and was unveiled by Ben's five-year-old son. The base of the monument is six feet square and tapers to a height of eighteen feet. Ben Kiehn's name appears in raised letters on each side of the stone just above an inscription honoring the slain banker. The marker was erected on the main street, next to the bank building where Ben was killed. It still stands today in honor of Ben Kiehn, the pride of Bessie, Oklahoma.

CHAPTER 23

Mayhem in Kay County

'Twas the Christmas season of 1930. Mr. and Mrs. J. F. Griffith's daughters, Zexie and Jessie, had spent the holidays with their parents who lived at Blackwell, Oklahoma. The girls had planned to leave Saturday afternoon and return home, but their ailing mother had asked that they stay over. A little before five o'clock, on Sunday morning, December 28, Mr. Griffith, the night captain of the Blackwell police department, helped his daughters carry their luggage to their car. After biding the girls adieu, he watched as they drove away.

Zexie and Jessie headed south in their Chevrolet coupe. The sisters had recently purchased the nearly new car, jointly. They were en route to Norman, where Jessie lived and was the supervisor of music in the public school. She was scheduled to sing a solo in church that Sunday morning. It was planned that after the church service, Zexie would take the automobile and drive on to Warner, Oklahoma, where she resided and taught school.

About nine o'clock that same Sunday morning, C. C. Woods and his sons were hunting rabbits when they came upon the bodies of two young women, on "the old river road," near the Salt Fork of the Arkansas. The corpses were found approximately one mile southwest of the river bridge on the highway just south of Tonkawa. Woods, who operated a furniture store

Zexie Griffith. (Author's collection)

Jessie Griffith. (Author's collection)

in Tonkawa, rushed back into town to inform Police Chief Charles Wagner of his grim discovery. Upon locating the Tonkawa police chief, Woods led Wagner and some followers to the scene of the crime. Kay County sheriff Joe Cooper was notified at Newkirk, the county seat.

When Police Chief Wagner arrived at the crime scene, he found the victims near the road, about a hundred feet apart. Each of the women had been shot in the head. The younger lady's undergarments had been torn from her body and thrown to the side. She had obviously been sexually assaulted.

As the police chief observed the facial features of the two casualties, he realized they looked familiar. After mulling a few moments, he recognized them as the daughters of Jeff Griffith, a fellow lawman whom he had known for years.

Sheriff Cooper, Kay County attorney Bruce Potter, and other officers from Newkirk joined Wagner at the crime site on Sunday morning. Jeff Griffith also arrived and confirmed that the two fatalities were his daughters, Zexie and Jessie.

Further examination of the crime scene revealed a large spot of dried blood with a tire track through it, not far from the place where Zexie lay dead. Her stockings had been scuffed through at the knees and the hem of her dress was frayed. Her knees were scratched and bruised.

The officers began to speculate that the attacker had first taken Zexie from the car and shot her, and that she had fallen where the blood-soaked ground revealed the passing of a car tire. They projected that Jessie had tried to run away; a scarf lay on the ground, and broken twigs revealed the suspected route of her attempted escape. The lawmen concluded that Jessie had been overtaken by her assailant at this point, stripped, raped, and then shot.

The officers surmised that Zexie had regained some degree of consciousness while Jessie was struggling with the villain. They supposed that upon hearing the commotion, Zexie realized that her sister was being molested. The lawmen further assumed that she tried to go help Jessie, but after crawling only a short distance she "had passed-out" beside the road.

The investigating officers presumed that after the brute had raped and murdered the younger sister, he was walking back to the car when he came upon Zexie. He then fired a final bullet into her brain that also passed through her hand, upon which her head was lying. The spent bullet lodged in the ground below, where the officers recovered it. Apparently the killer then went to the car and drove away.

The two bodies were taken into Tonkawa, where the Kay County medical examiner, Dr. J. A. Jones, sought to find clues about their demise. Dried blood and bits of flesh were found under Jessie's broken fingernails, evidencing her desperate effort to fight off her attacker. Doctor Jones determined that Jessie was alive at the time that she had been sexually assaulted.

Both of the women's purses had been found in the brush at the crime scene. When located, the handbags were unclasped and empty, except for some cosmetics and trinkets of no value. The officers thoroughly searched the area, but could not find any weapon.

The Griffith girls' car was located and identified on Sunday afternoon. It was found near Sears, a small settlement a few miles southeast of the murder site. The vehicle had a bullet hole just below the rear window. Evidence of blood was on the right rear tire, and the tread checked to be the same as the tread on the tire that had rolled through the large spot of blood at the crime scene. Next to the place where the Chevrolet coupe was found, there were tracks that revealed that another car had been parked, then driven away.

The officers speculated that the murderer had overtaken the sisters' car on the road and had fired a shot into their vehicle, causing them to stop. They concluded that he had left his automobile and had taken the girls in their car to the location where their bodies were found. It was assumed that after slaying the sisters, the attacker had driven their car back to where

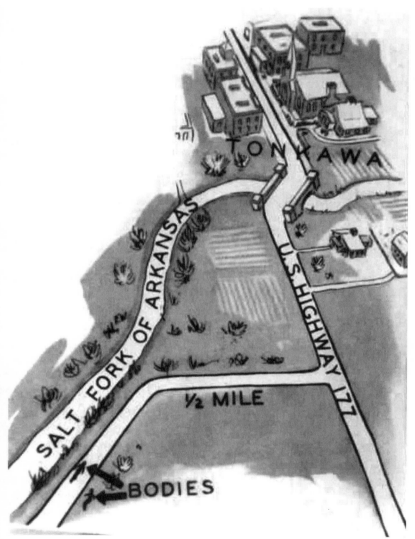

Sketch of the murder scene, south of Tonkawa, Oklahoma, between the Salt Fork River and U.S. Highway 177. (Author's collection)

he had left his vehicle. He had then parked the Chevrolet coupe where it was found and had left the area in his automobile. Apparently the girls had traveled only about fifteen miles from Blackwell when they encountered the killer.

The Griffith sisters were highly accomplished, fine-figured, dark-eyed beauties. Thirty-six-year-old Zexie was a talented musician as well a schoolteacher, and attractive twenty-four-year-old Jessie taught music. Neither of the ladies was married. They were both active in church and popular in social circles.

Prior to coming to Blackwell, Jeff Griffith had served in other Oklahoma communities as an officer of the law, and he was well known. The murder of his daughters caught the attention of the entire state. Gov. William H. Murray immediately announced a five-hundred-dollar reward for the killer or killers. With the Oklahoma City newspaper, the *Daily Oklahoman,* promoting the reward, it soon reached two thousand dollars.

A man had been seen early Sunday morning driving a car that resembled the Griffith girls' vehicle, not far from the murder site. He had been recognized as Lyman Constant of Blackwell, who until recently had been a patient in the state's mental institution at Norman. He was arrested and held for questioning. Lyman was able to establish his innocence and was released.

A visitor to the Salvation Army in Oklahoma City on the day following the murders became a suspect. He had prayed for more than an hour, then left two women's bloody handkerchiefs at the altar, which the attendants suspected as having belonged to the Griffith sisters. When the officials of the center tried to question the stranger about the hankies, he ran from the facility. The officials then called the law, and a short time later the man was located and taken in. He was able to prove an alibi that precluded his involvement in the double murder and was then set free.

Funeral services for Zexie and Jessie Griffith were held on

Tuesday afternoon at the First Baptist Church in Blackwell, and more than fifteen hundred people attended. Many of those who came to pay their respects could only stand in the churchyard. The sisters were laid to rest in the I.O.O.F. Cemetery, at Blackwell.

Shortly after the shocking news of these Kay County crimes had spread across the state, a young lady who lived at Muskogee came forward and told of an ordeal that had befallen her a few weeks earlier. The woman had not previously reported the encounter to the police because of the shame that it instilled in her. The recent rape and murders prompted her to forgo her feelings and report the attack in hopes that her experience might help locate the killer. Out of respect for the conscientious woman, neither the police nor the news media revealed her identity.

The reporting party related that she had recently visited relatives in Wichita, Kansas, and that the incident had occurred as she was driving home late in the evening. She stated that upon reaching a point just south of Tonkawa, a man who was driving a Buick automobile forced her off the road. She related that when she stopped to prevent a collision, the man pulled a gun and ordered her into his car. With her as his captive he started driving away. As she realized her predicament, she decided to try to escape by jumping from the moving vehicle. Grabbing for the door handle, she found it was missing. The man was watching as her hopes shattered and extensive anxiety setin; he then laughed and said, "They never get out of here."

Her captor turned onto a side road and drove to an isolated place where he stopped the car. To avoid becoming a casualty of the pistol, which the man held at her head and threatened to use, she submitted to his sexual attack. After assaulting her, he drove the young lady back to her car and let her out.

The anonymous lady's description of the place of her ordeal led the officers to believe that she had been taken to the same site where the Griffith sisters were delivered and killed. The lawmen assumed that her attacker was likely the same person who had committed the recent double murder.

Another story surfaced, which garnered a share of the publicity about the case. A few weeks before the Griffith sisters were murdered; a nine-year-old boy had been run over by a car and killed in Tonkawa. The automobile that was involved in that homicide had been driven by the daughters of a local wealthy oilman. Officers who investigated the accident absolved the girls of blame. It was reported that the victim's stepfather was not satisfied with that determination and was quoted as having threatened that "he would get even with those girls."

The car that had struck the boy greatly resembled the Griffith girls' vehicle, and there was some conjecture that they may have been the victims of mistaken identity. The stepfather was located and questioned about the recent homicides. He was able to fully establish that he was not involved with the death of the sisters.

About noon on Sunday, Virgil Davis, a young man from Blackwell, approached the police who were working the case. He advised them that as he was taking his girlfriend, Ruby Heard, home late Saturday night, they had encountered an unusual incident not far from the murder site. He said that the driver of a Buick automobile overtook them after first trying to run them off the road.

Virgil reported that he hoped to elude the offending driver by pulling into a farmhouse driveway but that the man followed, then got of out his car and drew a pistol. He told Davis that his name was Rogers and that he was a prohibition officer. He ordered the young couple into his vehicle. After driving about a quarter-mile he stopped and said, "I guess that you're not the people that I am looking for; you can go back to your car." The man got out and had the young couple exit on his side of the sedan. As the man drove away, Virgil and Ruby started walking back to their car.

Davis further reported that after delivering Ruby Heard to her home near Three Sands, he saw the car again. He said that as he was driving back to Tonkawa in the early hours of Sunday morning, he had seen the same automobile in a ditch, apparently stuck or broken down as a tow truck was being attached to it.

Wagner contacted W. S. Winchell, the local wrecker truck operator. Winchell advised the police chief that at about three-thirty Sunday morning he had pulled Earl Howard's Buick from a ditch at the location that Davis had cited.

Howard was a newcomer to the community and had recently moved into a rooming house in Tonkawa. He was unemployed and was suspected to be operating as a bootlegger. A woman who was thought to be Howard's wife lived with him most of the time, but often she was not present.

Police Chief Wagner went to the apartment where Howard lived, but the man wasn't there, and neither was his car. Neighbors who lived in the rooming house reported that they had heard Earl and his wife Jean loading up and leaving, early Sunday morning. The lawman left the apartment to work other aspects of the case.

Wagner was surprised shortly before noon on Monday when he was advised that Howard's wife was back in Tonkawa. He was told that Jean had driven home Sunday night and was again at the rooming house. The police chief immediately went to the Howard residence and began questioning her.

Jean related that she and her husband had left early Sunday morning, going to Wichita. She reported that after arriving in Kansas, they had argued and as the discord became more heated, she had left Earl in Wichita and had driven home alone. When advised that her husband was a suspect in the murder of the Griffith sisters, she responded, "Oh no, he couldn't do that; he's just a bootlegger."

Chief Wagner learned from Jean that her husband's surname was Quinn, not Howard as he had been using. She also

The "Dapper" Mister Earl Quinn. (Author's collection)

told the officer that Earl had served two sentences in the Missouri State Penitentiary, the first for "forgery," and the second for "assault with intent to kill". Wagner obtained a copy of Earl's prison record, which revealed that his most recent release had been in May of 1929. Quinn was of slight build and stood five feet five inches tall. He was known to be a sporty dresser.

Continuing their investigation into Earl Quinn, the officers learned that he was currently wanted for questioning in connection with various crimes in Wichita and Omaha. He was a suspect in a murder case at Kansas City, and officers believed that he was involved in the recent robbery of Tom Pendergast's home in that city. Pendergast was thought to be a local crime boss as well as a political kingpin.

When a picture of Earl Quinn was shown to the lady from Muskogee who had reported being assaulted, she identified him as the man who had taken her to the remote site and raped her. A check of Earl's car revealed that the inside door handle was missing from the passenger side of his automobile, just as the anonymous victim had described.

From that time forward, Quinn was the prime suspect in the Griffith sisters' murder case. His whereabouts was unknown. Officers throughout Oklahoma, Kansas, Missouri, and Nebraska were on the lookout for Earl Quinn. As the days and weeks passed, he remained at large. His wife was thoroughly questioned and constantly shadowed, but Earl Quinn was not to be located.

About a month after the sisters had met their doom, a lady named Lucille Price, who lived near Newton, Kansas, was murdered. Like Jessie Griffith, Miss Price had been sexually assaulted, slain, and left beside a lonely road. Earl Quinn was still at large and was thought to be in that area. He became the major suspect of that crime.

More than three months had passed since the double murder when, on April 1, Police Chief Wagner and Sgt. G. C.

Messenger discovered a .32-caliber automatic pistol. They found the gun buried south of the Salt Fork River, near the murder site. The pistol had started to rust, indicating that it had been cached in the sand some two or three months. The officers suspected that it was the weapon that had been used in the recent homicides.

One account of the discovery related that the police had been tipped that some bootleg whiskey was buried at that location, and they were searching for the illegal booze when they accidentally unearthed the gun. Another version reported that Jean Quinn had told Wagner where to dig to find the pistol. Ballistic tests of the gun confirmed that it was the murder weapon.

As the hunt for Earl Quinn continued, his wife moved to Kansas City and was under surveillance of the local police. On Wednesday, May 13, a Kansas City detective received a tip that Jean would be leaving by train to meet her husband. When the undercover agents learned of her destination and the train's scheduled arrival, they drove to Omaha and were at the Union Station when she came in, about seven o'clock Thursday morning.

The officers followed Jean to a hotel where she checked in, and they took up watch. About midnight Thursday, she came out of the hotel and got into a taxi. The detectives followed her back to the Union Station, where within a few minutes she met her husband. The officers stepped forward and arrested the "wanted man." Earl Quinn offered no resistance when taken into custody and appeared to be rather unconcerned about the matter. The officers hustled him back to Kansas City.

Oklahoma authorities were notified of Quinn's arrest, and Kay County officials prepared the legal papers to get him returned to the state. Governor Murray signed the documents, and Sheriff Joe Cooper departed on Sunday for Jefferson City, to present the request. Missouri's governor Henry Stewart Caulfield honored the requisition.

On Friday, May 20, officers brought Earl Quinn back to Oklahoma to be tried for murder. Nearly five months had passed since the crimes had been committed when the prime suspect was placed behind bars in the Kay County jail.

Earl Quinn's trial for the murder of Jessie Griffith began on September 22, 1931, at Newkirk. James H. Mathers was the defendant's lead attorney. Much of the state's case was based on the gun that Wagner had found; he testified that Jean Quinn had told him where it could be located. After eight days of presentations, the case went to the jury. That panel deliberated seventeen hours, then on Saturday, October 3, 1931, they voted that Quinn was guilty and sentenced him to be executed.

Jean Quinn and Earl's mother, May, were prominent each day at the trial. Both of the women showed a great deal of emotion when the guilty verdict was read. Quinn was the first person "sentenced to be electrocuted" by a Kay County jury.

Immediately following Quinn's conviction, Mathers started action to appeal the case. Earl had been on death row over a year when in November 1932, the State Court of Criminal

The "Not So Dapper" Earl Quinn, inmate #27567. (Author's collection)

Appeals ordered a new trial and granted him a change of venue.

Quinn's second judicial agenda was held at Enid and began in late February 1933. The Garfield County Courthouse had recently burned, and the trial was held in the Enid Convention Hall. As the case unfurled, the issues were presented and debated. Jean Quinn was noticeably absent from her husband's second trial. On Tuesday, March 7, 1933, the Garfield County jury convicted Earl Quinn for the murder of Jessie Griffith. They fixed his punishment at "death in the electric chair."

Earl Quinn was taken back to the Oklahoma State Penitentiary on March 25, 1933, and resumed his role as prisoner number 27567. The convict's occupation was listed as "bookkeeper" in his McAlester prison record, and the cause for his downfall was simply recorded as "he had been framed."

Again, Attorney Mathers filed an appeal in behalf of his client; however, this time it was to no avail. It brought no relief for the condemned man. Quinn contended that he had not received a fair trial and insisted that he was not guilty of murdering the Griffith sisters. As the appointed date for his electrocution approached, Quinn continued to staunchly claim his innocence. In the early morning hours of November 24, 1933, Rich Owens, executioner at the Oklahoma State Penitentiary, was at the controls and tending to all the details. Earl Quinn was buckled into the electric chair called "Old Sparky" and put to death.

In 1954, twenty years after Earl Quinn had been executed, his attorney, James Mathers, compiled a book titled *From Gun to Gavel: The Courtroom Recollections of James Mathers of Oklahoma.* Chapter 9 of his memoirs is titled "Framed." Even though the author changed the names of the characters in the story, anyone who is knowledgeable of the Griffith sisters' murder and the subsequent conviction of Earl Quinn, called Nelson Quady in the book, would easily recognize the true characters in that

Zexie and Jessie Griffith's tombstone. (Author's collection)

chapter. The attorney professed that his client had been convicted on inconclusive and faulty evidence. Mathers still
claimed that the dapper young bootlegger, who had lived in
nearby Tonkawa, was not guilty of "the rape and double murder
in Kay County."

CHAPTER 24

George Birdwell, Bank Robber

George Birdwell was Pretty Boy Floyd's confederate, for about two years. The outlaw career of Floyd has been well recorded in numerous books and magazine articles. Those chronicles have included little information about his cohort, Birdwell. The purpose of this chapter is to provide an insight into the life and death of George Birdwell, who was known as "Pretty Boy Floyd's lieutenant."

George William Birdwell was born in Texas, in February 1894. George's father James J. Birdwell frequently moved his family throughout Texas and Oklahoma as he sharecropped one farm, then another. His son took the role of a cowboy and grew to be six feet tall, slender and handsome. While growing up, George worked on ranches in the vicinity of wherever his father was currently farming. He participated in local rodeos, competing in both riding and roping events, and was considered to be a top hand.

One source reports that George Birdwell's first notoriety came in July 1913, when he was eighteen years old and was shot by a farmer, T. W. Jennings. The shooting occurred in the Mellette community near Eufaula, Oklahoma, when the farmer became suspicious that George had been philandering with his wife. Jennings found the prowling young man plowing a field. The irate husband pulled his gun and shot at George,

The only known photo in existence of George Birdwell, known as "Pretty Boy" Floyd's chief lieutenant. (Author's collection)

hitting him once in his leg. Young Birdwell soon recovered from the flesh wound, and thenceforth steered clear of Mrs. T. W. Jennings.

George Birdwell married Flora Mae (maiden name unknown), who was always called "Bob" by family and friends. Early in their married life, they lived on a ranch where George was employed. To provide for his growing family, Birdwell sought work in the oil fields, where he could earn more money. George was a good worker and became known as "a roustabout who could dig a hole as well as a gopher."

In March 1920, George and Flora were living in an oilfield housing settlement, in Shannon Township, Creek County, Oklahoma. At that time, they had two sons. The older boy, named Wade but called "Jack," was recorded as two years of age, and G. Q. was three months old.

The oil boom of the Seminole field attracted experienced workers. George became an employee of the Magnolia Oil Company and moved into Pottawatomie County. The Birdwell home was close to that of Bradley and Bessie Floyd, near Earlsboro, located between Seminole and Shawnee.

Charles Arthur "Choc" Floyd (later known as "Pretty Boy") had served three years in the Missouri State Prison and was released in March 1929. After kicking around and spending some time in Kansas City, he came to live with his older brother, Bradley. The younger Floyd also became an oilfield worker. Birdwell and the Floyd brothers got acquainted on the job. Being of similar ilk, the proximity of their homes promoted a close association. George Birdwell and Choc Floyd were daring young men, and each wanted to make some extra money. This hankering soon led them into the illegal liquor business. As time from their jobs permitted, the pair began "running whiskey."

The oil companies were trying to dispel their image of employing thugs, and when they learned that the younger Floyd had until recently been in the penitentiary, he was fired. Choc then became a full-time "rum runner." He established

Charles Arthur "Pretty Boy" Floyd. (Photo courtesy of the Archives & Manuscripts Division of the Oklahoma Historical Society)

contacts in Kansas City, which was commonly known at that time by those in the trade simply as "Tom's Town," in reference to Thomas Joseph Pendergast, a political boss who ran the city.

By 1930, two daughters, Mahota and Patty Lou, had also been born to George and Flora Birdwell. The depression reached the "oil patch" in the early thirties, and resulted in the work force being greatly reduced. A short time later George Birdwell was among the multitude of workers in the Seminole oil field who was laid off. About the time that George lost his job, his brother died. He then considered it his duty to provide for his brother's widow and their four children.

Feeling responsible to support this enlarged family of eleven, and now out of work, Birdwell began to associate more closely with Choc Floyd, who was renting a place in Shawnee. A man named Bill Miller had been "running booze" with Floyd, and when Birdwell made himself available on a full-time basis, the three began to plot a more lucrative course of crime.

On March 9, 1931, Choc Floyd, Bill Miller, and George Birdwell robbed the Bank of Earlsboro of about three thousand dollars. Birdwell took his share and paid family bills while hiding out in Pottawatomie and Seminole counties. After the bank robbery Floyd and Miller, with two "fast women" from Kansas City, headed east. A month later, the frolicking foursome got into a gunfight with police in Bowling Green, Kentucky, and Miller was killed.

By mid-summer Choc had returned to Oklahoma and was again staying with Bradley and Bessie. Both Floyd and Birdwell were anxious to get back into the bank robbing business. On August 4, 1931, they held up the Citizens Bank of Shamrock, but garnered only four hundred dollars. They hit the Morris State Bank, on September 8, and got two thousand dollars. On September 29, they robbed the First National Bank at Maud, Oklahoma, of an estimated thirty-one hundred dollars.

Typically, Birdwell wore his finest cowboy duds, and Floyd, who was now known as "Pretty Boy," was dapperly attired. They usually recruited someone to drive the car. Without masks but both well armed, the pair would enter a bank, grab the available money, and then take two or more hostages to the getaway car. To protect themselves in the event that a local officer was nearby and learned of their mission, or some gun-toting citizen became concerned, the hostages were ordered to stand on the running boards as the car sped out of town. When the robbers felt that they were clear of pursuit, the vehicle was slowed, and the hostages were dropped off. If all had gone well, and they were so inclined, the robbers would doff their hats to their hostages, as the bandits' car wheeled away.

While the outlaw pair was quite flamboyant in their operation, they seemed content with robbing banks in small Oklahoma towns. Seven months after robbing the Bank of Earlsboro, they hit it again. On October 14, 1931, Pretty Boy Floyd and George Birdwell applied their bank-robbing talents to that financial institution a second time, and got away with twenty-five hundred dollars. Their abandoned car was found that same evening in a dense growth of trees between Earlsboro and Maud. It had been stolen a few days earlier from James Granette, a Magnolia Pipeline employee who lived in Wewoka.

James Birdwell died during the night, following his son's second robbery of the Earlsboro bank. George was determined to pay his respects to his father, while the corpse was in the funeral home at Earlsboro. The outlaw suspected that the officers anticipated his visit to the local morgue and were awaiting his arrival, prepared to nab him.

He and Pretty Boy Floyd kidnapped Deputy Sheriff Franks on the street in Earlsboro, late in the evening of October 15, 1931. With the deputy as their hostage, the two wanted men went to the bier and viewed the senior Birdwell as he lay in death. Upon completing their call at the morgue, the outlaw pair drove to a nearby farmhouse and met with Pretty Boy's mother. When they concluded their visit with Mrs. Floyd, they drove back to the edge of Earlsboro and released the officer unharmed. After removing the cartridges, they handed Deputy Frank his pistol, and as the kidnapers drove away, they told the officer, "Now you be a good boy."

Most of those who had known George Birdwell when he was an oil-field worker thought of him, not as a bank robber by choice, but as a victim of the times and circumstances. Some of his former fellow workers and their families were thought to aid the bandits in evading the law. The outlaw pair was generous in sharing the proceeds of their projects with their friends. Mrs. Birdwell was a respected neighbor in the community. The

Birdwell children were well accepted by the other students at Prairie View, located between Earlsboro and Seminole, where they attended school.

Flora was approached by Oklahoma officials and advised that if her husband George would surrender, he would be charged only with the Morris bank robbery. It was reported that Birdwell was willing to give himself up, to be tried at Okmulgee on the one charge, but Pretty Boy convinced him to forgo the offer and continue their criminal activity.

The banks at Castle and Paden, merely twelve miles apart, were both robbed on January 19, 1932. This act prompted the State Bankers Association to solicit Governor Murray, to call out the National Guard and try to halt this rash of bank robberies. The insurance rate for small town banks in Oklahoma had doubled in recent weeks.

As their crime wave continued, E. A. "Erv" Kelly, a noted law enforcement officer of the time, formerly from McIntosh County, joined the search for Pretty Boy Floyd and George Birdwell. Kelly learned that Floyd's former wife, Ruby, was living with her parents, the Hargraves, near Bixby, and that the outlaw often visited Ruby and their son Dempsey (called "Jackie").

After darkness fell on Friday, April 8, 1932, Kelly and a posse stationed themselves beside the road, near the Hargraves place. Kelly believed that Floyd would arrive that night for a rendezvous with Ruby. At about two o'clock Saturday morning, while some of the posse was out of position having coffee, a suspicious car came down the road, and Kelly stepped forward to be in view of the approaching headlights, so that he could halt the automobile. From inside the car, gunshots spewed forth. Kelly triggered his machine gun, but immediately fell to the ground, mortally wounded. The two local farmers, who were Kelly's only backup at the moment, were unable to get their automatic rifles to fire. The car, carrying Floyd and Birdwell, turned around and got away. The vehicle was traced to the vicinity of Earlsboro but could not be located in that neighborhood. Erv Kelly was buried in the Greenlawn Cemetery at Checotah.

Usually, Floyd and Birdwell were able to pull off these robberies and get away from the small Oklahoma towns without being seriously challenged. However, on occasion they were strenuously pursued. One such close call resulted from their robbing the bank at Stonewall, on April 21, 1932. As they were being chased during their escape from Stonewall, they overtook Estle Hanson riding a motorcycle near Ada. The outlaws took the twenty-year-old Hanson with them and held him hostage until they escaped their pursuers. The next morning, Hanson was released unharmed.

A few hours later, it was reported that the outlaw pair was seen at a remote site along the Canadian River near Calvin. Authorities called for an air search of the area. One airplane, flown by the world-famous aviator Wiley Post, was dispatched from Oklahoma City, and another plane was sent from Norman. The aerial posse closely scanned the suspected site and the breaks along the river, but didn't locate the bank robbers.

Some weeks later, officers were tipped that Floyd and Birdwell were using a vacant farmhouse, southeast of Ada, as a hideout and were planning to rob the bank at Stonewall again. The suspects were seen at the abandoned house on June 7, 1932. A posse surrounded the deserted home, and their weapons burst forth when Floyd and Birdwell came out of the house with their guns blazing. Estle Hanson was with the posse and waved at the escaping outlaws. No one was injured in the barrage of gunfire, and upon reaching their car, the bandits returned Hanson's friendly gesture, as they sped away. Posse members, who fired more than a hundred rounds at the bandits, reported that they believed both men were wearing bulletproof vests.

The newspapers usually referred to the bank robbery suspects as "Pretty Boy Floyd and his lieutenant, George Birdwell."

Officers had no picture of Birdwell, which made identification most difficult. The outlaw pair went on to rob a dozen banks in small towns within fifty miles of Earlsboro, including Roff, Mill Creek, Konawa, and Meeker.

Between jobs, Floyd sometimes visited his former wife in Fort Smith and later in the Tulsa area; he also visited a lady friend, Beulah Ash, in Kansas City. Perhaps, curtailed by a lingering memory of "sowing wild oats" in the Mellette community, Birdwell did not normally travel to Kansas City with his cohort on those merry capers. He hid out in Seminole and Pottawatomie counties, to be near his family, and waited for Floyd to return, "Eager for another bank."

Floyd was partying with Beulah Ash in Kansas City when Birdwell became aware that Ruby had emergency surgery in a Tulsa hospital and needed money to pay for the operation. In the absence of Pretty Boy, Birdwell considered it his duty to raise the funds to pay the former Mrs. Floyd's hospital bill. He then concocted the plan to rob the Farmers and Merchants Bank at Boley, one of the more progressive of several towns in Oklahoma that had been predominantly settled by African Americans.

For this undertaking George Birdwell recruited C. C. Patterson and a young black man named Charley Glass as his companions. Patterson was from Kiowa, Oklahoma, and had previously been in trouble with the law. He was currently out on bond awaiting trial for having wounded police officer W. M. "Bill" Jones in a gun battle at Shawnee, during which a bystander, Sam Miller, had been killed. He also had criminal charges pending in Lincoln, Seminole, and Pontotoc counties.

Patterson was experienced with firearms and would work the bank with Birdwell. Charley Glass was to be the driver, as he had often visited women and gambled in Boley and knew the layout of the town. The three drove to the targeted bank during the afternoon of Tuesday, November 22. They finalized their plan that night, in the home of Charley's half-sister, Polly Crane in Earlsboro, with whom Charley lived.

The next morning, the trio arrived at Boley as planned. Birdwell and Patterson entered the Farmers and Merchants Bank. H. C. McCormick, a bookkeeper and assistant cashier, saw the armed men come in the front door. He slyly left his desk and entered the vault to get a shotgun that had been placed there for such an emergency. Upon seeing Birdwell enter the bank with pistol in hand, D. J. Turner, the bank president, defiantly sounded the alarm. Birdwell asked the white-haired gentleman if he had pulled the alarm, and when Turner acknowledged that he had, Birdwell fired four shots into the elderly bank official.

While Birdwell was engaged with Turner, and Patterson was grabbing money from the till, McCormick stepped from the vault with shotgun in hand. Neither robber had noticed the bookkeeper's activity. Just as the bank president fell from Birdwell's bullets, McCormick fired his well-aimed weapon, and Birdwell went down, mortally wounded. Patterson then ordered W. W. Riley, a bank cashier, and Horace Aldridge, a customer, to bring Birdwell along as he attempted to retreat from the bank.

The sounding alarm and shooting had alerted people near the bank that a robbery was in progress. When Patterson, with Riley and Aldridge lugging the body of Birdwell, reached the front door, a band of armed citizens were converging in the street. Upon seeing the gun-wielding Patterson lead the others out of the bank, the irate citizens began firing at the lone standing robber. When the bullets began to fly, Riley and Aldridge dropped Birdwell and ran for cover. Patterson was struck in his legs, hip, and neck, then sprawled on the sidewalk near his comrade, George Birdwell.

Upon hearing the first shots, Charley Glass had got out of the vehicle with his automatic pistol and started toward the bank to aid his companions. Seeing the barrage of gunfire by the vigilantes, and Patterson go down, Glass ran back and jumped into the car, started the engine, and began to drive

away. Several shots were fired at the roadster, which immediately rolled into a curb and stopped. Armed citizens approached
the bullet-pierced vehicle and found Charley Glass slumped
behind the wheel, dead. The seven hundred dollars that was
missing from the till was retrieved from the hand of the severely
wounded Patterson who lay on the sidewalk.

D. J. Turner died while being transported to Okemah. The
critically wounded Patterson was taken to the Okemah hospital. Birdwell's body was delivered to the Okemah morgue,
where he was identified by Seminole County sheriff Frank
Aldridge. At the morgue, officers obtained their first pictures
of George Birdwell and described him as follows: 5 feet 11
inches, 160 pounds, light complexion with light brown hair
combed straight back. Later his wife and mother made the pos-
itive identifications.

Birdwell's remains were then transferred to the Chadwick
Funeral Home at Seminole, and arrangements were made for
a private funeral service and burial. Only family and friends
were allowed to view the body and attend the funeral. Among
those in attendance were Bradley and Bessie Floyd; Ruby (the
former Mrs. Charles A. Floyd); and Estle Hanson (the kidnap
victim), from Ada. There were numerous unsubstantiated
rumors that Pretty Boy Floyd (disguised as a woman), attended
the funeral of his comrade. George Birdwell was buried in the
Maple Grove Cemetery, at Seminole, on Friday, November 25,
1932.

The body of Charley Glass had been taken to the Myers
Funeral Home at Wewoka. A friend, Bill Bruner, and Polly
Crane arranged for her half-brother to be interred at Wewoka.
Glass was buried the same day that George Birdwell's funeral
was held.

D. J. Turner, who had served as president of the bank since
it had opened in 1906, was buried at Boley, on Monday,
November 28, 1932. Bankers and business leaders from across
the state attended his funeral and paid their respects.

D. J. Turner, president of the Farmers and Merchants Bank in Boley, Oklahoma, was killed by George Birdwell during a robbery of this bank. Photos of author Ken Butler in the Boley cemetery at Turner's gravesite. (Author's collection)

George Birdwell's grave in Seminole, Oklahoma. (Author's collection)

Even during the depression, banks were usually able to survive these typical heists. The Earlsboro bank was robbed three times in one year, yet continued to operate. Less than a month after the foiled robbery at Boley, the bank was forced to close, not because of any monetary loss to the robbers, but because depositors withdrew their accounts. State Bank Commissioner W. J. Barnett announced that seventy thousand dollars had been withdrawn by friends of the late long-time bank president, which forced the bank to close.

The Ford roadster that the ill-fated trio drove to Boley had been stolen a few days earlier in Oklahoma City. Two weeks after the attempted bank robbery, the owner was permitted to reclaim his damaged vehicle in which Charley Glass had been shot and killed.

A couple of days after H. C. McCormick triggered his trusty shotgun, which ignited the armed resistance that thwarted the bank robbery, C. C. Patterson was transferred to the prison at McAlester for safekeeping and medical attention. His resemblance to Pretty Boy Floyd was quite noticeable and created speculation that he had been the party who had participated in some of the recent bank robberies with Birdwell and had been mistakenly identified as the noted outlaw.

After recovering from his wounds, Patterson was returned to Okfuskee County to be tried for the murder of D. J. Turner. Even though all of the newspaper accounts of the fiasco at Boley reported that Birdwell had fired the shots that killed the bank president, Patterson was convicted of the murder on September 12, 1933, at Okemah. He was sentenced to life imprisonment and served time in the state facilities at Granite and McAlester. C. C. Patterson was paroled on June 29, 1949, and was pardoned on May 9, 1956. After his release he operated a service station in Arizona.

Pretty Boy Floyd eluded the law for nearly two years after George Birdwell was gunned down. Law enforcement officers at East Liverpool, Ohio, killed the notorious outlaw on October 22, 1934.

CHAPTER 25

Kidnapped

Twenty-month-old Charles Augustus Lindbergh, Jr., was abducted on Tuesday night, March 1, 1932, from the upstairs nursery in the family home at Hopewell, New Jersey. Neither the child nor his famous father nor the kidnapper had any connection with the Sooner State, yet that crime would bring Oklahoma into the limelight. The kidnapping would instigate the enactment of a Federal law that would affect the state—the first in the union to implement such a law.

Abduction of the Lindbergh baby brought sadness to the populace of the nation, to whom his father was an idol. Charles A. Lindbergh was known as "The Lone Eagle" for his feat of having flown an airplane, The Spirit of St. Louis, nonstop, from New York to Paris in 1927. His solo flight across the Atlantic Ocean, the first successful accomplishment of such an undertaking, had made him "America's Hero." Without reservation, his popularity in the United States towered above all others.

The Lindbergh baby had been "put to bed" about 7:30 in the evening, but when the nurse checked on him at 10:30 P.M., she found that he was missing. On the sill of the opened window was a note, the content of which was not revealed to the public; however, it was assumed to have been a ransom demand. A three-piece ladder that was thought to have been used by the kidnapper to reach the second floor window was found about two hundred feet from the house.

The next day, after the baby had been taken, Lindbergh publicly announced his willingness to pay ransom for the safe return of young Charles. The presumed abductor contacted the Lindbergh family and demanded payment of fifty thousand dollars. Neither the information about this request for ransom nor Lindbergh's timely compliance was reported by the news media, at that time.

Even though the ransom was paid as ordered, the safe return of the baby was not achieved. The child was found dead, in a ditch about five miles from the Lindbergh home, on May 12, ten weeks after having been kidnapped. Examination of the small body indicated that the baby had been killed shortly after having been taken from the nursery.

A couple of days following the abduction, members of Congress began to proclaim that "there ought to be a Federal law" against kidnapping. Their response was indicative of the public's outcry about this dastardly crime. Congress and Pres. Herbert Hoover moved more swiftly than customary, and on June 22, 1932, the Lindbergh Kidnapping Law was enacted. It established that if an abducted party was taken from one state into another, the kidnapper would be subject to the Federal law, which provided a penalty of life in prison.

About eleven-thirty on Saturday night, July 22, 1933, two men (one toting a "tommy gun" and the other carrying an automatic .45-caliber pistol) burst through the screen door onto the sun porch of millionaire oilman Charles Urschel's home, at 327 Northwest 18th Street, Oklahoma City. Mr. and Mrs. Walter Jarrett, who lived nearby, were visiting and playing cards with Charles and Berenice (often misspelled as Bernice) Urschel, in their outdoor parlor, at the time that the armed strangers abruptly entered.

The larger of the intruders, the one holding the machine gun, asked, "Which of you men is Urschel?" Neither the host

The Slick-Urschel Mansion at 327 Northwest 18th Street in Oklahoma City, Oklahoma, as it appeared in 1933. (Photo courtesy of the Archives & Manuscripts Division of the Oklahoma Historical Society)

nor his guest acknowledged the question. Their silence prompted the stranger to retort, "All right, we'll just take both of you." The deadly weapons in the hands of the duo and their demeanor provided sufficient inducement for Urschel and Jarrett to conform to their dictates.

After ordering the women not to use the phone until they had driven away, the armed men took the two hostages from the Urschel home. Immediately upon hearing a car engine start and leave the driveway, the two women ran into the bedroom of Betty, Berenice's sixteen-year-old daughter. After locking the door and checking that Betty was all right, Mrs. Urschel called the police and reported the kidnapping. City police soon arrived at the Urschel home and began to learn the few details of the crime that the spouses could provide.

A little over an hour after having been abducted, Jarrett returned to the scene of the crime. The armed pair had taken their captives' billfolds, which revealed which of the two men was Charles Urschel. The kidnappers kept sixty dollars that they removed from Jarrett's wallet. Moments after determining which was their quarry, the abductors stopped their vehicle some nine miles northeast of Oklahoma City, on 63rd Street, and ordered Jarrett to "get out of the car." A few minutes later, the freed hostage caught a ride with a couple of obliging young men, and they drove him back to the Urschel home.

Walter Jarrett told the police the details of what had occurred, but he was unable to provide any key information. He was reluctant to talk with anyone other than Mrs. Urschel and merely related to her that the kidnappers had not abused either of the hostages. Jarrett confirmed that the men still had her husband in the automobile when they continued, after dropping him off.

Charles Urschel was an oil tycoon of the "Black Gold" era. As that colorful period unfolded, Tom Slick became known as "King of the Wildcatters," and during his heyday Urschel was his right-hand man. Slick's moniker appropriately implied that he had been extremely successful in the "oil patch." When Slick died in August 1930, Urschel began his own operation.

About a year after Slick's death, his sister, who was Urschel's wife, also passed away. In October 1932, Charles Urschel married Tom Slick's widow, which merged two major fortunes that had been developed from the Oklahoma oil fields. The new Mrs. Urschel had three children from her marriage to Tom Slick, and Mr. Urschel had one child from his previous marriage.

While being interviewed by the police, Mrs. Urschel related that when the armed men appeared, she first feared they had come to kidnap her daughter. Betty had recently reported that a pair of men had followed her on two occasions. Berenice acknowledged feeling some degree of relief when she realized that they were after her husband, not her daughter. She reasoned that Charles, being a mature man who was known to be

Charles F. Urschel, millionaire oilman. (Photo courtesy of the Archives & Manuscripts Division of the Oklahoma Historical Society)

extremely resourceful, would be better able to cope with such an ordeal than would a sixteen-year-old girl. Apparently, Mrs. Urschel was a logical-thinking person, as was her husband.

The Urschels were extremely wealthy and realized they were potential targets for such crime. They had previously received some threatening notes. Charles had employed an armed guard in their home until recently before the kidnapping.

One of the earliest leads indicated that Urschel was being held hostage in Missouri, which prompted the FBI to join the search. Agent Gus Jones, a former Texas Ranger, had been pulled from a lead role investigating the Kansas City Massacre, to head up the agency in this case. Several telephone calls came to the Urschel home, each claiming to have the hostage whom they would release if certain ransom were paid. The family (with the FBI) responded, as they deemed appropriate. Mrs. Urschel's desperate desire for her husband's safe return led her to be hoaxed out of a substantial amount of money in one or more of these cases.

The abductors' first confirmed communication was delivered by Western Union on Wednesday, July 26, to John G. Catlett, a Tulsa oilman, who was a close friend of the Urschels. Catlett immediately brought the papers that he had received (which included a handwritten letter from Urschel) to Arthur Seeligson (a brother-in-law of Tom Slick's and co-trustee of his estate) in Oklahoma City. As directed in the instructions, a dialogue was established between the family (and the FBI) with the abductors, via want ads in the *Daily Oklahoman*.

The kidnappers demanded a ransom of $200,000 be dropped from the train en route to Kansas City, which was scheduled to depart from Oklahoma City at 10:10 Saturday night, July 29. The party bringing the money was to come alone, sit on the observation platform, and toss the bag containing the ransom when the train passed the second small fire ablaze on the right side of the track.

Seeligson arranged for amassing and recording the bills

(the largest ransom ever demanded, to that date). John Catlett and Ernest E. Kirkpatrick (another close family friend who also lived in Tulsa) boarded the 10:10 train Saturday night in Oklahoma City, carrying the satchel containing the money. Proper signals to make the drop were never recognized by the messengers, and upon arriving at Kansas City, they checked into the Muehlebach Hotel (which the courier was to do, if delivery had not been made en route). In keeping with instructions, Kirkpatrick registered as E. E. Kincaid of Little Rock.

About 5:00 P.M. on Sunday, a telephone call to "Mr. Kincaid's room" directed him to take a taxi to the LaSalle Hotel, not far from the Muehlebach, then start walking west carrying the ransom satchel. Kirkpatrick followed the instructions, and shortly after getting out of the cab, he was approached by a husky fellow who asked for the suitcase. As Kirkpatrick stalled, insisting on being apprised of when the hostage would be released, he was trying to mentally record the stranger's features for future recognition. The man stated, "He can be expected home within twelve hours." Upon hearing those words, Kirkpatrick released the satchel, and the stranger walked away with the bag, containing ten thousand twenty-dollar bills. Kirkpatrick later wrote a book about the kidnapping.

Urschel did not return within the time period that had been promised. However, shortly before midnight on Monday, July 31, 1933, the bedraggled recently released hostage did appear at his Oklahoma City home. The constant tension of his last ten days had left Urschel in a trance-like stupor.

Following a series of family hugs and some much-needed rest, he began relating to the FBI items that he could remember. Urschel started by reporting that he had been blindfolded with adhesive tape most of the time. The tape was removed only to be renewed, except for a few minutes when he was ordered to write the ransom note to Catlett, again when he was permitted to shave just before being returned, and once more when he was dropped off at the outskirts of Norman. Urschel was able to provide a great deal of information about the house where he had been held blindfolded and shackled. He could remember conversations between the guards who watched over him and statements that he had overheard when the car made stops, as he was being transported.

The former hostage related many specifics of worthy information to the FBI, but his most astounding revelation came when he stated, "A plane flew over the house at 9:45 A.M. and 5:45 P.M. each day except Sunday morning." While Urschel was developing this clue, he would wait a few minutes after each flight, then inquire of his captors, "What time is it"? By calculating the pause before asking, he was able to fix the time of the plane's passing. To safeguard his secret he would frequently ask, "What time is it"? The routine question would be answered without suspicion.

Urschel reported that it had rained hard Sunday evening, just after they got to the site where he was held. He related that a strong wind had blown all day Saturday, and a rain had drizzled most of Sunday, the day before his release.

With these bits of information, the FBI agents began reviewing weather records and airline routes. They were able to identify one locality that had been subjected to the weather that Urschel had described. It was also on the path of an airline that made flights over that area. The proximity that fell under suspicion centered around Paradise, Texas.

When the American Airway was consulted, they confirmed that one of their planes passed over that locale each day at the times that Urschel had reported. They also advised that their pilot did not fly over that area on Sunday morning, because of a rainstorm in the vicinity. The airline's totally compatible responses convinced the officers that the home in which Urschel had been held captive was near the little town of Paradise, thirty miles northwest of Fort Worth, Texas.

To check out the area and hopefully locate the house where Urschel had been kept, the FBI "sat up a front." Agent Edward

Down began to canvas the suspected vicinity, pretending to be a representative of a finance company that was seeking to evaluate farm and ranch lands in the community, with a view toward extending loans. Agent Down had studied a list of notes and a map of the home where the kidnapped victim had been held. The data had been compiled by the FBI from information that the blindfolded and shackled hostage had been able to ascertain about his surroundings and recall to help identify the place.

While acting in the role of a financial representative, one of the homes that Edward Down visited was that of R. G. "Boss" Shannon, a well-known resident in the suspected locale. After talking with Mr. and Mrs. Shannon for awhile, the caller was invited into the home of their son Armon. Armon and his wife Oleta lived some distance from the residence of the senior Shannon, but it was on the same land holdings. Armon's house was at the end of a private lane that accessed the county road at the residence of Boss Shannon.

Agent Down related later that soon after entering the younger Shannon's home, he began to recognize features that coincided with the notes that he had studied. As he scanned the household he saw various particulars, which he recalled that the hostage had identified. Among them were the missing window pane that was covered with cardboard, the cracked mirror that the hostage had used to shave, the child's high chair with the broken arm to which he was often shackled, and numerous other items that Urschel had described in detail.

When Edward Down reported his findings to the Dallas offiicers, they too considered that he had located the place where Urschel had been held. The FBI investigated further and learned that numerous strangers had arrived in Paradise (Wise County, Texas) in recent months and that many were thought to be en route to Boss Shannon's domicile. They also learned that Shannon's stepdaughter Kathryn was married to George R. "Machine Gun" Kelly, who was known to the bureau.

FBI agents from Dallas and Oklahoma City along with eight

Mugshot of Kathryn (Mrs. Machine Gun) Kelly.
(Author's collection)

sharpshooters from various police departments met at Denton, Texas, to plan an attack on the Shannon ranch. Gus Jones was the leader of this special team, which included Charles Urschel. The heavily armed squad hit Boss Shannon's homestead just after daybreak on Saturday morning, August 12, 1933.

The officers, including Edward Down, arrested Boss and his wife Ora and two fifteen-year-old girls in the main house. One of the girls was Shannon's daughter from a previous marriage, and the other was a daughter of Kathryn Kelly, from a husband prior to George. Urschel, who was armed with a shotgun for this raid, immediately recognized Boss Shannon's voice as that of one of the men who had watched over him.

The surprising bonus of the raid was locating and arresting the party whom the posse found asleep in the yard, next to the porch. When they drove up and saw a person lying on a cot outside of the house, Gus Jones with two men rushed to the stranger's open-air quarters and covered him with their weapons. Within reach of the sleeping man lay a loaded machine gun and a pistol; also parked only a few feet away was a car filled with gas and "ready to roll." Jones immediately recognized Shannon's outdoor guest as Harvey Bailey, who was wanted by the FBI for numerous crimes including the Kansas City Massacre.

Officers found that the Shannon homestead was extremely well fortified, but fortunately those positions were not manned when they arrived. Only five people were present at the time of the raid, and no shots were fired.

After securing the captives and leaving guards on site, others of the posse drove to the son's house, a little more than a mile away, where they found Armon, Oleta, and her father. All three were receptive and cooperated with the officers. Urschel felt like it was "old home week" and identified (by feel) many items in the younger Shannon's house. By his voice, he recognized Armon as one of his guards. Gus Jones talked with twenty-three-year-old Armon, who readily admitted his role in the crime and identified his stepmother's son-in-law, George "Machine Gun" Kelly, as one of the abductors. The young couple and her father were arrested and taken along with the posse.

Little did Gus Jones think at the time that he had been pulled from the Kansas City Massacre case that within three weeks he would come upon a prime suspect of that mass murder, asleep in the yard, as he was leading a raid on the home of the suspects in his new assignment. No connection between the two crimes had been anticipated. It matters not how unlikely that logic would dictate the odds against such a strange occurrence; the fact is that "it came to pass," that Saturday morning at a rural homestead near Paradise, Texas.

A stash of the ransom money was found in Harvey Bailey's possession at the time of his arrest. This discovery persuaded the agents who were acquainted with his past operations to suspect that he was the "brains behind the kidnapping." Those arrested at the Shannon ranch were delivered to the Dallas jail, which was considered to be one of the most secure facilities in the country.

Officers working the case had been able to establish that Machine Gun Kelly and Albert Bates, who was already wanted by the FBI, were the armed men who had broken in on the card-playing couples at the Urschel home in Oklahoma City and kidnapped the wealthy host. Shortly after the raid on the Shannon ranch, Albert Bates was located and arrested in Denver, Colorado. Part of the ransom loot was found on him.

About the time that Bates was brought in, another clue developed. Several of the recorded twenty-dollar bills appeared in the Minneapolis-St. Paul area from various local transactions. This led the FBI to arrest five men in Minnesota. George and Kathryn Kelly had recently visited that region.

A hearing was held by Federal District Court judge Edgar S. Vaught in Oklahoma City on Wednesday, August 23, 1933, which resulted in twelve men and two women being indicted in the Urschel kidnapping case. Those charged with the crime included: George "Machine Gun" and Kathryn "Kate" Kelly, R. G. "Boss" and Ora Shannon, Harvey Bailey, Albert Bates, Armon Shannon, and seven others who were thought to have been involved to a lesser degree. Neither Oleta Shannon, nor her father, nor either of the fifteen-year-old girls was indicted.

Harvey Bailey had earned a reputation of being able to escape from the most secure facilities, including the Kansas State Penitentiary at Lansing, and some three weeks after being incarcerated in Dallas he managed to get out of that lockup. On Labor Day, September 4, 1933, he escaped and took a jailer captive. A few hours later, while driving his hostage's car, Bailey was recognized as he approached

Ardmore, Oklahoma. While trying to elude the Ardmore police, he wrecked the automobile in that city, and the pursuing officers were able to take Bailey into custody before he could get away. It was later determined that Harvey Bailey had manipulated his exodus from the Dallas jail by bribing a jailer.

On September 18, 1933, Federal Judge Vaught "called to order" the Court of the Western District of Oklahoma in Oklahoma City. Machine Gun and Kate Kelly were still on the lam and were not available for these proceedings, so twelve of the fourteen people who had been indicted in the Urschel kidnapping case were the defendants in this trial.

Prior to the court's opening session, those who were to be tried had been brought to Oklahoma City and jailed. As the court proceedings got underway, Charles Urschel received a letter from the Kellys (complete with Machine Gun's intentionally applied fingerprints), threatening death to him and his family if he testified against the Shannons. The letter did not deter Urschel from providing an exceedingly substantial testimony, when he was called to the witness stand.

While Judge Vaught was conducting the trial of those indicted who were in custody, agents continued their search to locate George and Kathryn Kelly. The wily couple had traveled more than twenty thousand miles trying to shake the FBI from their trail. They had frequently changed the color of their hair, often switched cars, and pulled many other shenanigans, but on Tuesday morning, September 26, 1933, the elusive pair was located in Memphis, Tennessee. When "Machine Gun" Kelly realized that morning that FBI agents had entered their quarters and had their weapons trained on him, he is said to have shouted, "Don't shoot, G-men," which coined the term that became a popular epithet for Federal agents; then without resistance he and Kate surrendered.

The Urschel kidnapping trial, the first to be recorded by movie cameras, had been progressing while the Kellys were being pursued. After their capture in Memphis, the Kellys were

George "Machine Gun" Kelly and his wife Kathryn embracing and wondering about their future. (Author's collection)

promptly brought to Oklahoma City to face Judge Vaught. They were in his courtroom on September 30 when the jury returned with verdicts to convict seven of the twelve people who had been tried. On October 7, 1933, Judge Vaught took time from George and Kathryn's trial to sentence Albert Bates, Harvey Bailey, and R. G. and Ora Shannon to life in prison. Armon Shannon had cooperated with the prosecution and was given a ten-year suspended sentence. The other two defendants, who had been convicted, were each assigned a five-year term.

After sentencing those who had been convicted earlier, Judge Vaught resumed the Kelly trial, which was proceeding smoothly. George didn't take the stand in his own defense. The husband and wife were convicted on Thursday, October 12, 1933. George and Kathryn Kelly were each sentenced to life in prison. That sentence completed the litigation of the Urschel kidnapping, which was the most publicized criminal case in Oklahoma (until the Murrah Federal Building was bombed on April 19, 1995) and brought to a close the first trial in the nation to invoke the Lindbergh Kidnapping Law.

CHAPTER 26

The Hanging of Arthur Gooch

As related in the previous chapter, Oklahoma had been the first state in the nation to implement the recently passed Federal act known as the Lindbergh Kidnapping Law. Seven months after the Urschel kidnapping trial, which resulted in six people being sentenced to life in prison, Congress amended the law. The amendment was enacted on May 18, 1934, and provided that if a subject (covered by that law) was harmed while being held hostage, the crime became a capital offense, and the death penalty could be imposed. There was no connection to the Urschel case; however, fate again handed the Sooner State the initial crime that brought this revision into Federal court. The legal proceedings that resulted from that first violation were processed in Oklahoma and led to a native son's falling victim to the hangman's noose.

Arthur Gooch was born in January 1908 at Mason, Oklahoma (Okfuskee County), and was raised in Okmulgee. As a young man, Arthur became a butcher. While working in a meat market he had married a local girl named Mary, and subsequently fathered a son, Billy Joe. Later, Arthur acknowledged that "drinking and late night parties" were his downfall. Those vices led him into trouble with the law and prompted his wife to seek and obtain a divorce.

In June 1931, Arthur Gooch, along with another young man

and a woman, became suspects in the theft of two cars in Okmulgee. One of the vehicles belonged to a deputy sheriff and had been towed away from the officer's home. The other automobile belonged to an oil-field worker. After maneuvering these cars to a secluded site, the thieves had stripped the tires and batteries from them, then abandoned the vehicles and sold the parts.

A few days after the vehicles had been vandalized, Gooch was arrested for his part in this crime and was charged with stealing automobiles. Before his trial was scheduled, Gooch pled guilty in a district court hearing at Okmulgee to a grand larceny charge. Judge Mark L. Bozarth sentenced the first-time offender to eighteen months in prison. Arthur Gooch was received at the McAlester Penitentiary on July 10, 1931. He served his time without incident and was released on June 7, 1932.

Sometime later, he was arrested again. On this occasion Gooch was to be charged for having stolen two saddles from a farmer's barn (located in the Newby community of southern Creek County). Again his case did not go to trial; instead, Gooch was presented before Judge C. O. Beaver at Bristow, Oklahoma, where he pled guilty to a grand larceny charge. He was sentenced to serve one year in the penitentiary for having swiped the riding gear. The former inmate was returned to "Big Mac" on February 8, 1933, and discharged in October 1933.

The next known accounting of Arthur Gooch was on August 20, 1934. About dawn that Monday morning, the police at Wetumka, Oklahoma, in Hughes County, received a telephone call alerting them that four suspects of a string of service station robberies were in a car heading toward Wetumka, on Highway 75. Immediately, Night Police Chief Curtis Lowder and Officer Glen Young started south in a car to intercept the robbers.

Shortly after Lowder and Young parked beside the highway

to watch for the suspects, an automobile passed which fit the description of the reported vehicle and which was carrying four people traveling in the appropriate direction. The chief and his driver sped after the car. They soon overtook and drove up beside the suspects' vehicle. At that point, Lowder, who was sitting on the passenger side with the window down, signaled for the driver to stop. When it became obvious that his effort was being ignored, he blew his police whistle and shouted for the occupants to halt. Instead of obeying the officer's command, the driver "put gas" to their car, trying to speed away as the suspects started firing their weapons at the officers. Lowder and Young returned the gunfire and continued their pursuit. Soon thereafter, gunshots disabled both vehicles.

The suspects' automobile stalled (both rear tires were punctured) some distance ahead of the place where the officers' car had quit (bullets had ruptured the radiator and flattened one tire). From the officers' car, the police chief and his deputy watched as two men and two women got out of the lead automobile and ran into a cotton field. Lowder, knowing that officers from McAlester and Holdenville, along with some trail hounds, were in pursuit of the suspects' vehicle and would soon arrive on site, decided that he and his partner should wait for the reinforcements.

The out-of-town lawmen did drive up within a few moments. The combined squad of officers, with the help of the bloodhounds, was able to find and arrest three of the suspects in short order. One of the men, Gooch, was hiding in a nearby farmhouse and was not located until sometime later.

None of the parties had been injured in the exchange of gunfire, and the four suspects were taken to Holdenville where they were booked into the Hughes County jail, to be charged with grand larceny. The men were identified as Arthur Gooch, twenty-five, and Bill Johnson, twenty-seven, both from Okmulgee, and the women were named as Maudie Lawson and Dosie Beavers. Each of the females was reported to be nineteen years old and lived in McAlester.

The night before being caught at Wetumka, the four miscreants had been on a wild spree of robbing filling stations. First, they robbed two stations at Arpelar (Pittsburg County) and took two attendants hostage. After being stripped of their clothing, the men were released near Stuart (Hughes County). A few minutes later, the hijackers stopped three youths who were in a car that had been following them from Arpelar. They robbed the boys of their meager money and forced them to disrobe, then released the trio, sans clothing.

From Stuart, the quartet drove to Calvin, Oklahoma (also in Hughes County), where they robbed Blaylock's Station. They took the station attendant a few miles out of town; at that point they made him strip off his clothes in the middle of the road, and then they drove on, leaving him with only the night to cover his nudity. These events had been the highlights of the wild crime party that the four roguish characters had been engaged in during the night prior to approaching Wetumka, where they were apprehended.

The accused men were still confined some two months later, when on Wednesday, October 24, 1934, Gooch and Johnson, along with one of the nineteen-year-old girls and three other inmates, broke out of the Holdenville jail. One of the other prisoners who got away that morning, was Ambrose Nix from Sardis, Oklahoma (Pushmataha County). Nix was being held in the Hughes County jail on a robbery charge when the opportunity to flee presented itself. At some point after leaving Holdenville, Nix and Gooch teamed up and left the others. Gooch and his new partner succeeded in eluding the officers who searched to round up the escapees.

A few days later, Gooch and Nix broke into a hunting lodge near Choctaw, Oklahoma, in Oklahoma County, and stole some guns. They left that crime scene without being caught, as probably they did numerous other sites in the coming days.

A month after they escaped from the Holdenville jail, the "wanted men" robbed a combination lunch counter and country beer tavern near Tyler, Texas, on Sunday evening, November 25, 1934. The robbers got away with nearly one hundred dollars in money and a stock of cigarettes. The thieves left the owner of the business and his employee bound and gagged. Shortly after their regular closing time, family members went to the tavern looking for the missing men, whom they found tied to a nearby tree. The released men were able to provide the police with detailed descriptions of the robbers and the vehicle that they were driving.

When Gooch and Nix stopped at a service station in Paris, Texas, the next day, their car was recognized as being suspiciously like the one involved in the recent robbery 120 miles south. City Police Officers H. R. Marks and R. N. Baker were on routine patrol in Paris when they spotted the automobile and drove into the service station to check more closely. Upon being approached by the lawmen; somehow Gooch and Nix were able to "get the drop on the officers" and forced them back into their police cruiser. While one of the outlaws held guns on the officers, the other transferred their weapons, including a machine gun, from their car into the officers' vehicle. The four then sped away from the service station in the police car.

The sedan that Gooch and Nix had driven into Paris, and which they left at the station, had been stolen on October 30 from Dr. Oscar Caldwell at Durant, Oklahoma (Bryan County). The vehicle was identified as the car that the robbers of the country tavern near Tyler were driving.

Probably, this escapade would have generated a great deal of publicity if the kidnappers had been caught with their hostages in tow, but because of the way it happened the incident garnered very little attention from the news media. The kidnappers stole another vehicle and ditched the police car shortly after racing away from the service station. That is one of the loose ends that was not covered in the brief articles written in the Oklahoma newspapers about this caper that occurred at Paris, Texas, twelve miles south of the Red River.

Some eighteen hours after having been abducted in Texas, the two policemen were released about twenty miles northeast of Antlers, Oklahoma, near Snow, both in Pushmataha County. Baker and Marks made their way to Antlers where they reported that they had been held at gunpoint throughout their ordeal. The Texas officers identified pictures of Arthur Gooch and Ambrose Nix as their kidnappers. After releasing their hostages in the remote region, the robbers had again slipped away and were not to be located for some time. At opening time on Saturday morning December 22, 1934, two banks in Okemah (Okfuskee County), were robbed simultaneous, and the thieves made off with seventeen thousand dollars. The robbers (three at each bank) had fled the area before authorities became aware that a crime had been committed. Numerous lawmen arrived in Okemah later that day, and the bank heists were thoroughly discussed, but it appeared that the robbers were long gone and had left no trace.

The following Saturday, while investigating the crimes, the authorities did receive a tip "that the bank robbers would gather that night at the farmhouse of Lee Mulky," located some three miles west of Okemah. More than a dozen lawmen waited throughout Saturday night, but no suspicious activity occurred at the Mulky place.

Most of the officers had left the rural home shortly after the new day had dawned; however, three lawmen were still on site about nine-thirty Sunday morning when an automobile with three passengers arrived. As soon as the car stopped, a girl jumped out and began yelling as she ran away. This action prompted the officers to begin firing at the two men as they were getting out of the car. Immediately, Ambrose Nix started shooting at the lawmen. One of the deputies' bullets struck and fatally wounded Nix. When Ambrose fell, Arthur Gooch, who had not fired a weapon, held up his hands, and the shooting ceased.

Gooch and Nix were not suspected of having participated in the double bank robbery at Okemah; however, they were wanted for questioning about numerous other crimes in that area. The tip, which advised that the bank robbers would gather at the farmhouse on Saturday night, had not been exact, but it had led to the shoot-out in which Nix had been killed and Gooch captured.

Lee Mulky was later convicted for harboring criminals. The car that the outlaw pair was driving that Sunday morning had been stolen on December 15 at Bristow, Oklahoma (Creek County).

After being arrested at the Mulky farm, Arthur Gooch was incarcerated in the county jail at Okemah. Later that same evening, after being placed in a car to be transported to Oklahoma City, he was attacked by an irate individual. As John Hopkins stood beside the automobile, he drew a pistol. He raised the gun, pointed it at the head of the sitting prisoner, then pulled the trigger. The weapon failed to fire, and deputies grabbed the attacker before he could trigger the derringer again. Hopkins was upset with Gooch because the pair of outlaws had robbed his filling station, some ten miles west of Okemah, the previous weekend.

Soon after he was confined in jail at Oklahoma City, it was determined that Gooch was to be indicted for having kidnapped the two officers in Texas and bringing them across the state line into Oklahoma. It was further claimed that one of the officers had been cut by a piece of broken glass, when he was pushed into a display case at the Paris service station. These were the two key factors that prosecutors felt they could prove, to convict Arthur Gooch of having violated the Federal Lindbergh Kidnapping Law, as amended in May 1934.

The prisoner was immediately transferred from Oklahoma City to Muskogee, where he was to be confined in the Federal

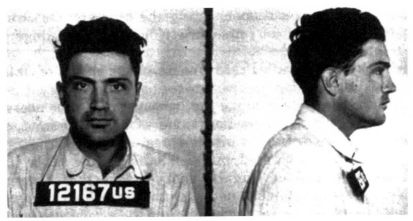

Arthur Gooch as a Federal prisoner in 1934. (Courtesy of the Oklahoma Publishing Company)

jail and prosecuted. When arraigned before U.S. Commissioner R. M. Mountcastle, on December 26, 1934, at Muskogee, Gooch pled not guilty to violating the Federal kidnapping act and the Dyer Motor Vehicle Law (stealing an automobile).

His preliminary hearing was first scheduled for January 16, 1935. There was a delay, and it was held on Tuesday, February 12, in the Federal court at Muskogee. Police Officers Baker and Marks had been brought from Paris, Texas, to testify before the grand jury. That hearing resulted in Arthur Gooch's being officially charged with violating the amended Lindbergh Kidnapping Law.

Arthur Gooch was later transferred to Durant, Oklahoma, some seventy miles from the place where the men had been kidnapped. His case went to trial in the Federal district court, a large room in the post office building, at Durant, on June 10, 1935. Robert L. Williams, a former Oklahoma governor, was the presiding judge. Gooch's attorney offered very little defense; he merely claimed that his client had not participated in any kidnapping.

Undoubtedly Gooch's trial was one of the shortest capital

offense cases on record in the Federal court system, taking less than eight hours to complete. On Monday afternoon, June 10, 1935, the jury returned with a guilty verdict against the defendant with the recommendation that he be sentenced to death.

The Federal district judge was not bound by the jury's recommendation. The magistrate had leeway in assigning the penalty. However, on June 19, 1935, when Arthur Gooch was presented in the Federal court at Durant, Judge Robert L. Williams sentenced him to be hanged. The next day, the prisoner was returned to the Federal jail at Muskogee. Execution of the doomed man was then scheduled to be carried out at that location on September 13, 1935.

Early Wednesday morning, August 7, 1935, Federal officers took Arthur Gooch from his cell at Muskogee and delivered him to the Oklahoma State Penitentiary at McAlester, where he was to be held as a "safekeeper." No explanation for this transfer was offered to the public; in fact, the news article that reported about the prisoner having been taken to McAlester stated that "Gooch had been secretly moved by three federal agents," and indicated that he would be returned to Muskogee for his scheduled execution. The new arrival was placed on death row at Big Mac along with fourteen state prisoners.

Gooch had not participated in the gunfight with the officers in which his cohort Nix had been killed. He had twice pled guilty (without going to trial) to the charges leveled against him. Gooch was accustomed to "paying the price" for the criminal acts for which he had been charged; but he could not fathom why he was to be hanged. He reasoned that since "he had not killed nor even shot at or hadn't really hurt anyone," surely it was not right for him to be "put to death."

Gooch's attorney appealed his client's conviction, and twice his arguments went to the U.S. Supreme Court. Neither occasion prompted that panel to rescind the "death by hanging" sentence. Following the second denial, the convict appealed to Pres. Franklin Delano Roosevelt to stay his execution.

Judge Robert L. Williams, sitting on the Federal bench at Durant, Oklahoma, on June 19, 1935, sentenced Arthur Gooch to death by hanging. (Photo courtesy of the Archives & Manuscripts Division of the Oklahoma Historical Society)

Arthur Gooch is seen in his cell at the Oklahoma State Penitentiary at McAlester, Oklahoma, during June of 1936, while awaiting exe-cution. (Courtesy of the Oklahoma Publishing Company)

While Arthur Gooch awaited the results of his appeals, a development at Trenton, New Jersey, made the national headlines. Bruno Richard Hauptmann, who had been arrested, tried, convicted, and sentenced to death for having kidnapped and murdered the Lindbergh baby, was executed. On Friday, April 3, 1936, four years after Charles Lindbergh, Jr., had been kidnapped; the man who had been convicted of that crime was electrocuted in the New Jersey State Prison. Hauptmann continued to deny guilt, even as he was being strapped into the electric chair.

Arthur Gooch was still being held on death row at McAlester when President Roosevelt's response was received. The president declined to interfere with the sentence that had been recommended by the jury, decreed by Judge Williams, and reviewed by the Supreme Court. The Federal prisoner then wrote a personal letter to Eleanor Roosevelt, pleading that she help him out of his predicament. It is not possible to report whether or not he received a written word from her. It is obvious that she did not accomplish the task that he asked of her. Even though the numerous attempts to avert Gooch's execution had not voided his sentence, they had delayed his hanging.

At some point during these appeals, it was determined by "the powers that be," that if the case cleared all hurdles, and if Arthur Gooch was to be executed, he would be hanged at the Oklahoma State Penitentiary. Rich Owens, the longtime executioner at Big Mac, had used "Old Sparky," his trusted electric chair, to execute more than fifty men in carrying out the death penalty as imposed by the state. However, he had never participated in a hanging.

When neither the high court nor the president provided any relief for the condemned man, Rich Owens could see that it was becoming his task to carry out the federally imposed hanging. The executioner then solicited help from the prison carpenter and blacksmith shops to build a gallows that could be assembled in sections and fabricated with a trap door.

U.S. Marshal S. E. Swinney of Muskogee was officially in

charge of the execution. Rich Owens did the planning and carried out the hanging. On Thursday night after the inmates had been locked in their cells, the gallows was brought into the prison yard and assembled under the watchful eye of Rich Owens. Two feet of earth was removed directly below the trap door to permit a maximum drop. At five o'clock on Friday morning, June 19, 1936, Deputy Warden Jess Dunn led Arthur Gooch, who was shackled between two prison guards and followed by three deputy U. S. marshals, from his death-row cell, nearly a quarter of a mile to the scaffold and up the thirteen steps.

Upon reaching the platform, there was a short pause while

Rich Owen, long-term executioner at the state prison, executed more than fifty men by electrocuting them using "Old Sparky"; however, Arthur Gooch was the only individual he ever executed by hanging. Gooch is seen (front and center) on the prison-constructed gallows—June 19, 1936. (Courtesy of the Oklahoma Publishing Company)

the cuffs were rearranged on the condemned man. Following brief formalities on the gallows, Rich Owens guided the prisoner into position, placed the black hood over the victim's head and the rope around his neck. After adjusting the noose, the executioner stepped back and tripped the lever. The trap door immediately sprang open, dropping Gooch downward so that his feet dangled within mere inches of the bottom of the pit. The extended fall had not, however, broken his neck, and almost fifteen minutes elapsed before the strangled victim was pronounced dead.

Immediately following the doctors' announcement of Gooch's passing, the rope was disconnected from the overhead beam so that the noose could be loosened and removed from the victim. The body was then taken to Humphreys Undertaking Parlor in McAlester to be prepared for delivery and burial at Okmulgee. As soon as the corpse was removed from the death-dealing rig, Owens and his helpers began dismantling the structure, which was removed from the grounds before the prisoners were allowed to enter the yard on Friday morning.

Two years after Congress had passed the amendment, which

Arthur Gooch's tombstone. (Author's collection)

STATE STANDARD CERTIFICATE OF DEATH

DEPARTMENT OF COMMERCE
BUREAU OF THE CENSUS

91

1. PLACE OF DEATH:

County __Pittsburg__ State __OKLAHOMA__ Registered No. __307__
Township __McAlester__ 6-178 or Village __Oklahoma State Penitentiary__ or
City __McAlester__ No. ____ St. ____ Ward.

(If death occurred in a hospital or institution, give its NAME instead of street and number)

Length of residence in city or town where death occurred ___ yrs. ___ mos. ___ days. How long in U. S., if of foreign birth? ___ yrs. ___ mos. ___ days.

2. FULL NAME __Arthur Gooch__ 2-00

Residence: No. __Muskogee, Oklahoma.__ St. ____ Ward. 61-259

(Usual place of abode) (If nonresident, give city or town and State)

PERSONAL AND STATISTICAL PARTICULARS | MEDICAL CERTIFICATE OF DEATH

3. SEX | 4. COLOR OR RACE | 5. SINGLE, MARRIED, WIDOWED, OR DIVORCED (write the word)

__Male__ | __White__ | __Single__ _Arnold_

5a. If married, widowed, or divorced
HUSBAND of
(or) WIFE of

21. DATE OF DEATH (month, day, and year) __June 19th,__ 193 6

22. I HEREBY CERTIFY, That I attended deceased from __June 19th,__ 193 6 to __June 19th,__ 193 6

6. DATE OF BIRTH (month, day, and year) __1909__

I last saw __him__ alive on __June 19th,__ 193 6; death is said to have occurred on the date stated above, at __5:18 A.M.__

7. AGE | Years __27 years__ | Months | Days | If LESS than 1 day, hrs. or min.

The principal cause of death and related causes of importance were as follows:

8. Trade, profession, or particular kind of work done, as spinner, sawyer, bookkeeper, etc. __GOV'T PRISONER__

" Legal execution by hanging "

9. Industry or business in which work was done, as silk mill, sawmill, bank, etc. __2 x 3__

10. Date deceased last worked at this occupation (month and year) | 11. Total time (years) spent in this occupation

(Other contributory causes of importance:)

__198__

12. BIRTHPLACE (city or town and State or country?) __Oklahoma__

13. NAME: __Gooch__

Name of operation ____ Date of ____

14. BIRTHPLACE (city or town and State or country?):

What test confirmed diagnosis? ____ Was there an autopsy? ____

15. MAIDEN NAME:

23. If death was due to external causes (violence), fill in also the following:

Accident, suicide, or homicide? ____ Date of injury ____ 193

16. BIRTHPLACE (city or town and State or country?):

Where did injury occur? ____

(Specify city or town, county, and State)

Specify whether injury occurred in industry, in home, or in public place:

17. INFORMANT (name and address)

__D. T. H. McCauley, McAlester Okla__

Manner of injury ____

18. (a) BURIAL, CREMATION, OR REMOVAL __6-19-36__ ____

Nature of injury ____

24. Was disease or injury in any way related to occupation of deceased?

19. UNDERTAKER (name and address) __Humphreys Undertaking Parlor__

If so, specify ____

(Signed) __J. H. McCauley M. D.__

19a. FILED __7-10-36__ __M. A. Emery__ Registrar

(Address) __McAlester, Okla.__

State Department of Health
State of Oklahoma
OKLAHOMA CITY, OKLAHOMA 73117

June 19, 2002

CERTIFIED COPY MUST BE
VALIDATED WITH 3 COLORS

John C. Bus
STATE REGISTRAR
OF VITAL STATISTICS

Arthur Gooch's death certificate. (Author's collection)

authorized that the death penalty could be invoked in Federal kidnapping cases, Arthur Gooch became its first victim. His execution has been the only legal hanging ever to be carried out at the Oklahoma State Penitentiary at McAlester, Oklahoma.

This chapter on the hanging of Arthur Gooch, and the previous chapter about the kidnapping of Charles Urschel, are accounts of the first cases in the nation to implement the Federal Lindbergh Kidnapping Law and its amendment. In the first instance, the victim (Urschel) had been kidnapped in Oklahoma and held hostage in Texas, while the second crime was carried out in the reverse order; the officers (Marks and Baker) were kidnapped in Texas and brought to Oklahoma. However, in each case, the charges were filed in Oklahoma, prompting the trials for both violations to be held in the Sooner State.

CHAPTER 27

Texas Officers Shot 'em Dead in Oklahoma

When the horseless carriage became available shortly after the turn of the twentieth century, both the outlaws and lawmen begin to adapt the new machine for their operation. By the mid-twenties, the horse had been replaced, and the automobile had become the standard means of transportation for those on each side of the law. This story relates an incident that occurred a decade later. It is about a car that had been specially equipped to help cope with the lawless characters.

The subject of this story is a Texas sheriff and his deputy, who proved to make a very effective team in disposing of bank robbers, even after they were well outside of the Lone Star State. This true account of the episode records the use of some rather unusual police equipment and procedures.

Shortly after 1:30 P.M. on Tuesday, July 10, 1934, two men robbed the First State Bank at Allison, Texas, located five miles west of the Oklahoma line. The robbers ran from the bank, hopped into a car, and fled. They were last seen a few miles southeast, speeding away from the small Texas Panhandle town.

The Wheeler County sheriff was out of the area and not available, so Hemphill County sheriff Walter Jones was notified of the robbery. Upon receiving the information at Canadian, Texas, about the bank heist, Sheriff Jones picked up Deputy Joe Oney, then raced toward Allison, thirty-five miles southeast.

After arriving in the little town, which was one mile south of the Hemphill County's southern boundary, the officers inquired extensively and learned what they could about the robbery.

"Lute" Funston owned the local telephone system, and the exchange was near the First State Bank. Funston talked with the officers and perhaps provided them some key information. The lawmen extended an invitation for Lute to join the chase and ride in their car, which he gladly accepted.

While at Allison, Sheriff Jones phoned Roger Mills County (Oklahoma) sheriff J. M. Bradshaw, and they discussed some details of the case. Apparently, Sheriff Jones had learned the identity of one of the suspects and had been apprised where the robbers might be located. Upon leaving the little Texas town, the officers drove some twenty miles southeast, crossing into Beckham County, Oklahoma, to the old Orteg homestead, which was located a couple of miles south of Sweetwater, Oklahoma.

When the Texas lawmen arrived at the Oklahoma farm where they thought the robbers might have taken refuge, they stopped to talk with a man who was working in the field, near the entrance gate. While thus engaged, the officers observed two men run from the Orteg house and get into a car that fit the description of the bank robbers' getaway vehicle. The lawmen raced their car after the fleeing automobile and were about one-half mile behind when the suspects reached the main road.

The lead car sped north, then turned right at the crossroads in Sweetwater. A couple of minutes later, the wanted men suddenly slowed their sedan. At that point, about one and one-half miles east of the small Oklahoma town, the bandits opened fire on the pursuing vehicle. The officers' car was fast approaching but was hardly visible in the cloud of dust that had been stirred up by the speeding vehicles. One bullet struck the windshield of the sheriff's car.

When the lawmen realized that they were under attack and

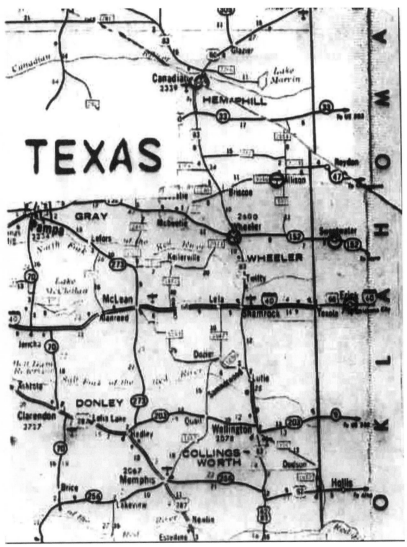

A 1934 map of the border area between the Texas Panhandle and western Oklahoma, showing the highways, byways, and towns patrolled by law enforcement from both regions. (Author's collection)

that the automobile they were chasing was stopping, Deputy Oney abruptly applied the brakes to his car. As the sheriff's vehicle came to a stop, the lawmen began to shoot at the bandits' car.

The sheriff's automobile was equipped with a bulletproof windshield, which protected the lawmen. This non-penetrable glass had two portholes, one at the lower right side and another near the center, just to the right of the driver. Though the porthole on the passenger's side, Sheriff Jones opened fire with a machine gun, which jammed after the first short burst. He then replaced it with a high-powered rifle and continued

Sheriff Walter Jones's car, a 1933 Chevrolet sedan, was equipped with a bullet-proof windshield with portholes and high-powered rifles—testimony for "Crooks to Beware!" Sheriff Jones preserved law and order in the Texas Panhandle by utilizing this auto in the pursuit and capture of criminals. (Author's collection)

the barrage, while Deputy Oney fired his pistol through the other porthole.

When shots ceased to come from the robbery suspects' vehicle, the two lawmen halted their shooting. After a brief pause, they cautiously approached the bandits' car and found both occupants badly shot up. The officers loaded the severely wounded men into the sheriff's car and rushed them back to Sweetwater, seeking medical attention. Finding no such facility in the small hamlet, they sped south trying to reach the closest hospital, fifteen miles away in Erick, Oklahoma.

The lawmen and their passengers arrived at the Erick Hospital around 5:30 P.M. There, doctors immediately pronounced both outlaws dead, and their bodies were delivered two blocks east, to the Fatheree Funeral Home. Neither Sheriff Jones nor Deputy Oney had been hit in the shoot-out, but their passenger in the back seat, Lute Funston, had received a minor scalp wound, having been struck by a bit of flying glass.

The dead men were identified as Wade H. Orteg and Buster Orr (some accounts listed the men as W. D. Ortag and Bert Orr). Orteg was nearly forty years of age and had previously resided in the Sweetwater community. Some of his relatives still lived in the area. In recent years, Orteg had moved to California, where he had met Buster Orr who was some fifteen years his junior. The two men had left the West Coast a few weeks earlier and come to Oklahoma. Neither man was known to have any prior criminal record. Orteg's sister-in-law owned the automobile that the robbers had driven.

Justice of the Peace J. O. Bell held an inquest at Erick on Tuesday night. The coroner's jury determined that Orteg and Orr came to their deaths from bullet wounds inflicted by Sheriff Walter Jones and Deputy Joe Oney, while the officers were in performance of their duty and the victims were resisting arrest. The amount of money found in the pockets of the outlaws' overalls totaled $124.22, which was almost exactly what the First State Bank had reported missing.

Less than four hours after stealing money from the bank at Allison, Texas, the bandits had been shot and fatally wounded on the road that divides Beckham and Roger Mills counties. Neither the robbery nor the subsequent action had occurred in Hemphill County, Texas, yet it was two officers from that county who had arrived at the scene of the crime, pursued the suspects (driving some eleven miles after leaving Texas), and killed both bandits about seven miles inside Oklahoma.

Wade Orteg and Buster Orr were buried in the Buffalo Cemetery, in northern Beckham County. Their final resting place is only five miles from the location where they made their last stand and their brief criminal careers came to an end, on a hot summer day, in a cloud of dust, on a dirt road, just east of Sweetwater, Oklahoma.

Tombstone marker of the two robbers, Buster Orr and Wade Orteg, located in the Buffalo Cemetery, Beckham County, Oklahoma. (Author's collection)

Personal Recollection by the Author

During the summer of 1934, I was seven years old and was living with my parents in Erick, Oklahoma. My father was driving a dump truck and was working for the Martin-Wright Construction Company. They had a contract to improve a few miles of the dirt road between Erick and Sweetwater. Both Bob Martin and Asa Wright, the owners of the firm, had lived at Reydon, as had Lute Funston and my family, the Butlers.

I recall one evening (obviously July 10, 1934) when my brother Gerald, who was fifteen months older than I was, jumped on the Model-A Ford dump truck (which had no cab, doors, or windshield, due to restrictions on the job) to ride with Dad down to the service station, to put some gas in the dual-wheeled dirt hauler. Dad asked my mother to bring the car along (that is, our 1929 Chevrolet coupe), as it needed gas as well. I rode with my mother.

As we approached the service station, we saw extra cars and activity at the Fatheree Funeral Home, which was directly north across the street (Highway 66) from the station. When my mother asked the attendant about the commotion at the funeral home, he replied, "Some sheriffs have just brought in a couple of outlaws that they killed up north of town."

My mother always had a hankering to observe anything of that nature and, with me in tow, she left the car at the gas pump. Dad and Gerald were aware that we were leaving the car and crossing the street.

As I recall there were several people in the funeral parlor when we arrived, but that did not deter my entry. Without hesitation, I demonstrated that natural talent of a seven-year-old boy, who is not hampered with manners, to get around in a crowded room. I hurriedly maneuvered my way to one of the objects of attention; then peeking over the end of a gurney, I found that I was gazing at a pair of bare, discolored feet, mere inches from my face.

That sudden sight startled me and sated my curiosity to see

the dead outlaws. I quickly left the funeral parlor and went into the yard, where I became interested in the sheriff's car that several people were looking at. Again, I had no trouble in gaining a position where I could witness the attraction.

Through the open door on the right side of the vehicle, I could see the porthole, which was being pointed at by a gentleman who also talked about the bulletproof windshield. He seemed to be well acquainted with the automobile. I then wangled my way to the driver's side and crowded in close, so I could get a good look at the weapon (some kind of carbine rifle) that was attached to the steering column. I also remember the porthole that was located to the right of the steering wheel.

During the intervening years, I occasionally thought of that evening in Erick. Those reflections always brought to mind my experience in the funeral parlor and my recollection of the sheriff's vehicle. Having never seen anything like it since, nor hearing of an officer's car being equipped in the manner that I recalled, I wondered if that car really had a bulletproof windshield with portholes, or if I as a kid had simply misunderstood and got the wrong impression.

A few years ago, I accidentally came upon a lengthy article in the *Cheyenne Star,* published at Cheyenne, Oklahoma, the county seat of Roger Mills County, and dated July 12, 1934, which reported the incident. This article confirmed and refreshed my memory. To learn more details of this episode, I sought out a copy of the *Beckham County Democrat* newspaper, which was published in Erick, Oklahoma, and also dated July 12. These two articles provided the basis for my writing this account, which was prompted by my desire to relate this childhood memory. Several years later, I happened upon an old nationally published detective magazine from the 1930s, and, to my astonishment, there was a photographic image of the very automobile that I had remembered, complete with bulletproof windshield and portholes. My childhood memory had traveled full-circle, and my faded vision had become a reality.

CHAPTER 28

Murray Humphreys, Crime Boss

Llewelyn Morris Humphreys, son of William Bryant and Ann (Wigley) Humphreys, was born on March 20, 1899, in Chicago, Illinois. Llewelyn's parents had emigrated from Wales to the United States in 1888, with hopes of providing a better life for themselves and their children—better than working and dying in the coal mines of their native land. By 1900, the Humphreys had lost three of their seven children to the harsh realities of disease and the rigors of childbirth; and, by 1910, only five of their ten children survived, or would survive, to adulthood. Llewelyn, the fourth oldest of the surviving five children, was one of only two sons.

The Humphreys family rented a modest house on Chicago's North Clark Street in a notoriously rough neighborhood known as "The Levee." It was all they could afford on William Humphreys' meager salary as a teamster. The entire area was inundated with saloons, gambling dens, and houses of prostitution; and when the elevated trains were constructed, encircling the Levee region, the name was changed to "The Loop." The Loop became even wilder and more notorious and would remain so for decades.

The Humphreys children attended public school for a while, but Llewelyn left the classroom at age seven to sell newspapers on the mean streets of Chicago—trying to make a small

Llewelyn Morris "Murray" Humphreys. (Photos courtesy of Brenda Gage)

financial contribution to his struggling family. He soon developed a "newsboys' culture" of streetwise hooliganism, spending every waking moment devising newer, faster, and easier ways to make money—by any means necessary—such as picking pockets, short-change artistry, burglary, hit-and-grab techniques, and hijacking.

At age thirteen, he was called to appear before Judge Jack Murray's court to answer to a slight digression, probably a larceny charge of some degree. However, after surveying the case, Judge Murray gave the youthful defendant a fatherly lecture and released him with conditions. The judge took the young Welsh lad under his wing, tutoring him in the ways of the judicial and political systems of the times. The boy was so impressed with the kindness of the benevolent old judge that Llewelyn Morris Humphreys changed his name to "Murray" Humphreys—a name that would soon be feared and revered by many in the world of gangsters, and by lawmen as well.

In his lifetime Murray ("The Hump," "The Camel," "Curly") Humphreys, as he was called, became one of the most notorious and ruthless gangsters in the annals of organized crime— a leader in one of the greatest criminal enterprises (the Chicago "Outfit") that this country would ever encounter. This is the story of a truly, big-time gangster and his close, personal, and lifelong connection with the state of Oklahoma.

The lectures, guidance, and assistance shown by kindly old Judge Murray could only go so far in reforming his wayward charge. When Humphreys was arrested and convicted for a jewelry heist at the age of sixteen, he was sent to the Illinois House of Corrections for sixty days. This was a relatively light sentence due to a lenient prosecuting attorney, who received a diamond-encrusted wristwatch for his understanding. Immediately upon his release, Humphreys returned to his old haunts and friends and discovered that he had a real knack for hijacking truckloads of merchandise and occasionally stealing a shipment of beer, or whiskey, which was easy to sell to an increasingly thirsty and appreciative populace. On one such foray, the driver of the truck, which Murray had commandeered at gunpoint, recognized him and reported the hijacking to his boss and owner of the shipment, Al Capone.

Al Capone, undisputed boss of the Outfit, ordered the streetwise offender to be brought before him for sentencing and punishment, which usually meant death. However, Al saw a toughness and brilliance in the young Welshman, and instead of inflicting physical retribution on him, he hired him as a driver in the organization. He drove delivery trucks, ran errands, and performed any job asked of him. When he was nineteen or twenty years old, while in the performance of his duties, he was seen committing a major infraction of the law, which, if he were caught and convicted, meant serious hard time in prison. Rather than sticking around and facing the music, he took off for parts unknown—to a land so different from his fast-paced urban environ that it was like an alien world. He traveled to rural Oklahoma to hide out and cool off.

He went to stay with his older brother Henry, who had moved to Little Axe, Cleveland County, Oklahoma, several years earlier, after being discharged from the military. By that time Henry was a civilian and ran a shop selling electronic products such as radios and phonographs. Llewelyn "Murray" Humphreys agreed to assist with his brother's business, which would give him something to do while biding his time. Besides, it was "good cover" and interesting work. While in Oklahoma, Murray went by the name Lew (or Lou) Harris.

Murray Humphreys' assignment was to demonstrate and sell Victrola phonographs to farmers and ranchers in the outlying regions of the county. On one of these door-to-door sales outings, he called on the Davis and Martha Brendle family near Pink, Oklahoma (Pottawatomie County). Humphreys met and fell in love with their beautiful, intelligent, and talented daughter, Mary Clementine Brendle, who was, at this time, home from her studies at the University of Oklahoma. Murray, using the name Lew Harris, made several excuses to return to the Brendle home to see her; and after a brief courtship, they ran off to Dallas, Texas, and were married on May 9, 1921.

Mary Clementine "Clemie" (or "Clema") Humphreys was half-Irish and half-Cherokee, which made for a most exotic combination—smart and witty, vibrant, energetic, and sophisticated. She majored in classical music and the humanities at the University of Oklahoma. By example, she instructed her new life-partner in the ways, mores, and customs of the upper social classes, and how to be accepted by them. Lew Harris was a "fast study" and absorbed completely all of the cultural and intellectually stimulating subjects presented to him.

With his bride by his side, and a more focused outlook on life, Murray returned to Chicago to begin anew. For a while, he worked at menial jobs, receiving only nominal compensation, but predictably, the old ways and his old friends eventually drew him back into the life of crime at which he was so adept. It is believed that Murray Humphreys returned to the organization as an enforcer in the protection racket and a man who could be counted on to get results. The top leadership of the gang listened to Humphreys and believed him when they saw the results that he attained. There were turf battles and gang wars, and Murray Humphreys' counsel always seemed to pay off.

The Congress of the United States passed the Volstead Act in January of 1920, which became the eighteenth amendment to the constitution. This new law prohibited the making and/or selling of most alcoholic beverages in the United States, creating a multimillion-dollar enterprise for the criminal elements in the society. Since there were plenty of hoods involved in the illegal liquor business (that is, the manufacturing, transporting, and distributing of beer and whiskey spirits to a rapidly growing market), Murray decided he could best serve the organization by establishing or taking over the labor unions. He started with the laundry industry, which he quickly controlled through force and intimidation. The laundry wars were bloody and brutal, but Murray Humphreys' ruthless, and sometimes, deadly, actions prevailed.

On February 14, 1929, the famous St. Valentine's Day Massacre occurred in Chicago, leaving several of the Outfit's rival gang members dead on the floor of a garage. Because of the "style" and "ingenuity" of the operation, it is believed to have been the plan—the "brainchild"—of Murray Humphreys. Al Capone had an excellent alibi. He was visiting with the Miami chief of police, in Florida, at the time of the shooting. Some even speculated that Humphreys might have actually been one of the machine gunners at the massacre. Not so coincidentally, the killing happened in the building next door to Murray's childhood home; therefore, he would have known the neighborhood inside and out. It was reported that the main target was supposed to be George "Bugs" Moran, leader of the opposition, who escaped the trap; however, one of the unfortunates lying dead on the floor that day was Humphreys' main rival in the takeover of the laundry unions. No one was ever convicted of the St. Valentine's Day Massacre.

Soon after establishing his control over the laundry workers' union, he began directing takeovers of all the other service-related businesses, such as: milk delivery drivers, bartenders, janitors, garbage collectors, garment workers, etc. Murray "the Camel" Humphreys, with full authority from the Outfit, used his wit, his persuasive personality, and every strong-arm means at his disposal to get the desired results, including assaults, destruction of property, bombings, kidnappings, and even murder. To achieve his goal, he never hesitated to perform the most horrendous acts of mayhem on anyone who stood in his way. By the early thirties, Murray controlled or directed the operations of almost all of the labor unions in the country. He made certain that "his people" held positions of leadership within the unions and answered *only* to him. His position of power within the organization grew, resulting in huge monetary benefits as well.

Clemie was considered an extremely able helpmate to her

Murray ("The Hump," "The Camel," "Curly") Humphreys, shown here in full gangster attire, on a typical day during his power growth years of the 1920s and 1930s with the Chicago "Outfit." (Author's collection)

husband in his business world dealings. She is reported to have been blessed with an amazing memory—possibly, total recall. She could remember and cite all the officers in all the unions that they controlled. She was the only female who was ever allowed to "sit in" on meetings of the organization, where notes were never taken; however, she was relied upon to remember and report the minutest details when needed. The Humphreyses were regarded as an outstanding couple among the upper echelon of Chicago's underworld; and with Clemie's tutoring and refining, Murray became known to the general public as an intelligent, suave, and debonair gentleman.

Murray committed one egregious error in his otherwise spotless criminal career. He failed to report fifty thousand dollars in kidnap ransom money as income, resulting in a charge of income tax evasion. He was never charged with the kidnapping—only for not reporting the "fee" that he received for intervening in the transaction and seeing that the kidnap victim was safely returned to his loving family. Murray pled guilty and was sentenced to eighteen months in Leavenworth Penitentiary, beginning on October 31, 1934. He rationalized the time away from his job as "going off to college"—taking some time off to study and hone his craft. Some speculated that the relatively light sentence, compared to the much greater one that Al Capone received, was due to some well-placed gratuities within the system. Murray served only fifteen months and returned to Chicago.

When the fledgling motion picture industry first began in the Chicago area, Murray Humphreys was right there to guide it with his unique expertise. Murray realized immediately the great financial benefits and enormous potential that one could gain by organizing the various trade unions involved in the making of motion pictures. When the industry moved to California because the West Coast afforded the moviemakers better weather to film, Murray and his union organizers were ever present. Not only did he control nearly a hundred labor unions across the United States, but the entire movie industry also answered to him. Long before Benjamin "Bugsy" Siegel, who is usually given credit for developing and controlling Las Vegas, even knew there was a state of Nevada out West somewhere, Murray Humphreys and his man in California, Johnny Roselli, were bribing, coercing, and manipulating the politicians in Nevada to pass pro-gambling and pro-union legislation. With Humphreys' control of the unions and the money in their pension funds Las Vegas was built.

For a short time, Murray and Clemie resided in Arcadia, California, wishing to be close to their Hollywood interests. During this period, only a month before Murray went to prison, the birth of their daughter, Mary Llewellyn

Murray, Clemie, and Luella Humphreys, posing in front of the fireplace in their Chicago home. (Courtesy of Brenda Gage)

Humphreys, occurred on September 21, 1934. She was called Lewella, or Luella. (It is rumored by some that the child was actually birthed by Clemie's younger, unmarried sister, an issue resulting from an affair the sister had with one of Lew's many associates.) Regardless, Murray and Clemie raised their daughter with all the love and worldly comforts that any parents could hope for their child.

While gangster life was Humphreys' natural vocation, he and Clemie maintained a relatively normal living arrangement back in Oklahoma, where her family and the locals knew him as Uncle Lew, and believed him to be "in the laundry business" in Chicago. Clemie's family were good, hardworking folk and claimed to be unaware of Murray's rather infamous background. Murray enjoyed returning to Oklahoma as often as possible, due to its laid-back, down-home atmosphere. He bought some land because he loved to hunt and fish, and even tried his hand at raising cattle. For obvious tax reasons, he usually purchased the land in his wife's name, or in the names of others. It is reported that he may have owned (controlled) as much as seven sections of land in and around the area known as Brendle Corner, east of Norman, Oklahoma. He built a very comfortable, native-stone house, landscaped with rock walls and flagstone patios and a swimming pool. The interior walls, cabinets, bookshelves, and doors were finished with highest quality, tongue-and-groove knotty pine and oak, throughout, and the finest imported marble and tiles were used on the floors and bathroom counters and fixtures.

The house, resembling a hunting lodge, was nestled deep within a grove of native blackjack oak trees, and the grounds were surrounded with a sturdy cyclone fence with steel gates, padlocked and guarded. A lookout tower was constructed and manned twenty-four hours a day, and an alarm system was installed to alert everyone in the compound of unexpected visitors. Local hunters, who occasionally strayed onto the property, or innocently set off the alarm, were quickly set upon and politely escorted off the premises.

Murray Humphreys, relaxing and enjoying life in the stone cottage that he built on a wooded acreage at Brendles Corner, east of Norman, Oklahoma. (Courtesy of Brenda Gage)

Frequently, friends and associates from Chicago, Hollywood, or Las Vegas were invited to enjoy the hospitality of the Humphreyses at their country retreat. Their guests would enjoy quail hunting, or horseback riding, or relaxing by the pool. The local people remembered the former Mary Brendle and often saw her and her husband, Lew, coming or going. Most of the hired help, who were needed to run the estate, such as groundskeepers and household domestics, were often chosen from the local Indian population, who were not of a gossipy nature, and in return were generously compensated. Murray, or rather Lew, was a very good, conscientious neighbor. He often took food baskets and gifts to many of the indigent Indian families in the area, especially on Thanksgiving and Christmas when he would load up the station wagon with turkeys and all the fixings, and deliver them, himself.

Occasionally, some members of Mary's family would travel from Oklahoma to visit with her and Lew in their Chicago home, where they were wined and dined and treated to a lifestyle that they could only consider as living "high on the hog." The relatives returned home thinking that Lew's laundry business was not only extremely successful but downright profitable too.

Luella was a bright student, attending various public and private schools. When she graduated from Chicago's South Shore High School in the early 1950s, her father asked her who she would like to escort her to the graduation party. She replied that she would like for Frank Sinatra to be her gentleman escort. Humphreys made a few phone calls, and sure enough, when graduation time came around, "Old Blue Eyes" himself showed up to escort Luella Humphreys to the dance. One can only imagine how the rest of the senior class reacted when the chauffeured limousine arrived with the famed entertainer and national heartthrob stepping out for the party with Luella on his arm. All the girls squealed and tried to get their pictures taken with the handsome singer/actor, who willingly accommodated many of them.

Luella was a talented pianist and, after graduating from high school, she studied music in Rome. She participated in three concerts with the Rome Symphony Orchestra, and traveled a great deal. Luella liked associating with the music and movie entertainers of the day. In 1954, she had a relationship with the very popular Italian actor, Rossano Brazzi. Brazzi starred in dozens of top-rated Hollywood movies, such as *The Barefoot Contessa, Three Coins in the Fountain,* and *South Pacific.*

Murray Humphreys with his grandson, George Brady, having a little family fun time. (Courtesy of Brenda Gage)

Luella would later claim that she and Rossano were married and had the marriage certificate as proof. However, since Rossano was already married at this time, and since divorce was not a recognized option in Italy until the 1970s, neither the Brazzi family nor the Italian government would ever acknowledge that this union took place. Regardless, when Luella returned to America, she gave birth, on July 14, 1955, to a son, whom she named George Llewellyn Brady—Brady being the anglicized version of Brazzi—who today lives in Oregon. She would call herself Luella Brady from that day forward.

Whatever the case, Luella's relationship with Rosanno Brazzi was of short duration. At about the same time as her breakup with Rossano, Murray and Clemie were also going through an amicable divorce, filed in Norman, Oklahoma, on

July 6, 1957. Within a year, Murray married Betty Jeanne (nee Niebert) Stacy, a beautiful, younger woman and an "entertainer," twenty-five years his junior. They established residency in Key Biscayne, Florida. In Florida, Humphreys was known as Lewis Hart, a retired oilman from Texas.

Murray maintained a good relationship with Clemie and Luella, keeping in touch with them on a regular basis in Oklahoma. Clemie had been an integral part of his criminal activities, as well as his wife for thirty-six years. She had "kept the books" as it were, and Murray continued to rely upon her in his business matters. Clemie was more than gracious, performing her tasks of bookkeeper and confidant. Murray had a penchant for using a multitude of aliases, which made her work that much more difficult, or interesting, as the case may be. The FBI tracked and traced Murray Humphreys by dozens of different names and titles.

For years, Murray had wanted to visit his family's ancestral home of Wales, where his parents (by then deceased) were born. Showing his grand power of diplomacy, he made the trip with his wife of three years, Betty Jeanne, and his first wife, Clemie. The three of them toured the countryside and had a very enjoyable time. Murray's marital problems continued, however, and he divorced Jeanne in Chicago on August 28, 1963. He paid her eighteen thousand dollars a month in alimony, and poor Clemie was only getting six thousand dollars a month back in Oklahoma.

Murray's innate intelligence and brilliant, problem-solving talents endeared him to his gangster associates, especially when it came to finding ways to invest their ill-gotten gains, which easily ran into the hundreds of millions of dollars. In the early days in Chicago, when a gang member had copious amounts of cash lying around, and didn't know what to do with it, the common solution was "take the money to Murray at his laundry establishment" and he would provide direction on how to best invest (or hide) it. This is how the term "money laundering" first appeared in the lexicon of criminal terminology. Murray schooled his miscreant minions on how to avoid answering questions in front of judges or law officers. Murray Humphreys instructed an entire generation of hoodlums, crooks, and criminals of the meaning of "taking the Fifth" and how to exercise one's "right" to the Fifth Amendment protection of self-incrimination. It had never been used in a criminal case until Murray Humphreys came along.

Murray Humphreys was at the top of the criminal world, controlling the unions, the politicians, the judges, and many law-enforcement officers as he served as the Outfit's chief advisor on all facets of their operation. He was referred to as the "Brainy Hood" and the "Einstein of Crime" and "the Fixer" of anything that needed fixing. He had Al Capone's jury "fixed" until the Feds got wind of it and changed out the entire venire at the last minute. When Capone was convicted and sent to prison in 1931 for income tax evasion, the Chicago press immediately dubbed Murray Humphreys as "heir apparent"— the leader of the Outfit, and Public Enemy Number One. Murray never liked the spotlight. He often chastised his brother gangsters for being too flashy and conspicuous, showing off their illegitimate spoils and calling attention to themselves.

Capone was sentenced to eleven years in Federal prison and fined eighty thousand dollars. He served his time at Alcatraz and was released in 1939. Al "Scarface" Capone had syphilis when he went into the penitentiary; and by the time of his release, the disease had crippled him both mentally and physically. He lived the remainder of his years in seclusion at his mansion in Miami, where he died in 1947.

The Outfit continued with its multifaceted, billion-dollar criminal enterprise, relying on a string of capable leaders, triads, and commissions. Murray Humphreys was always there when the important decisions were made about the operations and directions that the gang should take. The leaders met at one or the other's home, every Sunday, to eat and discuss future business and politics. Monumental decisions, concerning local, state, and national politics, were often made at these meetings. With their absolute control of all of the labor unions in the country, even presidential elections were decided upon and carried out at these informal gatherings.

Over five decades of power struggles between various regional criminal syndicates, Murray Humphreys remained a highly respected and active, integral part of the organization. Gang bosses and gangster soldiers came and went, sometimes in very violent actions; however, Murray not only survived, but thrived.

In May of 1965, a Federal grand jury was convened in Chicago to investigate organized crime. Although Murray appeared once to testify, as summoned, he failed to respond to a subsequent request. The FBI had lost sight of him and, therefore, they issued an order to all stations and agents to pick him up. On Saturday, June 27, 1965, Oklahoma agents located Murray around 1:00 P.M., at the Santa Fe railroad station in Norman. When arrested, he was inquiring of the station manager routes and time schedules for Mexico. Humphreys was taken to Oklahoma City and booked into the Oklahoma County jail on a Federal lockup order. Soon, he was on a plane back to Chicago in the custody of U.S. marshals. Upon arrival in Chicago, he appeared in front of the committee and joked that he wasn't even aware that they were looking for him to testify again. He immediately made bail for a hundred thousand dollars and retired to his penthouse apartment overlooking Lake Michigan.

On November 23, 1965, the FBI, fearing that Humphreys would disappear again, decided to rearrest him on charges that he had lied to the grand jury when he said that he didn't know they were looking for him. The Feds had surveillance photos of him in the train station at Chicago before he left for Oklahoma, reading a newspaper that clearly indicated he was sought. When the FBI agents arrived at Humphreys' apartment to arrest him and search the premises, including his safe, Murray came to the door with a loaded .38-caliber revolver in his hand. He refused to allow them to enter, or take the safe key from his pocket. The younger, much stronger agents wrestled the old gangster to the floor, disarming him and ripping his pants pocket in the process to get at the key. They seized twenty-five thousand dollars in cash from the safe, and a coded journal, which, allegedly, has never been deciphered. The agents claimed to have left Humphreys in his apartment, alone and unharmed; however, later that evening, the lifeless body of Murray Humphreys was discovered in the apartment by his brother Jack, who had let himself into the apartment with his own key that he routinely carried.

Jack reported that he noticed signs of a struggle—things strewn around in the room. The authorities had the deceased removed to a funeral home where, without delay, the body was embalmed, rendering an autopsy, which was performed later, practically useless in determining whether foul play was involved. One source states that a small laceration, or puncture wound, was detected just below his right ear, causing some to speculate that an empty hypodermic needle, filled with air, was injected into his veins, causing his death. The death certificate cites the cause of death as "acute coronary thrombosis," and his occupation was listed as "investment broker."

Numerous questions about Murray Humphreys' death still remain. Chief among them: Why did the agents not take him into custody, especially after having scuffled with him and having a warrant for his arrest?

When Clemie and Luella learned of Murray's death, they immediately flew to Chicago to make the necessary arrangements to have him cremated. They then returned to Oklahoma, taking his ashes with them. The remains of Murray ("The Hump," "The Camel," "Curly") Humphreys (aka Lewellyn Morris Humphreys), a Chicago "Crime Boss" of the first order, were buried beneath a marble crypt on a grassy knoll at the center of a wooded section near Brendle Corner, Oklahoma.

This is a photo of the beautiful blue-marble family crypt, located in the center of a section near Brendles Corner, Oklahoma, which serves as the final resting place for Murray Humphreys and his wife, Clemie (Brendle) Humphreys, and their only daughter, Luella (Humphreys) Brady. (Author's collection)

Mary (Brendle) Humphreys and Luella (Humphreys) Brady would live out their lives in the stone cottage built by their beloved husband and father. Mary "Clemie" ("Clema") Humphreys died on June 9, 1980, in the hospital at Norman, Oklahoma; and, Luella passed away on July 26, 1992, in the hospital at Shawnee, Oklahoma. The ashes of both ladies, Murray Humphreys' first wife and daughter, were interred with him beneath the crypt. The tomb, which is now surrounded by a trailer park development, is inscribed—etched deeply into the beautiful blue marble are only three names:

BRENDLE—HUMPHREYS—BRADY

Bibliography

Books

Berry, Howard K. *Moman Pruiett, Criminal Lawyer.* Oklahoma City, OK: Harlow Publishing Company, 1944.
————. *He Made It Safe to Murder: The Life of Moman Pruiett.* Oklahoma City: Oklahoma Heritage Association, 2001.
Butler, Ken. *Oklahoma Renegades: Their Deeds and Misdeeds.* Gretna, LA: Pelican Publishing Company, 1997.
Burton, Art. *Black, Red and Deadly.* Austin, TX: Eakin Press, 1991.
Chrisman, Harry E. *Fifty Years on the Owl Hoot Trail.* Chicago: Sage Books, 1969.
Dale, E. E. and Gene Aldrich. *History of Oklahoma.* Edmond, OK: Thompson Book & Supply, 1969.
Demaris, Ovid. *Captive City, Chicago in Chains.* New York: Lyle Stuart, 1969.
Fulton, Maurice G. *The Lincoln County War.* Tucson, AZ: University of Arizona Press, 1968.
Gibson, Arrell M. *Oklahoma, A History of Five Centuries.* Norman, OK: Harlow Publishing Company, 1965.
Hersh, Seymour. *The Dark Side of Camelot.* Boston: Little, Brown & Co., 1997.
Houts, Marshall, as told to by James Mathers. *From Gun to Gavel.* New York: Wm. Morrow & Company, 1954.

Jones, W. F. *The Experiences of a Deputy U.S. Marshal of the Indian Territory*. W. F. Jones: Tulsa, 1937. Reprint: Muskogee, OK, 1976.

King, Jeffery S. *The Life and Death of Pretty Boy Floyd*. Kent, OH: Kent State University Press, 1998.

Kirkpatrick, E. E. *Crimes Paradise, The Authentic Inside Story of the Urschel Kidnapping*. San Antonio, TX: The Naylor Company, 1934.

Kobler, John. *Capone: The Life and World of Al Capone*. New York: G. P. Putnam's Sons, 1971.

Koontz, Sammy and Rose Crawley. *The Saga of Oklahoma State Penitentiary*. Eufaula, OK: Cantrell Graphics Printing, n.d.

Lamb, Arthur H. *Tragedies of the Osage Hills*. Pawhuska, OK: Osage Printery, 1935.

McLoughlin, Dennis. *Wild and Woolly, An Encyclopedia of the Old West*. Garden City, NY: Doubleday and Company, 1975.

Mooney, Charles. *Localized History of Pottawatomie County*. Midwest City, OK: 1971.

———. *Doctor in Belle Starr Country*. Oklahoma City: The Century Press, 1975.

Morgan, John. *Prince of Crime*. New York: Stein and Day Publishers, 1985.

Murray, George. *The Legacy of Al Capone*. New York: G. P. Putnam's Sons, 1975.

Nash, Jay Robert. *Encyclopedia of Western Lawmen & Outlaws*. New York: Paragon House, 1992.

Owens, Ron. *Oklahoma Justice*. Paducah, KY: Turner Publishing Company, 1995.

———. *Oklahoma Heroes*. Paducah, KY: Turner Publishing Company, 2000.

Rainey, George. *No Man's Land, The Historic Story of a Land Orphan*. Guthrie, OK: Co-operative, 1937.

Roff, Charles L. *A Boomtown Lawyer in the Osage*. Quanah, TX: Nortex, 1975.

Russo, Gus. *The Outfit*. New York: Bloomsbury, 2001.

Shirk, George H. *Oklahoma Place Names.* Norman: University of Oklahoma Press, 1974.

Shirley, Glenn. *Law West of Fort Smith.* New York: Henry Holt & Company, 1957.

———. *Temple Houston, Lawyer with a Gun.* Norman: University of Oklahoma Press, 1980.

———. *Henry Starr, Last of the Real Badmen.* New York: David McKay Company, 1965.

Wallis, Michael. *Pretty Boy, The Life and Times of Charles Arthur Floyd.* New York: St. Martin's Press, 1992.

West, C. W. "Dub." *Outlaws and Peace Officers of Indian Territory.* Muskogee, OK: Muscogee Publishing Company, 1987.

Magazines and Periodicals

Barber, Devergne. "The Crimson Career of Tom Slaughter." *Startling Detective* (1935).

Bowman, Ruth Fisk. "Death by Hanging, The Crimes and Execution of Arthur Gooch." *Chronicles of Oklahoma,* Vol. 62, No. 2 (Summer 1984).

Cordry, Dee. "The Killing of Sheriff W. A. Williams." *Oklahombres Journal,* Vol. 4, No. 2. (Winter 1993).

Ernst, Leif. "The Day a Great Lawman Drowned." *Oklahombres Journal,* Vol. 6, No.1 (Fall 1994).

Farris, David. "Good Times at Keokuk Falls." *True West* Vol. 46, No. 9 (September 1999).

Hardcastle, Stoney. "Eufaula-Checotah War." *Real West* (n.d.)

Hatfield, Leon N. "The Love-Mad Slayer and the Doomed Beauties." *Startling Detective* (March 1937).

Mattix, Rick. "Machine Gun Kelly." *Oklahombres Journal,* Vol. 4, No. 1.

Myers, Olevia E. "Scourge of the Cherokee Nation." *Frontier Times* (June-July 1972).

Nolan, Paul T. "Ira Terrill, Lawmaker, Madman or Political Scapegoat." *Old West* (Winter 1966).

Shirley, Glenn. "The Case of the Scrambled Brains." *True West* Vol. 40, No. 5 (March 1993).

Shoemaker, Arthur. "An Outlaw and His Mother." *Old West* (Fall 1965).

Turpin, Bob. "Heck Bruner's Graveyard." *True West,* Vol. 24, No. 4 (March-April 1977).

Warrick, Sherry. "I'll Kill 'Til I Die." *True West* Vol. 25, No. 2 (November/December 1977).

Wellman, Manley W. "Solving the Baffling Murder of the Oklahoma Police Chief's Daughters." *Real Detective* (October 1937).

Newspapers

Adair County Citizen, Stilwell, OK, Aug. 30, 1923.

Altus Times Democrat, Altus, OK, Mar. 12, 1950.

Antlers American, Antlers, OK, Dec. 27, 1934.

Arrow Democrat (The), Tahlequah, OK, Feb. 23, Mar. 16, 1922.

Beckham Democrat, Erick, Roger Mills Co., OK, July 12, 1934.

Blackwell Morning Journal, Blackwell, OK, Dec. 29-31, 1930; Jan. 1-8, 13, 24, Feb. 12, May 16-21, 31, 1931.

Blackwell Morning Tribune, Blackwell, OK, Aug. 17, 1930; Oct. 18, 1932.

Buffalo Republican, Buffalo, OK, Mar. 31, Apr. 7, 14, 28, May 5, June 9, Aug. 18, Sept. 22, 29, 1921.

Chandler News Publicist, Chandler, OK, Aug. 6, 1916.

Checotah Inquirer, Checotah, I.T./OK, Jan. 11, 1907; May 29, June 19, 1908.

Checotah Inquirer, Checotah, I.T., July 26, 1907.

Checotah Times, Checotah, I.T., Sept. 14, 28, 1906; Feb. 22, Mar. 1, May 17, 1907.

Checotah Times, Checotah, I.T./OK, Jan. 25, 1907; June 19, 1908; Jan. 15, 1909.

Cheyenne Star, Cheyenne, Roger Mills Co., OK, July 12, 1934.

Chickasaw Enterprise, Pauls Valley, I.T., Dec. 9, 1893; May 24, 1894; Apr. 4, 25, 1895; May 30, Nov. 28, Dec. 5, 1901.

Chickasha Star, Chickasha, OK, May 15, 1930.

Commanche Reflex, Commanche, OK, May 15, 1930.

Cordell Beacon, Cordell, OK, Jan. 26, Feb. 2, 16, Apr. 19, 26, Dec. 26, 1928; May 30, 1929.

Curtis Courier, Curtis, OK, April 7, 14, 1921.

Cushing Daily Citizen, Cushing, OK, Apr. 13, 16, 18, May 11, 13, 1951.

Daily Ardmoreite, Ardmore, OK, Aug. 31, 1918.

Daily Ardmoreite, Ardmore, I.T., Jan. 17, 1898.

Daily Ardmoreite, Ardmore, I.T., May 22, 1894; June 23, Sept. 6, 1895; Apr. 16, Dec. 18, 1896.

Daily Ardmoreite, Ardmore, OK, Sept. 4, 5, 1933.

Daily Enterprise-Times, Perry, O.T., Mar. 20, 23, 1896.

Daily Gazette, Stillwater, O.T., Feb. 20, 1901.

Daily Oklahoman, Oklahoma City, OK, Dec. 24, 1934; Aug. 9, 1935; Apr. 4, June 18, 19, 1936.

Daily Oklahoman, Oklahoma City, O.T./OK, Jan. 17, 1894; Oct. 3, 1895; Jan. 18, 1898; Aug. 9, 1899; June 2, 1918; Nov. 6, 1921.

Daily Oklahoman (series of articles by Alvin Rucker), Oklahoma City, OK, June 7, 14, 21, 1931.

Daily Oklahoman, Oklahoma City, O.T., Apr. 25, 27, 28, 30, 1897; Nov. 6, 1907.

Daily Oklahoman, Oklahoma City, OK, May 3, 4, 7, 1930; Oct. 18-20, 1932; Dec. 4-6, 1933; Jan. 19, Dec. 4, 29, 1934; Jan. 4, 1935.

Daily Oklahoman, Oklahoma City, OK, Mar. 2, 7, May 13, 1932; July 23, 24, Aug. 1, 15, Sept. 4, 5, 16, 18, 30, 1933.

Daily Oklahoman, Oklahoma City, OK, Feb. 20, 25, 1917; Nov. 17, 18, 1920; Dec. 10-12, 15, 1921.

Daily Oklahoman, Oklahoma City, OK, Nov. 3, 5, 1913.

Daily Oklahoma State Capital, Guthrie, O.T., Jan. 18, 1898.

Daily Oklahoma State Capital, Guthrie, O.T., Jan. 24, 1894.

Daily Oklahoma State Capital, Guthrie, O.T., Jan. 10, 1891; Aug. 18, 1893; Feb. 19, Dec. 14, 1894.

Duncan Eagle, Duncan, OK, Aug. 4, 1948.

Duncan Weekly Eagle, Duncan, OK, May, 15, 29, 1930.

Durant Daily Democrat, Durant, OK, June 8, 10, 14, 1935.

Eagle Gazette, Stillwater, O.T., Mar. 9, 1894.

Edmond Sun, Edmond, O.T., Jan. 3, 1896.

Enid Daily Eagle, Enid, OK, Feb. 27, Mar. 7, 1933.

Enid Daily Wave, Enid, O.T., Dec. 13, 1899.

Eufaula Democrat, Eufaula, OK, Oct. 10, 17, 20, 1913; Nov. 27, 1914.

Eufaula Democrat, Eufaula, OK, Nov. 7, 14, 1913.

Eufaula Republican, Eufaula, OK, Mar. 28, 1913.

Eufaula Republican, Eufaula, OK, Oct. 20, 1911.

Evening Gazette, Oklahoma City, O.T., Dec. 10, 1889; Jan. 16, 19, 20, 21, 23, 26, 27, 1893.

Evening Gazette, Oklahoma City, O.T., Jan. 5, 1891.

Fairfax Chief, Fairfax, OK, Oct. 21, 1921.

Fort Smith Elevator, Fort Smith, AR, Aug. 4, 1893; Jan. 6, Apr. 6, 13, 1894.

Frederick Express, Frederick, OK, Dec. 28, 1928.

Grandfield Enterprise, Grandfield, OK, May 15, 29, June 5, July 3, 1930.

Guthrie Daily Leader, Guthrie, OK, June 9, 1908.

Guthrie Daily Leader, Guthrie, O.T./OK, Mar. 13, 1898; Jan. 23, 1912.

Guthrie Daily Leader, Guthrie, O.T., Aug. 24, 1893.

Guthrie Daily Leader, Guthrie, OK, June 9, 1908.

Harper County Democrat, September 16, 23, 1921.

Henryetta Free Lance, Henryetta, OK, Mar. 27, 1924.

Holdenville Times, Holdenville, I.T., Aug. 9, 1907.

Hugo Husonian, Hugo, OK, Dec. 21, 1916; Feb. 22, 1917.

Indian Chieftain, Vinita, I.T., Jan. 19, July 5, Nov. 15, Dec. 6, 13, 20, 1888.

Indian Chieftain, Vinita, I.T., Nov. 10, 1892; July 6, Aug. 3, 31, Dec. 28, 1893; Jan. 11, 25, Feb. 1, Oct. 4, 1894; Mar. 21, 1895.

Indian Journal, Eufaula, I.T., Mar. 1, May 17, July 5, 19, 26, 1907.

Indian Journal, Eufaula, OK, June 11, 1911; Nov. 1, Dec. 6, 1912; Mar. 21, Sept. 19, Oct. 10, Nov. 14, 1913; Nov. 14, 27, 1914; Feb. 19, June 4, 1915.

Indian Journal, Eufaula, OK, Aug. 30, 1923.

Indian Journal, Eufaula, I.T./OK, Jan. 18, 1907; May 14, June 5, 12, 19, July 10, 1908; Feb. 19, June 11, 1909.

Indian Journal, Eufaula, OK, Nov. 7, 1913.

Kansas City Star, Kansas City, MO, July 21, 1893.

Kingfisher Free Press, Kingfisher, O.T., July 23, 1891.

Lawton Constitution, Lawton, OK, Feb. 25, 1929; May 15, 1930.

Lindsay News, Lindsay, OK, Aug. 29, Sept. 12, 19, 1919.

Marlow Review, Marlow, OK, Sept. 10, 1992.

Maud Democrat, Maud, I.T., July 27, Aug. 10, 1907.

May Bugle, May, OK, April 14, 1921.

McAlester Daily News, McAlester, OK, Nov. 26, 27, Dec. 24, 1934.

McAlester News-Capital, McAlester, OK, Dec. 22, 27, 1934.

McAlester News-Capital, McAlester, OK, Jan. 20, 1914. (Interviews with Rice, Ritchie, and Foster).

McAlester News-Capital, McAlester, OK, June 24, 1921; May 25, 29, 1923.

McAlester News-Capital, McAlester, OK, May 14, 15, 16, 1936; July 11, 1952.

McIntosh County Democrat, Eufaula, OK, Nov. 6, 1913.

Muskogee Daily Phoenix, Muskogee, OK, Mar. 27, 1924.

Muskogee Daily Phoenix, Muskogee, OK, Jan. 17, Feb. 13, Aug. 8, 1935; June 20, 1936.

Muskogee Phoenix, Muskogee, OK, June 9, 1908.

Muskogee Phoenix, Muskogee, I.T., July 5, Oct. 8, Nov. 8, 15, Dec. 6, 13, 20, 1888; Jan. 10, 17, 1889.

Muskogee Times-Democrat, Muskogee, OK, May 4, 6, 7, 1907.

Muskogee Times-Democrat, Muskogee, I.T./OK, Aug. 5, 1907; Mar. 25, Nov. 5, 1913.

Muskogee Times-Democrat, Muskogee, OK, June 19, 1936.

Muskogee Times-Democrat, Muskogee, OK, June 8, 1908.

Muskogee Times Democrat, Muskogee, OK, Feb. 17-20, 23, 27, 1915; Dec. 5, 1916.

Nelagoney News, Nelagoney, OK, Oct. 19, 1921.

Newkirk Herald, Newkirk, OK, Sept. 17, 24, Oct. 8, 1931; Feb. 16, 23, Mar. 9, Nov. 30, 1933.

Norman Transcript, Norman, O.T., Dec. 28, 1894.

Norman Transcript, Norman, O.T., Jan. 19, Apr. 27, 1894; June 28, 1895.

Norman Transcript, Norman, OK, Apr. 15, 22, 1909.

Nowata Weekly Star, Nowata, OK, July 11, 18, Sept. 5, Oct. 31, 1918; Jan. 9, 16, 23, Feb. 27, Mar. 27, 1919; Nov. 18, 1920.

Okemah Daily Leader, Okemah, OK, Dec. 24, 1934.

Okfuskee County News, Okfuskee, OK, Nov. 24, Dec. 1, 15, 22, 1932; Sept. 14, 1933.

Oklahoma City Times, Oklahoma City, OK, Mar. 11, Oct. 14, 17, 1931.

Oklahoma City Times, Oklahoma City, O.T./OK, Dec. 19, 1893; Nov. 6, 1926.

Oklahoma City Times, Oklahoma City, OK, Aug. 14, 15, 22, 23, Sept. 4, 30, 1933.

Oklahoma City Times, Oklahoma City, OK, Jan. 24, 1928.

Oklahoma City Times, Oklahoma City, OK, June 11, 15, 19, 1935.

Oklahoma City Times, Oklahoma City, OK, April 4, 1921.

Oklahoma City Times, Oklahoma City, OK, May 3, 1930; Oct. 18, 1932; Dec. 5, 8, 1933; Jan. 5, 8-12, 23, 1934; Jan. 4, 1935.

Oklahoma City Times, Oklahoma City, OK, Nov. 7, 1908; Nov. 3, 5, 1913.

Oklahoma City Times, Oklahoma City, OK, Oct. 4, 5, 8, 1923; Mar. 26, 1924.

Oklahoma City Times, Oklahoma City, OK, June 1, 1911; Nov. 29, 1916.

Oklahoma Gazette, Oklahoma City, O.T., June 14, 15, 1889.

Oklahoma News, Oklahoma City, OK, Dec. 4, 5, 1933; Jan. 5, 7-11, 1934.

Oklahoma News, Oklahoma City, OK, Oct. 16, 1920; Dec. 29, 1921.

Oklahoma State Capital, Guthrie, OK, June 6, 1908.

Okmulgee Daily News, % Okmulgee, OK, July 4, 1931.

Okmulgee Daily Times, Okmulgee, OK, July 7, 10, 1931; June 17, 1936.

Osage Chief, Pawhuska, OK, Oct. 21, 1921.

Osage Journal, Pawhuska, OK, Oct. 21, 1921; Oct. 11, 1923; Jan. 3, 1924.

Panhandle Herald, Guymon, OK, Aug. 1, 1929.

Pauls Valley Enterprise, Pauls Valley, I.T./OK, Nov. 7, 21, Dec. 12, 19, 1907; Jan. 2, Dec. 17, 31, 1908; Apr. 15, 22, 1909.

Pawhuska Daily Capital, Pawhuska, OK, Aug. 21, Oct. 8, 1923; Mar. 20, 26, 1924.

Pawnee Courier Dispatch, Pawnee, OK, Sept. 10, Dec. 17, 1914; Jan. 14, 1915.

Perry Daily Times, Perry, O.T., Dec. 26, 1894.

Ponca City Courier, Ponca City, O.T./OK, Apr. 4, 5, 7, 11, June 17, July 21, Aug. 11, Sept. 19, Oct. 4, Dec. 7, 8, 1899; Jan. 19, 1900; Mar. 13, 1908; Jan. 13, 1910; July 6, 20, 1911.

Ponca City Democrat, Ponca City, O.T., Apr. 6, 1899; May, 17, 1900.

Ponca City News, Ponca City, OK, Oct. 18, 1921.

Purcell Register, Purcell, OK, Nov. 30, 1916.

Purcell Register, Purcell, I.T., Aug. 25, Sept. 8, 1893.

Ringling Eagle, Ringling, OK, Aug. 2, 1928.

Sapulpa Evening Democrat, Sapulpa, OK, Mar. 15, 16, 27, 1912.

Sapulpa Evening Light, Sapulpa, OK, Mar. 16, 25, 1912.

Sapulpa Herald, Sapulpa, OK, February 9, 1933.

Seminole Capital, Seminole, I.T.,/OK, July 19, 25, 1907; Nov. 5, 1908.

Seminole County Capital, Seminole, OK, Nov. 6, 1913.

Seminole Producer, Seminole, OK, Oct. 14-16, 1931; Mar. 24, Apr. 11, Nov. 23-25, 1932.

Sequoyah County Democrat, Sallisaw, OK, Feb. 25, Dec. 23, 1921; Feb. 24, Mar. 17, 31, May 19, 1922; Feb. 23, Mar. 2, 9, Apr. 13, 1923; Apr. 4, 1924.

Shawnee Daily News, Shawnee, OK, Nov. 5, 1913.
Shawnee Evening News, Shawnee, OK, Sept. 8, 29, Oct. 14, 1931.
Shawnee Herald, Shawnee, I.T., July 21, 23, 24, 1907.
Shawnee Morning News, Shawnee, OK, Jan. 15, 21-24, Mar. 12,
    27, Apr. 10, 22, 23, June 8, Nov. 24, 25, 26, 1932.
Stillwater Gazette, Stillwater, O.T., Sept. 30, Oct. 7, 1892; Feb. 20,
    1901.
Sunday Oklahoman (Orbit sec.) Oklahoma City, OK, Feb. 19,
    1978, "Ira N. Terrill, Lawmaker-Lawbreaker" by Orben Casey.
The Telephone, Tahlequah, I.T., Mar. 22, 1895.
The Times, Oklahoma City, OK, Jan. 15, 1910; Mar. 14, 1912.
Times Democrat, Pawnee, OK, Sept. 10, Nov. 27, 1914.
Times Record, Blackwell, OK, Nov. 3, 1921.
Tonkawa News, Tonkawa, OK, Apr. 2, 3, 1931.
Tulsa Daily World, Tulsa, I.T., Jan. 15, 1907.
Tulsa Daily World, Tulsa, OK, Oct. 12, 16, 18, 30, 31, Nov. 2,
    1920.
Tulsa Daily World, Tulsa, OK, Aug. 22, 1923; Mar. 26, 1924.
Tulsa Tribune, Tulsa, OK, Jan. 21, Feb. 20, 21, Mar. 14, 1922;
    Mar. 26, 29, 1924.
Tulsa Tribune, Tulsa, OK, June 23, 1930.
Tulsa Tribune, Tulsa, OK, Apr. 13, 18, 1951.

Waurika News Democrat, Waurika, OK, Aug. 3, 1928; Aug. 5, 1932.
Weekly Chieftain, Vinita, OK, July 29, 1910.
Weekly Journal, Eufaula, OK, June 2, 1911.
West Side Democrat, Enid, O.T., Dec. 12, 1893.
Wetumka Gazette, Wetumka, OK, Aug. 24, Oct. 26, 1934.
Wewoka Democrat, Wewoka, I.T., July 19, 25, Aug. 9, 1907.

Government Documents (Federal/State/County/City)

Copies of 127 pages of documents relative to members of the

Rogers gang, from the files of the Western District of Arkansas (Judge Parker's Fort Smith Court) from the National Archives, S.W. Region, Fort Worth, Texas.

Clyde Mattox: Federal court appeals record, 12 pgs.
Clyde Mattox: Federal prison record, 9 pgs.
Clyde Mattox: Executive (Federal) clemency orders, 2 pgs.
Clyde Mattox's parole by Gov. Charles Haskell.
Clyde Mattox's pardon by Gov. Lee Cruce.

1860 U.S. Census, Clark County, IL.
1880 U.S. Census, Grayson County, TX; Sedgwick Co., KS.
1900 U.S. Census, Cherokee Nation, I.T.; Chickasaw Nation, I.T.; Kay County, O.T.; Kansas State Penitentiary at Lansing, KS; Union Parish, La.
1910 U.S. Census, Jefferson Co., OK; Oklahoma Co., OK; Pittsburg Co. (OSP at McAlester), OK; Dallas Co., TX; Callahan Co., TX; Creek Nation.
1920 U.S. Census, Jefferson Co., OK; Oklahoma Co., OK; Shannon Twp, Creek Co., OK.

Cleveland County (Oklahoma) Land Records, Norman, OK.
Copy of Ira Terrill's affidavit filed with the land office.
Death Certificates: George Birdwell; Forrest Cunningham; John Cunningham; Ed Lockhart; Clyde Mattox; Ernest Oglesby; Elbert Cole Oglesby; Arthur Gooch; Ambrose Nix; Murray Humphreys; Mary Luella Humphreys Brady; Ira Terrill.
Duncan Cemetery Records, Duncan, OK.
Llewelyn Humphreys-Mary Brendle Marriage and Divorce Records.
Office of Communication & Archives, Federal Bureau of Prisons, letter dated Oct. 9, 1997.
Oklahoma Criminal Court of Appeals Records: Ernest Oglesby.
Oklahoma Department of Corrections.

Oklahoma Department of Corrections, Inmate Records.

Oklahoma Department of Corrections, letter dated June 8, 2001.

Oklahoma Department of Health, letter dated October 2, 2001.

Oklahoma Historical Society, Archives and Manuscript Division, Fred Barde Collection on Ira Terrill, 5 pgs.

Oklahoma State Penitentiary Records, McAlester, OK: Ed Lockhart; Joseph Heirholzer; Charles Brackel; Bennett Highfill; Thomas Dickson; C. C. Patterson; Arthur Gooch; John Oglesby; Ernest Oglesby.

U.S. Census (IL-OK): 1900, 1910, 1920, 1930 (re: Humphreys/Brendle families).

Index

Burwell, Benjamin F., 76
Bush, Lawrence, 253
Bush, Lewis "Brushy," 44-46
Bussey, Hess, 93
Butler, Gerald, 337

Caddo (land), OT, 131
Caddo County, OK, 251
Caldwell, Oscar, 319
California, 61, 76, 98, 335, 346
Callahan County, TX, 243
Calvin, OK, 121, 293, 318
Campbell, Gerald "Jerry," 246-47, 249-50
Campbell, R. D., 255
Campbell, Ralph, 235
Campbell, Webb, 247, 250-51, 253
Canadian, TX, 91, 331
Caney, KS, 86
Cann, Herman, 55
Cannon, Rufus, 91
Canton, Frank, 90
Canton, TX, 247
Cantrell, W. C., 221
Canyon City, CO (prison), 56
Capone, Al "Scarface," 342, 344, 346, 353
Carey, Jack, 220
Carlisle, PA, 127
Carney, Jack, 221
Carolian, Peter, 182
Carr, Abe, 23-24
Carr, Bill, 90
Carroll, John, 25
Carter County, OK, 196-97
Casey, Bert, 132, 135-36; gang, 139
Casharego, James C., 123-26
Castle, OK, 292
Cathey, Randolph, 105-6, 108, 110, 113
Catlett, John G., 305-6
Catoosa, IT, 29
Cattle Annie. *See* Annie McDoulet
Caulfield, Henry Stewart, 282
Cave City, KY, 203
Cedarvale, KS, 202

Centralia, OK, 196-97
Chamberlain, J. B., 56
Chancellor, Mayre, 255-56
Chandler, OK, 95-96
Charlie, Matt, 216
Chautaugua County, KS, 202
Checotah, IT/OK, 24, 93, 145, 148-50, 153, 165-67, 169-73, 235, 293
Chelsea, IT, 30, 36
Cherokee, 124, 145, 213, 343
Cherokee County, OK, 214, 220
Cherokee Indian Police, 29-30
Cherokee Nation, 27-29, 32, 36, 38, 213
Cheyenne, OK, 338
Chicago, IL, 243, 339; "The Outfit," 341, 343-44, 346, 348-50, 352-55
Chickasaw Nation, 99; legislature, 100-101, 104, 131, 135-36
Childers, IT, 25
Choctaw City, OK, 116, 118
Choctaw County, OK, 199, 318
Chouteau Trading Post, 115
Christie, Ned, 27
Chuculate, Perry, 215, 217
Cimarron, KS, 86
Circle Bar Ranch, 145
Civil War, 42, 48
Clark, Bill, 150
Clark, George, 143-44
Clark, J. D., 71
Clark, John, 244
Clayton, NM, 240
Cleveland, Grover, 72
Cleveland County, OK, 108; court, 110
Clifton, Charles "Dan," 88
Clifton, Dynamite Dick, 88, 91-93
Clinton, OK, 263-64
Clothier, A. E., 238-39, 242
Cobb, Lula, 234-35
Coffeyville, KS, 33, 86
Colbert, Bynum, 28
Cole, Charles, 159
Colorado, 240
Colorado State Penitentiary, 56